BEPPINA AND THE KITCHENS OF AREZZO

Beppina and the Kitchens of Arezzo

Life and Culinary History in an Ancient Tuscan City

Elizabeth Romer

PROSPECT BOOKS
2020

First published in 2020 in Great Britain and the United States
by Prospect Books, 26 Parke Road, London, SW13 9NG.

©2020 Elizabeth Romer.
©2020 Illustrations, various, see list of illustrations on page 274.

The author, Elizabeth Romer, asserts her right to be identified as author of this work in accordance with the Copyright, Designs & Patents Act 1988.

No part of this publication may be reproduced, stored in a retrieval system, or transmitted in any form or by any means, electronic, mechanical, photocopying, recording or otherwise, without the prior permission of the copyright holder.

BRITISH LIBRARY CATALOGUING IN PUBLICATION DATA:
A catalogue entry of this book is available from the British Library.

Typeset and designed by Catheryn Kilgarriff and Brendan King.

Cover design by Prospect Books.

ISBN 978-1-909248-66-3

Printed and bound by the Gutenberg Press, Malta.

For Arezzo with great affection and respect.

Contents

Preface   9

Introduction   11
Aretine food and culinary philosophy. Local produce seen as an expression of culture, enjoyment, identity and pride.

Chapter One
Finding Beppina   19
Life and food in the prosperous Arezzo of the nineteenth century. Pellegrino Artusi's cookery book and its influence. Beppina and her recipes, which are still prepared in Arezzo today.

Chapter Two
Bishop Tarlati's Soup   93
Culinary History – fact or fantasy? The Aretine passion for jousting. Francesco Gaudentio and *Il panunto toscano*. Francesco Redi and the exquisiteness of chocolate in the Baroque Period.

Chapter Three
The Land and the City   143
Arezzo's market, from the thirteenth century, via Napoleon, to the present-day market gardeners of the province. The city consumes the gastronomic delights that the farmers provide.

Chapter Four
Sustenance   159
Our *Alimentari*, a grocery at the centre of our lives, its secretive customers and what they really eat each day. Historic Aretine food. Etruscan *prosciutto* to *baccalà*.

Chapter Five
Pleasure   189
The *Aretini* at table. The true dish of Arezzo identified. Dinner served overlooking the city. Aretine cooks and lovers of good food: Gaudentio, Magi, Beppina and Aretino. 'Vivi Felice' – Live in Happiness.

Chapter Six
Recipes 213
Everything from *Crostini Neri* to *Frittata di Ceci*, *Pappardelle all'Aretino* to Drowned Trout, Artichoke Tart to *Agnello alla Casentinese* and on to *Pinocchiata* and Vin Santo.

Acknowledgements 271

Select Bibliography 272

List of Illustrations 274

Index of Recipes 276

General Index 278

❋ Preface ❋

Strange to relate it was partly the weather that was responsible for the beginning of my long attachment to the ancient city of Arezzo. For many years our beautiful, largely unaltered farmhouse near the borders of Tuscany and Umbria had been a base in Europe for our peripatetic lives spent working on archaeological sites in Egypt, and travelling while film-making. There in that peaceful valley our beloved neighbours the Cerotti family, about whom I wrote in *The Tuscan Year, Life and Food in an Italian Valley*, kept a kindly eye on us.

Some thirty years ago, while we were on an unusual winter stay at the house, one cold but sunny morning there came the sound of a tractor and then a knock at our old front door. There stood Orlando Cerotti, wrapped in a stout woollen jacket; with a smile on his face he unloaded a large pile of wood onto the pathway and said without explanation: 'You'll have need of this tomorrow.'

We were slightly puzzled as to why he had suddenly brought us such a very abundant load of logs. All became clear the next morning when we rose to find that near two feet of snow had fallen in the night; we were, in fact, stranded on the side of the hill. Orlando, with his lifetime of experience and strong adherence to the rules of the Lunar Calendar, knew this would happen and was concerned for our safety. That winter was indeed to become unusually cold, the water that came from the spring at the edge of the forest froze in the pipe which had in past times been laid under the fields. Even olive trees were damaged by the severely low temperature. With our water supply blocked, life in the house became impossible in spite of the fire that roared in the vast chimney place. This was one reason which induced us to find a second place to live when reasonable weather did not oblige in the winter countryside; another was my avid curiosity about how life was really lived in a Tuscan city.

We were fortunate to find a small apartment in an ancient house in the city of Arezzo, and it was there that I began once more to learn from my new neighbours and friends about their particular cuisine and culture. This book is about the other side of the Tuscan coin, the city, nourished by its surrounding countryside by means of the produce of generations of farmers and families like that of the Cerotti's. Town and country were – and still are – indivisible.

✻ INTRODUCTION ✻

Even if the discourtesy of the sea, almost seeming to envy your kindness, did not consent to my seeing or enjoying the goods which you sent me and which are much to my taste; I still render you that gratitude which a soul who seeks to please a friend deserves, that generosity which is yours. But if I could have your power, which up to now I would attribute to princes, I would implore you to do justice to the extravagance of your gift and my expectations. To be angry with the inconstancy of the waves who leave in peace those who with their silks and their gold jewellery defraud the taxes but castigate those who carry cheeses and sausages for which the tax is paid. The sea should be angry with the winds which disturb it, and not with me, who is more angry than the storms with all their battles; he should be angry with the spoilers of the sausages and the cheeses which he carries. Certainly it is right to say so, because it is not the sea's fault but the fault of the winds and the way they behave that I cannot eat here the things which I can no longer eat in Rezzo, and perhaps do not need to eat away from there as their taste resides in my memories and affections. They form the flavour of my memory.

Letter from Pietro Aretino to Francesco Albergotti
Venice, 3rd November 1541

The domestic food of the Tuscan city of Arezzo is inspired by fundamental ties to its surrounding land and an ancient culinary heritage. In this book, you will find beloved recipes and opinions about food that strongly express the character of Arezzo's citizens, both past and present, plus ways of preparing food considered so essential to the Aretine way of life that they have been preserved throughout the city's long and often turbulent past.

The quotation above is from a letter written in 1541 by Pietro Aretino, one of Arezzo's most famed citizens, to Francesco Albergotti, a member of a distinguished Aretine family. It well illustrates the nostalgia of an Aretine for his city and his native cuisine. That feeling for home, the Aretine countryside and the produce it provides, continues to thrive.

My writing of this book was encouraged by the discovery of a collection of handwritten recipes that I found by chance in an antique shop in Arezzo. The fragile sheets of paper, I later discovered, dated from the last two decades of the nineteenth century to near the end of the First World War, and were collected by a woman called Beppina. On further study of the recipes and a comparison with some of those of the distant past, as well as many from the present day, a pattern began to emerge of what was – and largely remains – genuine Aretine food. Beppina's recipes form a link in the ancient chain of Aretine culinary tradition.

One of the underlying themes of this book is that the preparation of food is one of the chief expressions of any culture. Traditionally prepared food provides stability and identity to the individual family, as well as to the society of a region or nation. Modern Italians are the inheritors of thousands of years of civilisation of a complex order and, in turn, Italian food accurately reflects this intricate legacy. Every area of Italy has its own culinary traditions.

> When you find yourself far from home never commit the error of asking for a speciality of your own birthplace. Cuisine varies from place to place because the quality of the water is different, as is the land and the pastures, but

Introduction

above all it is different because one cannot improvise a tradition that each region has conserved for itself over millennia. *(Non commettere mai l'errore trovandoti lontana dalla tua regione di chiedere una specialita della tua terra. La cucina varia da luogo a luogo perche varia la qualita dell acqua, varia il terreno, varian le pasture, ma sopratutto varia perche non s'improvisa una tradizione che ogni luogo conserva da millenni.)*
Arnoldo Miniati. Florence 1971

These myriad local dishes, which are nevertheless all Italian, are, as is intimated in the quotation above, the product of the diverse geographies and climates of Italy, which in turn define the type of agriculture possible in a particular area. They are also the result of the markedly different dispositions of Italians living in diverse parts of the peninsula, all with their local predilections, attitudes, pride in and love for their birthplaces, and their particular histories. The food of Italy was and yet remains an intense and delicate mosaic that cannot be reduced to simplicities.

Italians – and the Aretines are no exception – are still passionate about their food; they habitually talk about it and its preparation. To discuss food is both a *divertimento* and a demonstration of one's own particular cultural inheritance, something of which to be proud.

During my years in Italy, I have observed the influence of the modern food industry on the culinary habits of urban Italians. International manufacturers, giant supermarkets and the publicity that they generate in the mass media, plus price cutting, have all had an effect.

Fortunately, this industrial onslaught on traditional local produce and cookery has long been recognized and is vigorously questioned. Some of the strongest opponents of industrial food in the city of Arezzo are Aretine women who fiercely defend their ways of preparing food, those rules and methods which they have inherited from their forebears. Then there are movements such as the *Coldiretti*, the Association of Farmers, whose aim it is to protect both traditional Italian agriculture and genuine regional food. On each Wednesday morning, a group of local farmers bring their fruit and vegetables, and together with local producers of cheese, bread, preserved meats and honey, gather in the town to sell their excellent produce. Added to this, there is the strong presence in Tuscany of the now world famous 'Slow Food' movement, founded by Carlo Petrini. The celebrated chef and writer Alice Waters is vice president of the movement. Slow Food aims to preserve the cultural heritage of local cuisines along with their associated plants, seeds and farm animals. The very latest fresh food enterprise in Arezzo, however, is a market which was opened in December 2015 in the historic Logge del Grano, where in the past grain was sold. Here one can buy traditional produce of excellent quality, for example, *abbucciato aretino*, a *pecorino* cheese made from unpasteurised sheep's milk, a cheese good enough to meet the sternest standards of Aretine women. The name *abbucciato* comes from the old word to darken, as this cheese when matured grows a thin dark skin. Due to the unaltered quality of the milk, its flavour, gentle,

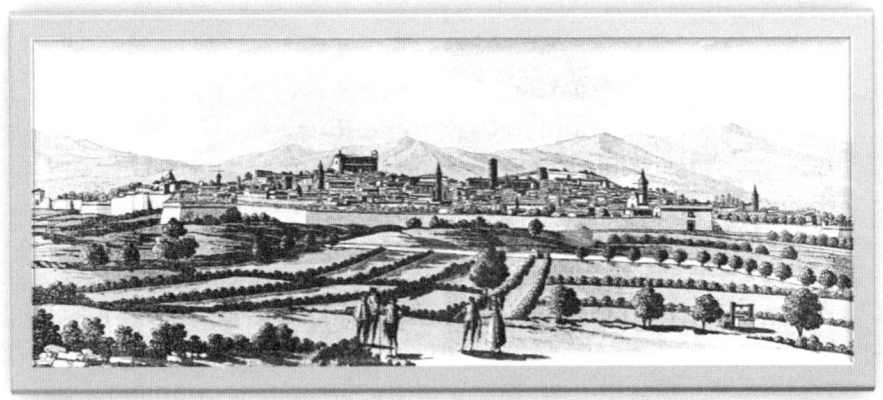

The walled city of Arezzo in the early nineteenth century when it was still surrounded by fields.

Introduction

creamy but with a hint of bitter sweet dry leaves, is redolent of the mountain herbage on which the sheep have grazed. Its origins are extremely ancient, in the eleventh century there is mention of it in documents written by the monks of Camaldoli who received it from its makers, the hermits of the nearby and famed Casentino valley. In Le Logge del Grano there is, too, an abundant choice of locally made foods, olive oils, fresh vegetables and rare fruits like the *mela roggia*, a delicious apple, anciently grown in the Tiber Valley.

Despite the activities of the modern food industry, if Beppina, one of the inspirations of this book, were to miraculously reappear in Arezzo today, she would still recognise some of the shops in the *centro storico*, and many of the goods that they sell – but she would have to walk outside the city walls to visit the market, where the vegetables would be larger than she remembered, and doubtless she would be overwhelmed by the confusion of roads and industrial estates which now cover the verdant fields of her day. Happily though, in countless households, she would still be able to sit down for dinner and recognize dishes that were served at her own table: dishes like *fegatelli*, parcels of liver perfumed with wild fennel flowers, *arista*, roast loin of pork spiced with garlic, nutmeg and cloves, *pappardelle alla lepre*, home-made pasta dressed with a hare sauce, *fagioli di Sant'Anna*, green beans cooked with *pancetta* (salt cured pork belly) and tomatoes, savoury *frittata*, a slowly cooked egg dish, much like the Middle Eastern *eggah* filled with diverse ingredients such as wild asparagus, zucchini, spinach, *pecorino* cheese and all manner of herbs.

Although the exact taste of a piece of meat might differ from era to era, because of the fodder that a pig, a lamb or a chicken might have habitually been fed and the manner in which the flesh, once slaughtered, was stored and for what length of time, the inherent characteristics, the biochemistry of the various meats, remain unaltered and recognizable in these recipes, which have been transmitted through the years – and in some cases centuries. The method of preparation of many dishes has remained much the same, too. These are treasured recipes made with genuine ingredients that have provided both sustenance and pleasure to the people of Arezzo.

Bearing in mind the influences of the modern food industry even in a conservative Italy, I have in this book observed the characteristic tradition of domestic cooking in Arezzo, viewing it as a genuine manifestation of culture. I have compared currently popular recipes with those of Aretine cooks of previous centuries. I have listened to conversations around me in groceries and heard echoes of the nineteenth century, seen what has remained constant in the Aretine kitchen for hundreds of years, what has evolved and what, under the pressure of our increasingly industrialised, globalised and regulated world, is changing.

The food of Arezzo has been shaped by the agriculture of its surrounding countryside in times of plenty and of famine, by historical events, religion, war, occupation, politics and fashion. However, it still clearly expresses the essential culture of this Tuscan hill town. Here there is a respect for the quality and purity of the ingredients, the simplicity with which they are traditionally handled and the spare elegance of the resulting dishes: plain food, good enough to stand up for itself without unnecessary adornment. *Senza fronzoli,* as the Aretines themselves would say!

And to quote again one of the greatest of Arezzo's citizens, Pietro Aretino, who wrote as well about food as he did about other pleasures, he too was an advocate and forbear of this Aretine notion of simplicity:

> Regarding he who laughs at me for eating such simple

❋ Introduction ❋

and rustic food, one laughs more at his boasting of feeding on regal fare, tell him, nay, swear to him, that it is true that he eats better than me, but I will live longer than he, because death is the cook of elaborate food, life is the cook of that which is simple. (*Se colui che si e riso nel vedermi mangiare cose si roze e cosi rustiche, se ne ride piu con il vantarsi del suo pascersi di vivande regie, ditegli, anzi giurategli, che in vero egli mangia meglio di me, ma ch'io vivero piu di lui, imperoche de I cibi delicati e cuoca la morte, e dei semplici la vita.*)

Pietro Aretino, Venice, August, MDXLVIII
Letter 538, Book 5

Pietro Aretino.

Chapter One

Finding Beppina

I came upon the above-mentioned collection of nineteenth- to early twentieth-century recipes in 1990, while on a walk from my apartment at the summit of the old city of Arezzo down through the Via Madonna del Prato, which skirts the church of San Francesco. At the time, this narrow lane, edged by the massive church and silent *palazzi*, had a few small food shops which served the quarter. A bread shop sold saltless Tuscan bread, home-made *grissini* flecked with sesame seeds, hard almond biscuits stored in glass jars, and little else. Further down the lane was a seed shop that also dealt in pulses; coarse hessian sacks of dried beans, peas and lentils filled the windows. Next to that was a greengrocer, his wares piled onto orange crates from Sicily. In winter, cardoons were hung like heraldic devices from the iron brand holders driven into the stone façade of the shop, iron rings that once held blackened oily flares to light the concealing shadows of the street. His shop was usually full of talkative housewives who came twice a day to buy fresh vegetables, the *odori* for the *sugo*, or seasonal fruit, always sufficient for just one meal. Twenty-one years later, however, in 2011, perturbing statistics gathered by Censis (Italian Centre for Social Investment Studies) and *Coldiretti* announced that roughly 60 per cent of Italians – and 60 per cent of those female – shopped for food once a week, 27 per cent daily and 10 per cent once a month. The habits of society were changing.

❋ Beppina and the Kitchens of Arezzo ❋

Today, a simple greengrocer's has become a rarity in the *centro storico* of Arezzo, and now some of the shops in the lane are specialist purveyors of fine ice cream, clothes, flowers, and perfume. Close to the now long-vanished store that dealt in seeds and pulses there was a small antique shop. The window was full of pretty oddments, *Stile Liberty* china, Venetian glass, small pieces of silver. Inside, the fifteenth-century vaulted room was lined with bookshelves, because its owner was mainly a dealer in antiquarian books. That evening I stepped into the shop to escape the cold and to enquire if there were any old cookery books for sale. I was shown a copy of the fifth edition of *La scienza in cucina e l'arte di mangiar bene* (*Science in the Kitchen and the Art of Eating Well*) by Pellegrino Artusi, which was first published in 1891, thirty years after the Unification of Italy. The fifth edition published in 1900, with 35 new recipes, brought the number of printed copies of Artusi's book to 10,000. Copies of the first edition of Artusi are extremely rare and those of later editions printed in his lifetime not commonly found – this for the simple reason that cookery books such as this were consulted in the kitchen and have been consumed by time and handling. Between the index and the back cover of the volume lay something of exceptional interest, a bundle of papers covered in copperplate handwriting. I established later that these were recipes which had been collected by the original owner of the Artusi edition, a woman called Beppina, probably a diminutive of Giuseppina – Josephine. Beppina, then, was one of the thousands of Italians who, by the turn of the nineteenth century, in a climate of an ardent middle-class interest in domestic cookery, had bought a copy of this influential work. Here in my hands I had a microcosm of Aretine middle-class culinary taste at a very particular period of time.

It became apparent from the sort of recipes Beppina collected that she was a member of the city's comfortably situated *borghesia*, witnesses to this being the elegance of the handwriting

Chapter One – Finding Beppina

and the many recipes for costly meat dishes, cakes, biscuits and liqueurs intended to be served to guests.

The recipes were written on thin pieces of paper, an old invitation card, and insurance policies; the dates, which by good fortune remained on the re-used sheets, stretched from 1884 to the 19th of January 1917. Some were in different handwriting and came from households in Milan and Rome, where it seems that Beppina had been a guest. The invitation was engraved by Pineider, an elegant and expensive stationery company which has been selling its refined wares in Florence since 1774. It came from one Eugenia Perelli, the widow of a Senator Tami, and was in celebration of the marriage of her daughter Bianca to L'Ingenere Mario Gherardi. Sadly, although the place and date of the wedding were recorded as Rome on the 27th July, the year was missing. Most unromantically, the recipe written on the reverse of the card is for making soap.

Gradually, as I read on, the personality and culinary preoccupations of Beppina and her circle, the upper middle class of *Belle Époque* Arezzo, began to emerge and I started to notice the similarities between Beppina's recipes and the food that I was eating at Aretine tables in my own time. There were differences too, but these resided more in the equipment used in the kitchen than in the style of the food served. I started to inquire into the history of Beppina's city, particularly that of the last third of the nineteenth century.

After the Unification of Italy in 1861, that fundamental and visceral change in the political composition of the peninsula, Arezzo was jolted awake from the rhythm of its millennial agrarian way of life and entered into a fresh age of innovation and relative prosperity. There was money to spare and an ambition to remodel the ancient city in a manner more fitting to the burgeoning energy of a new industrial age. Just as a dense central area of mediaeval housing in Florence was demolished and transformed into a modern city square – the Piazza della Repubblica – so in 1862 Arezzo's ancient Via de Bacci (now Via Cavour) which ran from the central spine of the *centro storico*, the ancient Borgo Maestro (now the Corso Italia), to the Church of San Francesco, was widened by means of razing mediaeval housing to the ground. The resulting space was lined with large houses sufficient to the needs of the rising upper middle class, and new shops were opened. Still today 'Alfredo', a first-class butcher's shop, continues to flourish and provide genuine Aretine specialities and excellent meat from the Val di Chiana and the Casentino valley. The venerable Caffé dei Costanti – initiated in 1804 by the French during Napoleon's occupation – which had been hidden in a side street found itself, with the aid of these developments, in a commanding position in the new Piazza Umberto I (now Piazza San Francesco), where, apart from a few short interludes, it still flourishes as a fashionable society café. The Costanti has recently been declared a national monument, one of a select band of historic Italian cafés.

In 1864 the railway from Florence to Rome was fast approaching Arezzo and this coming event promised well for the rebirth of the old city. In 1866 the railway station was inaugurated. Regulations put forward by the brand-new Kingdom of Italy made it easier to organize the modernisation of Arezzo and an urban plan for Arezzo was ready by 1867. The cattle market, an ancient focus of the largely agricultural municipality, had been moved and replaced with the new railway station. Then a wide access road was laid out between the station and the elegant new Piazza Umberto I, already created in 1862. This enabled Arezzo's theatre, the Teatro Petrarca built in 1830, to have a grand new entrance on the new street. By enthusiastic public request, and in the interests of opening the mediaeval city to the new Italy and letting fresh air and light into the *centro storico*, the ancient walls were demolished in several places, and a new barrier in the form of an elaborate iron fence was built to allow wide access to the station and other main thoroughfares.

❋ Chapter One – Finding Beppina ❋

The *barriera* at the station was furnished with large gates and it was here that taxes were collected on any merchandise brought into the city. These arbitrary taxes imposed upon foodstuffs were, unsurprisingly, a source of discord all over the new Italy. However, the Aretines were used to taxes since they had been paying them from at least 1327, according to the Statute of that date! In 1895 hanging lamps lit by electricity were installed in the principal streets and squares, which at that date was an extremely forward-thinking innovation.

This new post-Unification period of success and affluence furnished the upper middle classes of Arezzo, Beppina amongst them, with a brand-new stage on which to ride in their carriages, display their finery and amuse themselves.

And it is against this background of progress and prosperity towards the end of the nineteenth century, whose wealth, it must be underlined, did not extend to all classes of society, that we should consider Beppina and her recipes. She owned as we have already seen a well-used copy of Pellegrino Artusi's cookery book *La scienza in cucina e l'arte di mangiar bene*; and it is clear from the recipes she personally collected that her style of cooking was in tune with that of Artusi. Therefore, at this point it might be profitable to examine a little more closely the career, ambitions and effect of such an important cookery writer at that particular era in Italian history.

Pellegrino Artusi.

Beppina and the Kitchens of Arezzo

Pellegrino Artusi, whose formal occupation was to be that of a cloth merchant specialising in silks (with the addition of some private banking), was born in Forlimpopoli in the Romagna in 1820 but spent nearly sixty years in Florence, where he died in 1911. Having dipped his toes in the waters of the Arno for numerous decades he may be said to be Tuscan by adoption. His house, in his time number 25, now civic number 35, was in the elegant late nineteenth-century Florentine Piazza d'Azeglio, which had been designed on the model of a London Square and built by British businessmen. This was where, on his early retirement from the cloth trade, he compiled and sold what has become known as the classic cookery book of the new Italy. Fondly dedicated to his two cats, Biancane and Sibillone, the first edition was published in 1891 and went into fourteen editions during his lifetime, the last of which, still edited by the 91-year-old Artusi, was issued in 1911, the year of his death. The book was, and has continued to be, an authoritative bestseller. Since the work fell out of copyright in 1981, myriad editions have been issued by diverse publishing houses and a great majority of Italians either own a copy of Artusi or are acquainted with the book. When I once bought a nicely bound example from Rossi Mattei, a small stationers opposite the church of San Francesco in Arezzo, the owner and his wife volunteered the information that they themselves had been presented with a copy when they were married in the 1950s, as it was considered to be the very best book for teaching young urban brides how to cook.

Artusi's work has given rise to an ample range of scholarly books and articles discussing his life, culinary philosophy and his effect on the domestic cookery of Italy. His collection of recipes emanating from diverse areas of Italy indeed goes a considerable way to demonstrate the intricate fabric of the culinary culture of the peninsula. At this point it is important to realise that from the very earliest mediaeval examples of cookery treatises up until near the close of the nineteenth century, such books had largely been written by professional

Chapter One – Finding Beppina

cooks who had been employed in the kitchens of royalty, the nobility, and later, the wealthy. The purpose of many of these historic works is the provision of banquets rich in expensive and exclusive foods, suitable for the entertainment of the elite. Artusi was a non-professional in the sense that he did not cook for a living and wrote for the burgeoning ranks of middle-class Italian women who, besides aiming to entertain guests, wanted to provide good, healthy food for their immediate families. Artusi's recipes are intended for the domestic kitchen and do not address professional cooks working in either rich households or restaurant kitchens.

Artusi's book can be viewed as an expression of the gathering together of the various city states of the peninsula into a single country, which to some extent had meant a lessening of the influence of the powerful Papal State. Artusi was anti-clerical, and this is partly evidenced by the intricate title of his cookery book, which emphasises science and hygiene in the kitchen, both concepts of fresh concern at the end of the nineteenth century when the emerging influence of modern scientists created a conflict between their world view and that of the traditional church. Artusi's political opinions too were in favour of the Unification of Italy. As food is arguably one of the most important manifestations of any culture, it would follow that this new state must have its characteristic cuisine – that is, Italian food. And some modern scholars have indeed gone to great lengths to assert that Artusi's book codifies a national style of cooking.

However, with regard to food itself, Artusi's book is perhaps more accurately described as a compendium of good recipes gathered over many years from various cities in Italy, with a distinct bias towards Artusi's home territory, which ranged from the Romagna to Tuscany. The first edition of *La scienza in cucina* contains 475 recipes and the last edition 790. The additional recipes are largely the result of a lively correspondence between

Artusi, his epicurean friends, and readers residing in various areas of Italy, who sent him their favourite local recipes, which he enthusiastically tested and, when he found them satisfactory, included in subsequent editions of his book. This is, to be sure, an informal gathering of Italian recipes. There are, however, large areas of Italy whose cooking is not represented at all in his book and there are many recipes which originate in countries other than Italy, possibly emanating from members of the foreign community in Florence. Having said that, today, 128 years after its first appearance, the book has by its own merits become 'a national cookery book'. However, whether it is habitually consulted now by the majority of Italian home cooks is a moot point. It is certainly kept in many middle-class homes by middle-aged women, and read as an authoritative source on the correct methods of preparing various special dishes. In general, Artusi's long-lived popularity is perhaps partly the result of a nostalgia for the past; plus another factor, something that does unite all Italians – an interest in and appreciation of good food.

Whether Artusi actually set out to systematically produce a book that described the food of the new Italy *per se* is unclear.

Galantina di Fagiano alla Vallière.

His tastes were catholic: he included recipes from various Italian cities and geographic zones, and also foreign recipes, without fear or favour, in no particular order, and he made no attempt to formally classify them by provenance; the recipes are simply arranged by the course in which they were intended to be served, the chief method of preparation, and the principal ingredient. The book was distributed through Italy, initially by Artusi himself from the Piazza D'Azeglio, at a time when people largely lived all their lives in their native towns or the surrounding countryside, and in this manner he made Italians all over the peninsula aware of what their co-nationals were eating in far-off areas of Italy. Here, there is no attempt to make all Italians eat 'Italian' food, but rather an effort to encourage all Italians to eat enjoyable meals that were beneficial to their health and well-being, made with fresh produce that was obtained locally. Artusi greatly approved of and enjoyed the markets of Florence.

Artusi made a major contribution to the new Italy in the clear language he used in his writing. However, French culinary terms were very fashionable in the Italy of the nineteenth century; at this time French expressions were used in royal,

Galantina di Pollo all'Inglese.

noble, high bourgeois and official government kitchens, in the capital as well as in local municipalities. Italian culinary writing of the period – compiled by chefs in their menus, and by authors and journalists – was, to the great annoyance of Artusi, wont to employ a strange mixture of *gergo francioso*, 'Frenchified' culinary jargon and Italian. On the other hand, normal middle-class urbanites, artisans and country people discussed food in their own particular dialects. The difference in language used in the kitchen signified a difference in social class, and evidenced a divide in the style of the cookery of the peninsula.

Artusi wrote his recipes in a clear, friendly manner, adding anecdotes and quotations in places. To make his instructions comprehensible to every cook, Artusi rendered local terms for various dishes and ingredients into words that could be readily understood by all. At that period not only was an united Italy a new concept, so was what is now known as the Italian language. As we have seen above, the diverse zones of the peninsula used their own dialects and in some cases different languages. And to add complication to Artusi's work, sometimes the same word was used in diverse areas of Italy to describe totally different dishes. Traces of this diversity in language still linger. Indeed, in the early 1970s we were asked by neighbours in Tuscany whether we understood the Italian that was spoken on news programmes from the national broadcaster RAI TV, which in their view was very different to their manner of speaking. Artusi wrote in Tuscan Italian, the language of Dante; his words lean towards Florence where since 1582 the Accademia della Crusca, the guardian of the purest Italian language, has thrived. He comments on the subject of language in his recipe number 455 for *Cacciucco*, a fish stew:

> After the Unification of the country it seemed logical to me to think of the unification of the language, which few considered and many hindered, perhaps through mistaken

CHAPTER ONE – FINDING BEPPINA

pride and perhaps also from the old and ingrained habit of expressing themselves in their own dialect.

Artusi's main aim, however, was to teach the uninitiated to cook well, by means of instilling in them the necessity of loving good food, using only the best quality ingredients available to them, and paying great attention to detail. He upbraids those in contemporary *alta borghese* sections of Italian society who followed a fashion for despising any obvious interest in cooking. 'Nobody, apparently, wants to accord any importance to eating and it is easy to understand why: but hypocrisy apart, everyone laments a bad supper and the indigestion that results from ill-prepared food. Nutrition is a primary need of life, so it is reasonable to try to satisfy this need as well as possible.' Indeed, Artusi had the genial idea of starting a Culinary Institute in Bologna, that city of master cooks. It would be the best in all Italy, he opined, training young people, especially women, in the art of the kitchen, thus providing them with sure employment and in so doing benefiting many bourgeois households who were afflicted by the annoyance of bad cooking.

Artusi's motto was 'Hygiene, Economy and Good Taste', hygiene in its strict sense being of vital importance in those days when cholera and typhoid outbreaks were not unusual and effective medicines were few. But by the word 'Hygiene', Artusi also meant health-giving and thus, by association, scientific. Artusi was also concerned that his readers should practise 'Economy', providing for their families the best ingredients that their circumstances allowed. He encouraged his readers to use fresh produce and to eat according to what the particular season provided, setting a good example in his house and garden in Florence. There, with the help of his maid Marietta Sabatini and his cook Francesco Ruffilli, he procured the best meat and the freshest fruit and vegetables from the market in Florence, and produce from his own land in Emilia Romagna and the Marche. Using the finest materials possible was an important concept at a period when the adulteration of food was much practised. It was easier, perhaps, for the comfortably situated, to whom Artusi's book was directed, to buy the best, but at that period and all over Europe, groceries often expanded their profits by, for example, mixing coffee with ground chicory, extending butter and cheese with potato flour, putting sand in brown sugar and many other such sad devices. Very often this adulterated food ended up on the tables of the poorer families, who were thus cheated of both their money and their health. Of course food is still adulterated today, but in rather more subtle ways.

In using the term 'Good Taste', Artusi refers to the pleasure that can be derived from well-prepared food of excellent flavour, made from good ingredients. But in using the term he also refers to the art of cookery, the appetising arrangement of food on a plate and the pleasing beauty which can be achieved by means of a well-presented table.

Artusi's appreciation for dishes was not confined to the borders of Italy nor a spirit of *campanilismo* (parochialism). He happily included in his collection any recipe if it proved to be enjoyable and appetising, but with the proviso that the dish was chosen for its innate qualities and not driven by the blind and, at that period, fashionable mania for all things foreign. In Artusi's recipe number 277 for *Piccione all'inglese o piccion paio* (Pigeon Pie) he starts by stating:

> I tell you here once and for all that in my cookery I do not make an issue of names and I do not give any importance to bombastic titles. If an English person says that this dish, which is also known by the strange name of Pigeon Pie, is not cooked according to the methods used in his country, I do not give a fig; it is sufficient that it is judged to be good, and then all is equal.

So, with this in mind, in his book we can find such delights

✻ Chapter One – Finding Beppina ✻

as *Krapfen* (doughnuts), Roast-Beef, *Kugelhupf* (a cake baked in a circular mould) and *Gâteau à la Noisette*. It is, however, interesting that for a country which has usually been castigated for its indifferent cooking, several English recipes appear in Artusi's book, as they do in the later editions of *La Cuisinière de la campagne ou la nouvelle cuisine économique* by Louis-Eustache Audot (1783–1870), another writer on cookery who was not a professional chef. *La Cuisinière*, one of the few cookery books that Artusi possessed, was first published in 1818 and reissued continuously until the early twentieth century. It prefigures *L'arte di mangiar bene* in the sense that both books were intended to instruct the middle-class housewife in the art of making enjoyable food. Audot's work gives a good selection of English methods of roasting meat and game, and also has a separate section of English Entremets. He comments that although British meat dishes were mostly roasts and any vegetables were plainly served with melted butter or a white sauce, puddings were far more varied. He places Plum Pudding at the top of his list, giving minute instructions upon its preparation. Cabinet Pudding, which is a simple bread pudding, and Rice Pudding also find favour, plus various fruit tarts and apple fritters.

Artusi's English dessert recipes are fewer and concentrate mostly on simple desserts such as stewed blackcurrants, although he too gives recipes for Plum Pudding – which he explains does not contain any plums – and Plum Cake. His *mele all'inglese* is a succinct version of a cinnamon perfumed apple pie and in his recipe for *zuppa inglese*, a common or garden English trifle, he explains the difference between the single cream favoured in Tuscany and that required to make a trifle, *crema pasticcera*, which is a confectioner's custard made with milk, eggs, flour and sugar, scented with vanilla. *Zuppa inglese* is now one of the most ubiquitous of Italian puddings and is considered to be a national dish. Artusi was also of the opinion that *rosbiffe* (roast beef), now commonly found on Italian tables, was a suitable dish to serve to male diners as it was something they could sink their teeth into, whilst ladies invariably preferred *bricciche*, by which he meant something lighter, a trifle, in the other sense of the word.

In his *Lesso Rifatto all'Inglese*, he tackles Toad in the Hole, and points out that the art of cooking might also be called the art of finding strange and capricious names, adding that if the dish was not delicious it would be an insult to name it after the toad. The recipe differs from that given by Isabella Beeton in her *Book of Household Management* (1859–61), as Artusi employs leftover boiled meat, which is cut into thin slices and heated up on both sides in a pan with butter. The meat is then flavoured with salt, pepper and spices, and sprinkled with Parmesan. The batter, made of eggs, flour and milk, is poured over the dressed meat and allowed to solidify on top of the stove. Mrs Beeton, on the other hand, specifies pouring the batter into a buttered baking dish, then adding slices of well-seasoned cold mutton and either kidneys, oysters or mushrooms, before consigning the dish to the oven to bake for about an hour.

The first edition of Isabella Beeton's work – she became a journalist on her marriage to a newspaper proprietor, and like Artusi and Audot was not a professional cook – was published in twenty-four monthly parts between 1859 and 1861, during which year it was re-issued in one volume. Coincidentally, 1861 was also the year of Italian Unification. The first edition of Artusi's book was issued in 1891, although his recipes were collected over many years and not, as in Beeton's case, largely garnered from other published cookery books. However, both Beeton's and Artusi's books were directed at a then newly rising middle-class of urban tradespeople and professionals, in Britain and Italy respectively. Both writers produced domestic cookery books for a new society, and both books are, in one form or another, still in print. However, Artusi, in his attitude towards – and fondness for – good food, is perhaps better likened to Eliza Acton, whose *Modern Cookery for Private Families* was published in 1845.

❋ Chapter One – Finding Beppina ❋

Indeed, Acton's Preface to the 1855 edition of her book predates Artusi in the manner in which she recommends a healthy diet and careful preparation of food as being essential to the well-being of all. Acton too rejoiced in the same fascination for food as did Artusi, with both carefully preparing or overseeing the preparation of agreeable and healthy food, both testing recipes which they collected from the sources at their disposal. And here one must make further comment on the origins of many of the recipes given in domestic cookery books of the period. If Isabella Beeton plagiarised recipes on a large scale in her *Book of Household Management*, using thinly disguised recipes from such writers as Hannah Glasse, Charles Elmé Francatelli, Alexis Soyer and Eliza Acton, Acton herself was not innocent of this practice, which was common at the time. Her recipe for Truffles *à L'Italienne*, not to mention that for Truffles with Champagne Wine, is a clear, near verbatim copy of the recipe given in Louis Eustache Ude's *The French Cook: A System of Fashionable and Economical Cookery Adapted to the Use of English Families*, the first edition of which was published in 1813 and the tenth in 1829. Interestingly, Acton's earnest instructions for the preparation of truffles for cooking departs from that of Ude, in that she tries too hard to eliminate the earth clinging to the truffle. Her instructions to soak them for an hour or two in fresh water would imperil the flavour as well as the dirt. Ude, however, writes as a professional – his method is to 'wash them well with a brush in cold water'. But it is Acton's markedly sincere efforts to provide workable recipes that has perhaps endeared her to her many distinguished culinary fans. Isabella Beeton (who also borrowed from Ude) is now regarded by many students of culinary history as an able journalist who was influenced by her husband, and that both were motivated as much by a profitable business as by simply aiding women to provide decent food for their families.

Artusi's great strength partly lies in the fact that his recipes – which were judiciously tested in his kitchen and then published – largely emanated from real people, from his own culinary experience, and from readers in many parts of Italy who shared with him the recipes that their families had been preparing for generations. These were often recipes that were carefully handed down from mothers to their daughters or daughters-in-law, and which were typical of the area of Italy from whence they came. In the later editions of his book, however, there are also to be found dishes which were noted in important historical manuscripts but which have also survived in the kitchens of Italy: *arista*, spiced and roasted pork loin, is one of them, *zuppa regina* is another, as is *biancomangiare* and *panata*.

Amongst the wide-ranging selection of recipes in Artusi's book are to be found four which emanate from Arezzo. This places our city amongst those Italian cities which Artusi cites and which are more famed for their cuisine, like Naples, Milan, Genoa and Bologna. Artusi went to the heart of Aretine cooking and chose *Pappardelle all'Aretina*, partnered with *Anatra domestica in Umido*, the latter providing the sauce for the former as it still does in Arezzo's kitchens today. From the way he writes it is clear that he has obtained this recipe through personal experience, not literary sources. He begins his instructions with a slightly disparaging comment, but continues to describe a rich and delicious sounding dinner.

Pappardelle all'Aretina (as given by Artusi)

I do not give you this recipe as a refined dish, but it will serve for the family.

Take a domestic duck [as opposed to a wild duck], put it into a casserole with a piece of butter, flavour it with salt and pepper and when it has taken on some colour add a finely chopped *battuto*, mixture, of *prosciutto*, onion, celery and carrot. Leave this to soften under the duck, stirring it often. Next, pour away the excess oil which has come from the duck as it is indigestible. Continue to cook the

CHAPTER ONE – FINDING BEPPINA

> bird adding a little broth or water from time to time but in sufficient quantity to serve as a sauce for the *pappardelle*.
>
> Procure a piece of veal or beef spleen, open it and scrape away the interior with a knife then add this to the pan as another ingredient for the sauce, the addition of some tomato and a little nutmeg would also not be a bad idea.
>
> Roll out a sheet of dough made with eggs, to a thickness such as that used for *tagliatelle* and with the frilled edged pastry cutter cut strips as wide as a finger. Cook them lightly and then season them with the sauce to which you have added the duck liver cut into pieces, Parmesan [grated] and if needed a little butter. The *pappardelle* will serve as the first course and the duck as the second.

Here indeed is a comfortable domestic meal, the pasta sauce enriched with the intense meaty taste of spleen, something which is probably unknown on British and US tables today, though it is still much and rightly appreciated in Arezzo, where it is also traditionally employed in the making of chicken liver *crostini*.

Artusi also chose *Agnello Arrosto all'Aretina*, spit-roasted lamb, outlining precise instructions on a method of giving a fresh sweet taste to the meat by means of a mixture of olive oil and vinegar applied with a stalk of rosemary, which herb could also be inserted into the flesh here and there to improve the flavour. This recipe nicely shows the constraints with which cooks had to contend in the late nineteenth century, when the lamb purchased from the butcher might have a lingering taste of the stable about it and may well have been verging on mutton when it was slaughtered. The diverse methods of conserving food practised through the centuries have also clearly exercised a strong influence on the flavour of various foods. One is able to surmise the difference between the lamb of Artusi's time and the odourless and discreetly flavoured refrigerated lamb which we expect to eat today.

❋ Beppina and the Kitchens of Arezzo ❋

The topic of how the taste of different foodstuffs has altered through time is an interesting one. It is impossible to know the exact flavour of a fish caught in Lake Trasimeno in the 1400s and cooked over an open wood fire, or that of a lamb killed and roasted in Florence in the 1880s. All we can say is that apart from the inherent characteristics of the flesh – the biochemistry which characterizes that particular creature – the pasture on which the sheep grazed and the quality of the waters in which the fish swam were certain to have affected the flavour of the resulting dishes. Just as it does today: a summer lamb raised on a Welsh hillside, for example, where the herbage is of the finest, and a lamb grazed on a salt marsh on the northern shores of the Gower Peninsula (also in Wales), where salt-tolerant herbs and grasses like samphire and sea lavender grow, will have a very different flavour from that of a lamb that is simply milk fed. All three are ovine, but each have very particular flavours.

Another typical Aretino dish that Artusi described is his recipe number 383, *Fagiuolini dall'occhio in erba all'Aretina*:

> Trim the beans at each end and cut them into three parts. Put them into a casserole with two whole cloves of garlic, the juice of raw tomatoes and enough water to make sure that the beans are covered. Flavour them with oil, salt and pepper, then let them simmer slowly until they are done making sure that there remains enough sauce to render the dish pleasant. They can be served as a side dish (served between main courses) or as an accompaniment to boiled meats.

Fagioli dall'occhio (long green beans of the genus *Vigna unguiculata sesquipidalis*) are also known in the Arezzo area as *fagioli di Sant'Anna*, and are traditionally eaten by country dwellers on the 26th of July, which is the day devoted to Saint Anne. Today they are often cooked in a richer manner than that suggested

Chapter One – Finding Beppina

by Artusi: that is with the addition of cubed *rigatino* (a form of *pancetta*) which together with garlic is browned in a little olive oil. Then the trimmed beans are added to the pan and allowed to cook over a high flame for a few minutes before peeled and chopped raw tomato is added. The pan is then left to simmer over a low heat with the further addition of chopped parsley, some basil leaves and salt and pepper. The beans will be cooked through in about three-quarters of an hour. A little water can be added if the sauce should dry out.

Printer's flower from the first edition of Artusi's renowned cookery book, which was dedicated to his two cats.

In Artusi's discourse on *Fegatelli in conserva*, he mentions that although many people knew how to make these parcels of liver wrapped in caul, scented with fennel seed or bay leaves and either grilled, spit-roasted or cooked in a pan, not many were aware of the fact that housewives in the countryside around Arezzo were in the habit of preserving *fegatelli* in lard, thus enabling the meat to be kept for long periods of time. This method had the advantage of it then not being necessary to eat all the offal of the newly killed pig immediately before it went off. A careful, but also a tasty solution, which emanated from the traditional parsimony of country dwellers, especially those of Arezzo. In fact, Artusi makes it clear that what he appreciated about the true Aretino style of cooking was that it was robust, honest and excellent for feeding families.

Since ancient times, animals, foodstuffs and ingredients used in the preparation of food were carried for long distances.

❋ Beppina and the Kitchens of Arezzo ❋

Sheep, grains, olives and grapes entered Egypt in pre-dynastic times from the Levant and the hillsides edging Mesopotamia. This was not a trade for the delectation of the wealthy, but a slow expansion of the single most important step ever taken by humankind, evidencing the leap from hunting and gathering to the hard world of agriculture. Wheat entered Europe via Anatolia and Greece around 6000 BC and thence spread reaching Italy, France and Spain by 5000 BC. The Etruscans salted hams which were then exported widely to the north; indeed, they did so in Arezzo, one of the twelve chief Etruscan cities. During the Roman period in Italy, peppercorns and spices like silphium were imported from the East and North Africa and carried all over the Roman Empire. In the Mediaeval age foodstuffs like *insaccati* (cured meats) and wine and salted fish were traded all over Europe and beyond. Astonishingly, even in these early times, foodstuffs – born on boats, by donkeys, on horseback and then on carts – were almost as international in the old world as items purveyed in supermarkets today. The division of what could and could not successfully travel lay within the limits of the perishable nature of the foods in question and the distance that they were required to travel.

And, in turn, at the time of Artusi and Beppina – a period when the new Italy was but thirty years old – aided by the spread of a new method of transport, the railway, it became far more convenient for local foodstuffs and specialities from diverse areas to be carried all over the peninsula. Food shops that catered to the middle classes prided themselves on being able to provide their clients with a variety of seasonal produce, cheeses, hams, and particularly prepared items procured from all over Italy, as well as many from abroad. As we have seen above, during these years when both Artusi and Beppina were collecting recipes, there was a vogue for using foreign terms for well-known Italian dishes, a fact which irritated Artusi intensely. In his recipe for *Passato di Patate*, he testily says that if he did not speak like a foreigner – he uses the word *barbaro*, barbarian

Chapter One – Finding Beppina

– when discussing food, no one in Italy would understand him. Instead of the old-fashioned term *passato* (pressed through a sieve) one had to use foreign words like purée or the even cruder expression, mash! One wonders what he thought of such publications as *La cucina classica,* an extraordinary translation by Giacomo Giardini into the '*idioma Italiano*' of a work written by the head chefs of the royal house of Prussia, Urbano Dubois and Emilio Bernard. This two volume treatise was paid for by the Society of Milanese Cooks and was issued in Italy in 1877. The volumes contain menus from many of the royal houses of Europe and Russia and recipes for the predominantly lavish dishes served at the regal tables. The translated names of many of the dishes are delightful examples of the Italianisation of foreign culinary terms, for example, *Pudingo di pannckets alle albicocche*, presumably a pudding of pancakes flavoured with apricots; *rizzole* for rissoles and *gigotto* for *gigot*. *Un nonnulla di noce moscato*, on the other hand, is a graceful Italian term, here it describes the merest hint of nutmeg.

Title page of the 1877 edition of La cucina classica.

✻ Beppina and the Kitchens of Arezzo ✻

Beppina, after reading Artusi for inspiration, very probably shopped in a famous Aretine store called Giacomo Konz & C. which was established in 1856 in the Corso Vittorio Emanuele (now the Corso Italia). In one of their advertisements in a turn of the century guidebook they present themselves as a *drogheria*, that is a purveyor of spices, maker of liqueurs, biscuits, chocolate, and jams; they imported and roasted coffee and were sellers of scents and cosmetics, luxurious wines and champagne. They also sold household goods and dyes. Another branch of the company outside one of the city gates dealt in olive oil, imported goods, even petroleum, sulphur and ammunition for hunters.

Konz, trading under the name of Gli Svizzeri ('The Swiss'), its nineteenth-century nickname, provided delicate *pasticceria* and was one of the city's more elegant coffee shops until it sadly closed in 2007. Its rebirth in February 2012 as the Bar Pasticceria Stefano, run by a truly skilful family of pastry cooks of the same name, whose delicious cakes and tarts have been pleasing the *Aretini* for years, was eagerly awaited by many in Arezzo. Regrettably, in early 2018 the Bar Pasticceria Stefano closed again, due to the death of its master baker, but in June of that same year it was again revived.

Beppina may well have bought her *pastasciutta* at another store in the Corso Vittorio Emanuele, Andrea Corsi, who stocked the products of the famous Buitoni factory at Sansepolcro in the Province of Arezzo. Buitoni, one of the first manufacturers of pasta outside of the Naples area was founded in 1827 by Giulia and Giovanni Battista Buitoni and remained a family business for generations; the company was a sternly patriarchal, respected employer of many local people, but in 1985 was purchased by the industrialist Carlo de Benedetti. In 1988 Buitoni was bought by Nestlé and thereafter became submerged into the modern food industry. The emphasis of the company's products now seems to lie with frozen vegetables and pasta sauces rather than with the simple dried pasta of the past.

❋ Chapter One – Finding Beppina ❋

In Beppina's day, in 1882, to cater for an enlarging clientele the Buitoni factory imported a *Molino a Cilindri* from Hungary which was able to grind 100 *quintale*, ten thousand kilos, of high gluten hard grain a day. Hungarian expertise had invented a mill which used cylindrical rollers firstly of ceramic and then of steel which were much more efficient in the production of fine flour.

One of Buitoni's specialities was *pastina*, tiny pasta shapes for using in soups. They were packed in elegant boxes of various dimensions and were recommended for children and invalids. Also for the nourishment of invalids they proposed their *Pastina Iperglutinata Buitoni alla Somatose*. This was a mixture of flour and 10 per cent *Somatose* which was a meat extract made by Friedr. Bayer e C. of Eberfeld in Germany. The name *Somatose* probably derives from a supposed substance named osmazome, which in the late eighteenth century had been mistakenly thought, even by such as the great Brillat Savarin, to contain the good flavour associated with meat soups and the surface of roasted meats. Here we are near the beginning of food chemistry, mass-produced products and also the pharmaceutical industry.

Traditionally, cooking for invalids was of common concern and much attention was paid to providing suitable nourishment for delicate children and the sick. In the home, meat bouillon was thought to be of great benefit to the indisposed being both palatable and easily digested by the patient. Manufacturers of meat extracts like Liebig – and thereby creating a long believed culinary myth – emphasised in their advertising their extract's virtues by claiming that all the 'goodness' from a large quantity of raw meat which a sick person could not possibly eat could be extracted into a concentrated form which when diluted made a drink that was extremely nourishing and pleasant for a patient to consume. It is true that such extracts contain B-group vitamins and tend to stimulate the appetite but they were nowhere near as efficacious as their manufacturers claimed. However, in an age when effective medicines were few any perceived advantage was not to be spurned. Artusi includes in *L'arte di mangiar bene* a brief section on food for those with weak stomachs and a tendency to indigestion. However, one detects a tone of impatience in the way he writes. He clearly thinks that if one were to follow sensible rules such as chewing one's food thoroughly, eating lighter meals during hot weather, eschewing too many cakes and puddings and indulging in a modicum of healthy exercise, problems of indigestion would not exist. Nowadays in the West in our age of antibiotics, vitamins and sophisticated healthcare, invalid cookery as such is largely a non-subject. But, still today in Italy, rules for the suitable feeding of the unwell and hospital patients most certainly still apply, *pastina* in a meat broth is commonly served on many hospital wards. One might add here that in the Arezzo of the late 1600s a recipe for sustaining the sick was written by a Jesuit cook, Francesco Gaudentio, it described a delicate dish of 'great nutriment and refreshment to the sick', made from white of eggs, goats' milk, sugar and rose water. Artusi thought that a chicken broth was more appropriate for the delicate stomach, closely followed by *castrato* and veal, but all three were to have the fat removed before serving. Artusi, needless to say, heartily disapproved of commercial products intended to replace home-made stock.

Another of Arezzo's famous citizens Francesco Redi who was physician to the Medici in Florence in the later 1600s also often advocated the use of a *brodo* and a particular diet to accompany the medicines that he prescribed. Here, he writes to a friend in Arezzo, one Giulio Giannarini who it seemed suffered from problems of a digestive nature:

> Whilst you are taking the medicine. In the evening for supper take nothing other than a soup in which you can put either some lettuce or some borage or sorrel or other green herbage, particularly asparagus. Eat a little boiled meat and some fried testicles and brains, lamb's liver or that of goat or other similar things. As accompaniments,

Chapter One – Finding Beppina

you could take either strawberries, or asparagus or some sprouts of chicory, or a little salad of cooked lettuce dressed with vinegar, oil, sugar and salt. I would warn you, however, and you must listen well, that the strawberries must be washed with your very good sweet white wine, and further to that they need to be well, very well, sprinkled with sugar. The doctor [Redi himself] eats them like that and believes that prepared in that way they are good for those who are sick. And if the strawberries are not from the garden the recipe will not be good. The doctor eats them in the morning and in the evening gives them to the Grand Duke, who compares them to the large arbute berry, *corbezzola*. Please understand that the *corbezzola* is that fruit which in Arezzo is called *rosella*; I am telling you this so that you do not think that the doctor has forgotten the vocabulary of his home town.

...then try and live happily and this summer take some *brodo*.

Andrea Corsi's shop, which Beppina could have afforded to patronize, besides the attractive packages of Buitoni pasta, also sold *coloniali*, goods imported from the colonies, such items as coffee and sugar. His prices, his advertisements inform us, were moderate and he gave a discount of 2 per cent to his clients.

Beppina's recipes echo those of Artusi in that they are also eclectic. It seems that she was eager to carry home recipes that she had enjoyed on her travels outside Arezzo. In her collection, there are among other recipes from Milan, two for meat dishes *alla Milanese* as well as a version of *Manzo alla California*, a recipe also given by Artusi. Beppina's version of the dish differs from Artusi's in some particulars which would suggest that she did not copy it from his opus. *Manzo alla California*, moreover, did not spring from a trip to America. It may have been part of Beppina's collection of recipes from Lombardy as the dish originated in a dairy farm in a tiny *frazione* of Lesmo, Brianza, which was

❋ Beppina and the Kitchens of Arezzo ❋

called California, probably so named by returning Italian émigrés from the United States in the late nineteenth or early twentieth centuries (see page 69). Surprisingly, there are many places called California in Italy, mostly to be found in northern Italy.

Interestingly, Beppina's Milanese dishes are the fruit of a social visit to a household there. Milanese cooks were famous for their skill and at that time the well-to-do in that very bourgeois city much preferred to entertain at home. Indeed, to entertain in restaurants was seen as an admission that one was not sufficiently well established to employ a cook. One of the most treasured possessions of such prosperous Milanese families was their personal cookery book. This was handed down from generation to generation and enlarged and enriched with recipes gleaned from generous friends and relations. The Milanese penchant for eating at home was echoed in Arezzo where, as we will see, traditional Aretines tend to eschew restaurants. Possessors of the famously Tuscan virtue of parsimony, many older Aretines have been brought up to regard eating in restaurants as an unnecessary extravagance only to be indulged in at very significant moments of life, such as an engagement to marry, the baptism of children and first communions. In the years after the war, up until the 1970s and in some cases beyond, it was permissible for a respectable middle-class family to enter a restaurant but it was unthinkable to be seen in an *Osteria*, an inn or public house patronised mostly by men from the working classes. Women drinking wine in public, was also frowned upon and consequently was a very uncommon sight in polite society.

In spite of Artusi's lamentations over high society's lack of enthusiasm for the table, in Arezzo in Beppina's day it would seem from the press that interest in food was lively. Local newspapers printed recipe columns and in the society sections not only did they list the guests at evening parties and balls but they also listed the courses eaten at dinner and, as was the

Chapter One – Finding Beppina

fashion of the times, at the very grandest or official evenings the menus were written in French and the dishes and wines that were served also came from France. This latter would not at all have pleased the historian and commentator on food and wine Dr Giuseppe Ferraro. In 1891 (that year of culinary events, see page 60), Ferraro published the manuscript of a judgement of Italian wine written in 1536 by the great Farnese Pope, Paolo III, and his *bottigliere* (wine steward), Sante Lancerio, and in his preface castigates his contemporary Italian vintners for not refining, promoting and exporting the excellent wines of their native land, so allowing the wines of France, Germany and Spain to be given pride of place in Italy.

Bourgeois Aretine dinners of Beppina's period had a reputation for being elaborate, it was important to make a *bella figura*, so it was essential to serve many courses; a banquet for members of this class of society often consisted of upwards of ten. Still today in Tuscany there is a strong tradition of serving numerous courses for dinners and of course wedding feasts. A friend, Mariella, who is decidedly Aretine and an accomplished cook, will serve many differently flavoured *crostini*, a potato *tortino* enriched with Parmesan and made in a manner similar to the potato tart of Beppina's day, two sorts of pasta with contrasting sauces, then two different meat dishes with accompanying vegetables, before ending the meal with cheese and fruit and a tart or diverse *dolcetti*. She is a busy professional, but in her household good dinners must have many courses, all carefully designed to complement each other. One of her excellent and traditional Tuscan recipes is for roast rabbit stuffed with artichokes. Appropriate wines are served with each course and at the end of the meal there will be a *vino di contemplazione*, a serious red wine and cognac, plus good whisky for those who enjoy spirits.

However, in contrast to the tendency towards luxury which was to be noted in most bourgeois and upper-class societies of

❉ Beppina and the Kitchens of Arezzo ❉

Beppina's period all over Europe, there was also, as we have observed, a strong down-to-earth feeling for moderation or parsimony in the Tuscan kitchen. Recipes for the using up of *avanzi*, leftover food, were also published in the newspapers and Artusi gives many in his book as does Beppina in her handwritten collection of receipts. One of Artusi's friends and correspondents, also a companion at epicurean dinners, was Olindo Guerrini, better known in his day by his pen name Stecchetti, under which he wrote clever social commentary in an anti-conformist manner in the dialect of his native Romagna. He was librarian at the University of Bologna and also had an interest in the history of food, transcribing and publishing rare manuscripts on the subject (see pages 74–5). However, his chief interest to us at this point is his remarkable book, sadly only published after his death, entitled *L'arte di utilizzare gli avanzi della mensa* – the art of using leftovers from the table – in which his collection of delicate recipes, written perhaps with a gentle irony, rather belie their seemingly utilitarian provenance. He gives several versions of the ubiquitous *polpettone*, and *polpette*, meat loaves and meat balls, which were recommended ways of using up leftover pieces of boiled or roasted meat. Today, one of our Aretine neighbours, still recalls her family recipe for *polpette* which, however, were made to be given to the less fortunate.

At this point we should remember that in Arezzo and other Italian cities of the period, as well as Britain and Europe at large, the poor were in the majority and had great difficulty in obtaining sufficient nourishment for themselves and their families. The contrast between the menus of the well-to-do and the food found on the tables of the poor was immense. For example, here is a menu for Christmas at Osborne, the country retreat of Queen Victoria. As in the Italy of the late nineteenth century, the courses are expressed in a strange mixture of languages, in this case English with French, Pudding de Cabinet being a prime example!

❋ Chapter One – Finding Beppina ❋

Purée of Celery à la Crème
Cream of Rice à l'Indienne
Purée of Pheasant à la Chasseur

❋

Soles Frites, Sauce aux Anchois

❋

Woodcocks à la Robert
Quenelles of Fowls à l'essence
Salmi of Widgeon à la Bigamade
Border of Rice garnished with a purée of Pheasants

❋

Filet de Boeuf
Roast Turkey à la Périgord
Roast Goose à l'Anglaise

❋

Faisons
Gelinottes

❋

Plum-pudding
Mince-pies à l'Anglaise
Pudding à la Gotha
Pudding de Cabinet
Nougats de Pommes
Tourte de Pommes à la Cobourg
Gelée de Citron

❋

On the sideboard:
Boar's Head
Baron of Beef
Woodcock Pie

❋

WINES
Sherry or Amontillado
Dry white wines
Champagne and Moselle
Burgundy and Bordeaux
Malmsey, Madeira
Liqueurs
Port, sherry, Madeira, claret

(Balmoral whisky and Apollinaris for the use of her Majesty, who takes nothing else.)

Menu from *The St James's Gazette*, 24th December 1895.

✻ Beppina and the Kitchens of Arezzo ✻

In contrast, here is one of Artusi's luncheon menus for the month of August, aimed at his middle- and upper-middle-class readers:

Minestra in brodo. Zuppa regina n. 39 (Chicken soup)

Lesso. Arigusta con salsa maionese n. 476 (Lobster with mayonnaise)

Umido. Petti di pollo alla saute n. 269 (Sautéed chicken breast)

Erbaggi. Sformato di zucchini n. 451 (Zucchini flan)

Arrosto. Anatra domestica, Piccioni e insalata
(Duck, pigeon and salad)

Dolci. Pesche ripiene n. 697 (Stuffed peaches)
Gelato di lampone n. 756 (Raspberry ice cream)

Frutta e formaggio, popone, fichi ed altre frutti di stagione
(Fruit and cheese, melon, figs and other seasonal fruit)

There are indeed menus for the numerous European poor, but these are to be found in the charitable *mense* which in some cities were organised for the unfortunate. The following excerpt from *A Plain Cookery Book for the Working Classes*, published in 1861 and written by Charles Elmé Francatelli, a high-society chef and, for a brief period, chief cook to Queen Victoria, may be instructive. Francatelli in his little book was addressing 'the working classes', in this particular case, rural families with access to a small garden:

Recipe No. 90 Economical Vegetable Pottage
In France, and also in many parts of Europe, the poorer classes but very seldom taste meat in any form; the chief part of their scanty food consists of bread, vegetables, and more especially of their soup, which is mostly, if

Chapter One – Finding Beppina

not entirely made of vegetables, or as is customary on the southern coasts of France, Italy and Spain, more generally of fish.

The most common as well as the easiest method for making a good mess of cheap and nutritious soup is the following: – If you are five or six in family, put a three gallon pot on the fire rather more than half full of water, add four ounces of butter, pepper and salt, and small sprigs of winter savoury, thyme and parsley; and when this has boiled, throw in any portion or quantity, as may best suit your convenience, of such of the following vegetables as your garden can afford:- Any kind of cabbages cleaned and split, carrots, turnips, parsnips, broad beans, French beans, peas, broccoli, red cabbage, vegetable marrow, young potatoes, a few lettuces, some chervil, and a few sprigs of mint. Allow all this to simmer by the side of the hob for about two hours, and then, after taking up the more considerable portion of the whole vegetables on to a dish, eat one half, or as much as you may require, of the soup with bread in it, and make up your dinner with the whole vegetables and more bread. The remainder will serve for the next day. Let me persuade you, my friends, to try and persevere in adopting this very desirable kind of food, when in your power, for your ordinary fare. I, of course, intend this remark more particularly for the consideration of such of my readers as are or may be located in the country, and who may have a little garden of their own.

However, life for the urban poor midway through the nineteenth century was much crueller. The impoverished in the city had no gardens to grow vegetables nor fireplaces and cauldrons to slowly cook their soup, as this extract from Henry Mayhew's study of the London poor makes very clear:

Of the life of an orphan girl, a street seller [of flowers]
During the summer months, I take 1s. 6d. per day which

is 6d. profit. But I can only sell my flowers five days in the week – Mondays there is no flowers in the market: and of the 6d. a day I pay 3d. for lodging. I get a halfpenny-worth of tea; a halfpenny-worth of sugar; one pound of bread, 1 ½d; butter, halfpence. I never tastes meat but on Sunday [and that provided by her charitable landlady].

Mayhew's flower seller ends her story as follows:

What I shall do in the winter I don't know. In the cold weather last year, when I could get no flowers, I was forced to live on my clothes, I have none left now but what I have on. What I shall do I don't know – I can't bear to think on it.

In the mass of the London poor, many like this orphaned flower seller lived in perpetual poverty and fear, fear of hunger, cold and sickness and the most dreaded misfortune of all, becoming so destitute as to have to go to the Union – or as it is now more commonly known, the Workhouse. The shame of which was bitter, as to enter that establishment meant that one was of no use to anyone, least of all one's self. The menu for many of the unfortunate was simple. Bread washed down with tea made from used tea leaves, which were collected up by unscrupulous grocers, processed and sold again to the impoverished.

In Italy too, charitable arrangements were made for the poverty stricken, often in the shape of public *mense* where meals were served, but a corresponding shame was attached to them as well. In central Italy, bread formed the main portion of the country dwellers' diet and further north there was the far less healthy polenta, made with maize. In Milan, on the 15th December 1883, a public 'soup kitchen' was inaugurated, specifically to counteract pellagra, a disease whose symptoms are dark rashes which become worse when exposed to the sun, diarrhoea, even dementia and finally death. Pellagra affected the poorest in

Chapter One – Finding Beppina

society due to their daily diet being deficient both in quantity and substance. Constructed near the railway station, the Milan soup kitchen was the first enterprise of this sort to be built in the city. The refectory could seat 160 people.

As ever, the underprivileged who lived in the countryside around Arezzo managed better than their counterparts in the town. They, at least, had access to pieces of land on which to grow produce and raise farmyard animals. Since Mediaeval times and on to the slow end of the *mezzadria* (crop-sharing contract) in 1964–74, country dwellers who worked the land owned by Lords or Monasteries, and later the wealthy, were allowed areas around their houses to grow vegetables, the basis of their diet. Francatelli's recipe above for an economical vegetable pottage would not have seemed alien.

For the most part, the country dwellers in Beppina's time ate large quantities of home-baked bread, vegetables grown around the houses, and wild greens like *luppoli*, hop shoots, *vitalba*, briony, and *insalata di campi*, wild salad greens of many varieties such as wild valerian and rocket, plus *funghi* in their season. All of which provided sustenance but very often those, at that period unidentified, vitamins and minerals essential for human health were not contained in much of the food available to the poor. In north and central Italy, where citrus does not grow unless it is protected under glass or in walled gardens during the winter, which is the prerogative of the wealthy, the population had to rely on other fruits and vegetables for an adequate supply of Vitamin C. Where too the staple grain was maize, not wheat, and the system used in the Americas of mixing the maize with alkaline lime water which releases the nicotinic acid content, was unknown, chronic Vitamin B3 deficiencies were common, and as we have seen above, many of the poor thus suffered from pellagra. Added to this, zein, the protein found in maize, does not contain the amino-acid tryptophan out of which the body by itself can make nicotinic acid. To further compound the problem, little meat and few eggs which contain another source of nicotinic acid were eaten by the poorer families. This was because eggs were a precious resource for the impoverished country dwellers as, when sold at market, eggs provided a rare source of ready money which was used to purchase household necessities.

However, for family celebrations and religious feasts, country dwellers did occasionally enjoy poultry, such as chickens and geese, *l'ocio* (as the goose is known in Aretino dialect) being the prized dish at the celebratory grain harvest meal. Beef was eaten rarely, as the great white oxen used to pull the ploughs were treasured work animals and were kept to serve in that capacity for as long as possible. Male calves were sold to city butchers and their meat was bought by the well-to-do of the city, the money raised by the farmers in this way making a most valuable addition to their precarious finances. In fact, the cheapest cuts of boiling beef were the only type of butcher's meat ever afforded by country dwellers and that infrequently. However, there was the pig, killed in the winter months to aid its preservation, which provided both fresh and preserved meat, but this was carefully eked out and merely garnished a family's staple dishes. Not a scrap of the animal was rejected, except perhaps for its toenails, and the housewife's ingenuity went into preparing dishes from parts of the animal now long disregarded. Supper for a numerous country family could consist of large quantities of home-made bread cut into small pieces, which were then dipped into a communal pan containing a '*ntintino*', an Aretine dialect word for a sauce. The sauce could consist of the fat from a few pricked sausages, one for each person, that had been fried in the pan and whose fat and scrapings being deglazed, that is carefully mixed with a little water, with the addition of a sprinkling of salt then made a thin but tasty condiment When no scraps of meat were available, a handful of sage leaves could be slowly fried in a little fat to make another savoury dip for the mainstay of the

Chapter One – Finding Beppina

diet, bread. As in most societies living mainly on plain staples, ingenuity was exercised in creating small amounts of highly flavoured condiments to render basic foodstuffs palatable. Bread when stale was revived with a ladle of broth or when placed at the bottom of a bowl made a *zuppa di pane*, a soup made up of the vegetables grown around the house, similar to that advised by Francatelli.

Bread was also used as a base for *acquacotta*, whose contents were simple – whatever could be foraged and cooked in water – wild *funghi*, birds' eggs, herbs; a seminal dish, it is said, of shepherds during the process of transhumance when they walked with their sheep and cattle across Italy from pasture to distant pasture, from the Casentino Valley, in the instance of Arezzo, to the Maremma. But the ancient activity of transhumance and the food associated with it should not be romanticised. Leaving their mountain homes in September and walking to the far distant western coast, where they spent the winter so that their animals could graze, was a hard, difficult life and not less so for their families who were left alone for months in the icy winter mountains. It was only in May, when the danger of contracting malaria became imminent as the temperature rose and mosquitoes began to appear that the shepherds could return to their homes, traversing the rough road gouged out over centuries by cattle and the wheels of the carts that had carried their meagre supplies. One of their songs fiercely castigates the Maremma:

> Everybody says Maremma, Maremma but to me it seems a bitter place, the bird who goes there loses his feathers and I have lost a person dear to me. Everyone says Maremma, Maremma, but curses be on you, Tuscan Maremma. (*Tutti dicono Maremma Maremma a me mi pare una Maremma amara, l'uccello che ci va perde la penna, io c'i ho perduto una persona cara. Tutti dicon Maremma Maremma sia maledetta Maremma Toscana.*)

❋ Beppina and the Kitchens of Arezzo ❋

In a similar manner to the shepherds, the woodsmen and the *carbonai*, charcoal burners, worked in the forests and rarely visited home for provisions. The supplies they took with them to the wilderness were invariably bread which when stale and rock hard could be revived with water; oil, some hard cheese and perhaps strings of onions, which gave flavour and would keep for long periods of time.

The fundamental characteristic dishes of Arezzo and its Province can be divided into three distinct groups. Firstly, those, like *acquacotta, maccheroni co'l'ocio, carline* or *gobbi fritti*, fried wild thistle or fried cardoon, and various simple dishes made from the carcasses and produce of farmyard animals, wild fruits and greens, eels and frogs, come from the land surrounding the city: the land which for millennia had sustained the city dwellers.

Secondly, there are the dishes which originate in the city and are the products of low level commerce. For the numerous city poor, there were public butcher shops; in Arezzo there was one in the Via Bicchieraia where horsemeat was sold, the flesh sometimes coming from a carriage horse that had been injured in an accident then taken to be butchered in the old slaughterhouse in the Via Porta Buia. Here too could be bought for very little, *grifi*, the muzzles of cows or pigs, which when cooked slowly have an excellent flavour and provide much nutriment. Then there were *nervi*, cartilage and tendons, which form the basis of another of the characteristic dishes of the city. *Trippa*, too, tripe, whether it was white or *lampredotto*, the darker variety of the cow's second stomach, was utilised. All these made nutritious and economical dishes for families.

Paradoxically, many of these '*piatti poveri*' are now greatly appreciated at the tables of the well-to-do and are also served in the more traditional of the city's restaurants. For instance, *insalata di campo*, a collection of edible wild salad plants, is

Chapter One – Finding Beppina

now the most expensive salad to be purchased in the city greengroceries. What once was by many considered to be the food of the poor is now seen as redolent of local culture and of historical importance. And to support these latter observations is the fact that the '*piatti poveri*' are in themselves delicious. The exquisite qualities of wild salad have been appreciated by wise Aretines for centuries. A witness to this is a letter written by Pietro Aretino on the subject of one of his favourite foods.

To A. M. Girolamo Sarra, Venice, November 4th 1532

As soon, my brother, as your gifts of salad became less I was driven to imagine, to guess, to divine the reason for your keeping back your usual gifts of that food which is to my taste. But if I had squeezed my thoughts in an olive press it would never have occurred to me that you had ceased to bring me those provisions because of the *erba cedronella*, lemon balm, which you find so delightful to your palate and I find so disagreeable to mine.

Who can say from whence quarrels come – they even come from two rows of that plant which you can't stop yourself from sending me and I can't stop throwing away. What the devil would one of those who drinks no wine and eats no melons do when someone takes away gifts from a good companion at the behest of an orange-coloured dame who rampages through all gardens? Surely she must have cast a spell on you and left you in the arms of a witch or a Sibyl from whom you are taking orders. Alas, I shall have to become used to the loss, and I hope I can do so, after all I became accustomed to being without a penny, though that is different from opening one's mouth and swallowing a joke. But I will get used to it.

Please return to sending me those things that your goodness and courtesy has impelled you to do. I enjoy the fruits that come from the seeds sown in March in the soft earth for the amusement of the merchants who sell them.

❋ Beppina and the Kitchens of Arezzo ❋

Ask the illustrious Fortunio and the servant who fetches them what pleasure I receive, what praises I give and what a welcome I extend to the mixed salads you send me.

I perceive how you temper the bite of some salad greens with the sweetness of others. And it is not a simple task to know how to mitigate the bitter and sharp taste of some leaves with the flavour of others which are neither bitter nor tart, thus making an agreeable mixture that satisfies the palate. The blossoms sprinkled amongst the fine leaves whet my appetite and with their beauty tempt me to smell their perfume and touch them...

...I cannot remember which pedant made a face at one of the salads you sent me and started to laud lettuce and endive which have no flavour at all, he ranted on until Priapus the god of gardens become so cross that he thought of brutally kicking him out, because a fistful of wild radicchio together with a little *nepitella* is worth more than any domestic lettuce or endive could ever be...

And to finish I say that the good memory of the cedronella was diminished because there was too much of it. So let tomorrow be the first day when I can again enter into the pleasures of your garden. But avoid the deadly rue because when I come upon a salad that has been well sprinkled with oil and then doused in vinegar fit to melt stone I will rebel at the smell of it.

As we have observed above, just because a dish has humble origins does not mean to say that it is unappetising or unworthy of a place on the grandest of tables. This puts one in mind of the old Tuscan saying in which the landowner is urged not to tell the *contadino* how good the *pecorino* cheese tastes with a pear; the riposte being, the *contadino* is no fool, he already knows. And here again we can refer to the wit of Pietro Aretino with reference to the wisdom of country people. In a letter to Federigo Padovano, he describes the following scene:

❋ Chapter One – Finding Beppina ❋

To Al Federigo del Padovano. Letter 639 Book 5

I must write, my dearly loved one, that the two *pan pepati*, spiced breads, were beautiful and good, and when I broke off several mouthfuls, I started to laugh fit to break my jaw and so not to appear to have lost my mind I had to explain the cause for my laughter thus.

A *contadino* in Arezzo was permitted a place at the foot of the table of he who employed him, and there were served, one after the other, ever more delicious dishes. After modestly tasting each one there appeared before the happy countryman some *panunto*. At the other end of the table the grander guests were roaring with laughter at the amazement of the rustic fellow and they asked him if he liked the delicacy of the flavour. But to defend himself from their laughter the clever peasant said the following. "Leave me this dark bread if you please, because we do not eat white bread in the country." Regarding food the rustic philosopher had the wit and sarcasm to defend himself worthily... March, in Venice. MDLII.

To make the countryman's witticism clearer it should be borne in mind that at that period and indeed until surprisingly recently (the mid-nineteenth century in the UK) white bread was reserved for the tables of the nobility and then the well-to-do and rough brown bread was eaten solely by the lower classes. In this case, however, the *panunto* was a slice of the aristocratic white bread which had been darkened by toasting then frying in butter and afterwards exalted with the addition of fresh cheese, butter, rose water and spices. No fool he, the Aretino *contadino*!

And to return to the notion of the excellence of pears eaten with good *pecorino*, beautiful fleshy sweet pears have for centuries been appreciated by Aretines of all walks of life from country dwellers to Grand Dukes as witnessed here in the day book of

✳ Beppina and the Kitchens of Arezzo ✳

Francesco Redi for the 15th of November 1693:

> I record here that my brother *Balì* Giovanni Battista Redi, sent me from Arezzo, as usual, pears to give to the Most Serene Grand Duke, I did so and they were pears grown from grafts which in some years the most Serene Grand Duke had given me. When the coachman returned to Arezzo, I sent with him, for use in the Villa of the Gardens, four very large and very beautiful plates of Savona ware, two salvers of similar ware and a very beautiful Savona ware basin.

In the nineteenth-century city, however, life was certainly harder. For many, finding their daily bread was a continuous struggle. In spite of the prosperity produced by the arrival of the railway and the industry that came with it, Arezzo was still heavily dependent on agriculture. Apart from farming, viticulture and the production of olives, the main industries were the raising of silk worms and the preparation of silk, the weaving of linen and hemp, this done by outworkers, usually female, who had their own looms. There were tanneries with their accompanying foul smell, hat makers, dye works and printers too. Not to be forgotten was the pasta factory of Vincenzo Silei outside the Porta Santo Spirito who with a steam engine produced seven *quintali* – a *quintali* was equal to a hundred kilos – of pasta a day. Until 1875 Arezzo had its own brewery, making beer, seltzer water and fizzy pop.

The Fonderia Bastanzetti opened in Arezzo in 1889, a branch of a company which operated in Udine. They installed themselves near the bastion of the ancient Porta Buia and cast ornamental items in bronze such as medallions for the Vatican, vases and beautifully decorated church bells. In iron they produced equipment for pressing grapes and olives, distilling, and various tools for farmers. They also manufactured what was to become an essential of the domestic kitchen – the *cucina economica*. A wood or coal fired cast iron stove for institutional and eventually domestic use. In 1890, for the first time in Arezzo, Bastanzetti made massive kitchen stoves, their first went to the Collegio S. Caterina of Arezzo, then others to the Bishop's Seminary, the Convent of Sargiano and also to the girls' school of San Andrea, in Bibbiena. Stoves for domestic kitchens were to follow in the early years of the new century.

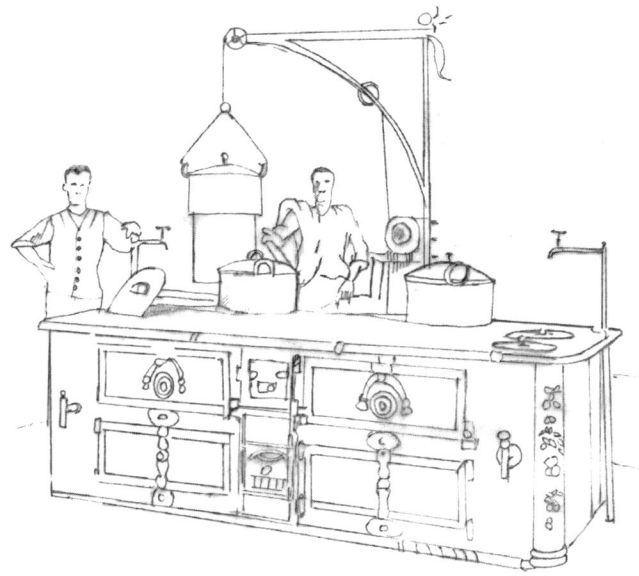

A 'cucina economica' cast and assembled in 1890 by the Arezzo foundry of Bastanzetti for the kitchen of the Convitta – the boarding school – of Santa Caterina.

In 1898, an ice factory was opened in Arezzo, the second one in all of Tuscany. Ice collected in the winter months had been conserved by the traditional method of placing it in an ice house. A method, however, which left something to be desired as far as hygiene was concerned. At that period before the advent of the domestic refrigerator, adequate food conservation was a constant preoccupation. Bottles were kept cool by burying them in buckets of damp sand which was in turn covered with salt, and fresh milk was scalded to prevent it becoming sour in the summer's heat. Initially, Arezzo's ice factory made use of various gases and compressors in a valiant but not always victorious attempt to provide a clean supply of ice for domestic purposes. However, by the turn of the century, technological problems were solved and the factory continued its work successfully. The ice was purveyed in large blocks and kept in ice boxes and cellars. It was not until the 1930s that the now indispensable domestic refrigerator made its first appearance in, to begin with, the kitchens of the well-to-do.

In spite of these diverse industries and activities, it seems that there was still unemployment in Arezzo, but had jobs been for the taking, finger-wagging contemporary journalists complained that there was a tendency amongst the poor to indolence and drunkenness; beggars both professional and those who were genuinely unfortunate were attracted to the city streets and there are press reports that they were sometimes aggressive and turbulent. Arezzo, in a determined effort to feed the poor, organised a public kitchen. The *Società per le Cucine Economiche* was installed in the Via Tolletta in 1891, incidentally, the same year in which Artusi first published his cookery book. In this city which had strong republican and anti-clerical tendencies, the new society was not the traditional charitable work organised by the church and the monastic orders, which latter, in addition to Napoleon's attentions, had been further suppressed in 1866, but was a lay organisation supported by several groups such as the Workers' Society, the *Fraternità dei Laici*, a truly ancient charitable organisation founded in 1262 which still exists in Arezzo to this day, the Bank of Italy, the city council and also private individuals. Perhaps Beppina was one of the people who contributed to the expense involved? The kitchen was open from the 1st of December to the end of April and served nearly four thousand meals a month, at a cost of ten *centesimi* each, or in some cases without charge. The meals consisted

Chapter One – Finding Beppina

of a *minestra* or *pastasciutta*, then meat or fish, pulses, as much bread as was wanted, and wine. A menu which was both varied and nourishing.

Finally, the third group of traditional Aretine recipes are those employed in the kitchens of the *benestante*, the households of noble Aretine families and the *borghesia*, and they stem from both city *palazzi* and country estates. Beppina's recipes come in this third category and contrast sharply with the meagre, although often flavoursome, food of the poor. One of her preoccupations was to find new ways of exalting expensive cuts of veal and beef, using spices, conserves, egg and lemon sauces, milk and cream, to be accompanied by intricately prepared vegetable dishes. Included in this third group of traditional recipes are those that have emerged from town records and literature and whose uses are the result of antiquarian tastes and, sometimes, political motivation.

Beppina's Recipes

The majority of Beppina's recipes are for meat dishes suitable for serving to dinner guests, using expensive cuts of meat, and they largely employ the *arrosto morto* method of cooking. Roasted meat had traditionally been cooked on a spit over or in front of an open fire, and in this manner the meat was in frequent, if not constant, movement. However, *arrosto morto* remains motionless, or dead in its pan. The method used in Beppina's time and also today involves rolling and tying the meat into shape, heating a little butter and/or olive oil in a large casserole or pan, then placing the meat in the pan and allowing it to seal and brown on all sides in the hot oil before adding a very small amount of meat broth to prevent the joint drying out and adhering to the casserole. The pan is covered and left on a very low flame to cook gently, the cook checking at intervals to be sure that the liquid has not completely evaporated. The meat is best salted when it is halfway cooked. This basic method was embellished with various additions, such as a glass of wine, a little vinegar, cream or milk, tomato, and diverse herbs and spices. The small sauce produced in the pan from the meat juices plus the additional ingredients, was collected and served sprinkled over slices of the meat. As Artusi observed, whilst meat roasted in this manner does not have the scent and flavour of meat roasted over an open flame, it is more tender and delicate.

Some of Beppina's meat recipes are for more domestic or possibly charitable use, but there are none for preparing offal. However, as we shall see in the next chapter, offal was not disdained at grand Baroque period tables and is still prepared today in traditional kitchens and the results greatly appreciated. Beppina also collected recipes for cakes and biscuits, intended to be served to callers together with liqueurs and Vin Santo, an important tradition which still survives in both town and country.

Amongst Beppina's recipes there are vegetable dishes which express the fashion at that period for flans and *sformati*, moulds. These *sformati* are still regarded as favourites on the Aretine table and serve to demonstrate the skill of the cook. Beppina also kept a recipe for preserving tomatoes, which warns of the need for care in case the fruit should ferment. Tomatoes even at that date were still not as ubiquitous in Italy as they are now and emphasis was laid on their successful and safe conservation. Recipes for making household necessities such as soap also appear, an activity that today not many people would contemplate.

I have translated Beppina's recipes in the spirit in which they were written, without putting them into a modern form and giving the modern equivalents of timing and quantity. Beppina uses ounces and pounds, *oncia* and *libbra* as measures, as well as kilos and grams, sometimes using both systems in the same

❋ Chapter One – Finding Beppina ❋

recipe. In Tuscany at the period in which she was writing, in spite of the Napoleonic introduction of the metric system in 1813, the *libbra* (which usually in Tuscany weighed about 317 gms) and the *oncia* (which was a twelfth part of the *libbra*, that is around 26.4 gms) were still commonly used as a system of measurement. Weights and measures in Italy before the gathering together of the various city states and kingdoms had since early times not been uniform and universal and it is common to see on the walls of many ancient Italian *Comune* buildings examples of their own specific measurements and the required sizes of such things as roof tiles. Beppina used other more esoteric measures too, such as how much of a certain ingredient could be bought, for example, for ten *centesimi*. Very often, she does not specify quantities unless they are vital for the success of the dish. The idea of combining this with that or using a new method is sufficient to remind her of the essence of the new recipe.

Where I have made an explanatory comment I have used squared parentheses [ ], but when the parentheses are part of Beppina's recipe I have employed the curved variety ( ).

Sformato di Tafacche
(Signor Tafacche's Potato and Parmesan Flan)

This recipe for a rich *sformato* is the one that reveals Beppina's name. It was written by Signor Tafacche himself, and has a lively, slightly flirtatious air about it. He is following, it seems, albeit modestly, in the footsteps of that other citizen of Arezzo, Pietro Aretino.

> As to the quantity, dear Beppina, decide it for yourself…
> Peel the potatoes and boil them in salted water, as soon as they are cooked pass them through a sieve then season them with salt, pepper, Parmesan and a little béchamel if you like it, egg yolks two or three. Serve it with a little

sauce that you have made specially, in that way it will be delicious. Remember to butter the mould and sprinkle it with breadcrumbs, cook it in the *bagna maria*. For the accompanying dish all you need is a good appetite and a beautiful woman to serve you at table…

And that, dear Beppina is all.

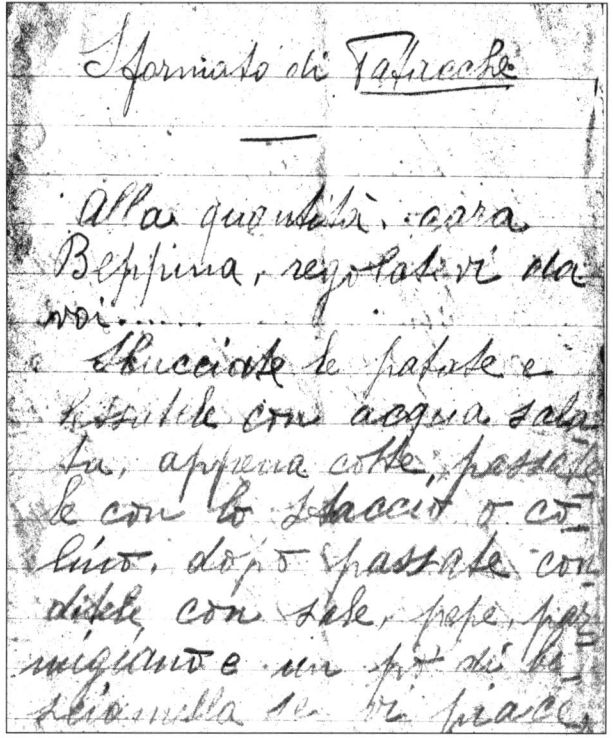

This is the recipe that introduces us to Beppina: 'Sformato di Tafacche' (Mr Tafacche's Flan).

Vitello in Fricandò (Veal Fricassé)

Milanese Dishes. At the Toniolo residence of dearest memory in the year 1915. The Cook P.D. (*Cuccini Milanesi, Casa Toniolo di carissimo ricordo, anno 1915. La Cuoca P.D.*)

Put the veal in a pan or casserole with butter and an

❈ Chapter One – Finding Beppina ❈

onion cut in half. Cover the pan and let the meat cook for 1 ½ hours being careful to add a little water in case the meat dries out. When it is cooked, cut into slices and arrange them carefully on a serving dish and pour over it the following sauce. Mix together an egg yolk with the juice of one lemon, pour this into the boiling liquid in the casserole being careful to stir it around and then pour it immediately over the veal. Serve hot.

Although the first two recipes given in this group come from Milan – so it's not surprising that they include butter – Beppina uses butter in a great many of her dishes and this rather belies the idea that Tuscan cookery has invariably relied upon olive oil. On the other hand, the Aretine journalist, cookery historian and writer Guido Gianni stated in his works about the food of Arezzo that butter was never at home in the city, so Beppina's inclusion of it in her recipes might indicate the middle-class curiosity of her period about all things foreign. At that time, butter would have been made in a wooden churn. These churns, as opposed to metal ones, were difficult to clean thoroughly and traces of rancid fat impregnated the wood, radically altering the flavour of the butter. *Burro di zangola* was until recently to be found in Arezzo; it has a faint flavour of cheese and dishes cooked with it taste completely different to those cooked with the sweet butter to which we are accustomed today. The flavour gives a strong impression of being from a different age, although it is not unpleasant.

Scaloppe alla Milanese

This recipe is also from Milan, but is not contained on the sheet of recipes from the Toniolo residence.

Cut some slices of veal, flour them and put them into a pan with butter letting them take on colour on both sides, then bathe them with some Marsala turning the slices frequently until the liquid has evaporated. Next add half a glass of stock or less if you are using *sugo di carne* [a concentrated meat essence], let the slices cook until the juice has almost gone.

VITELLO ALLA SCHNITZEL
(VEAL IN THE MANNER OF SCHNITZEL)

This is not a flattened schnitzel but a large piece of veal covered in egg and breadcrumbs and cooked slowly.

Salt the piece of veal well on both sides and dip it first into beaten egg then into breadcrumbs then seal it on all sides in a pan in which you have melted some butter. Cook the meat slowly with the pan covered adding a little water a bit at a time. Half an hour before it is cooked add half a glass of vinegar and the juice of a lemon and finish the cooking. Cut the meat into slices and arrange on a serving dish. Over this pour the boiling pan juices.

FRICANDÒ

As an additional note to this recipe, to make the *soffritto* – the base for many Italian sauces – chop the onion and garlic finely and gently fry the mixture in some oil in a casserole.

Take a piece of lean beef preferably *girello* [a cut from the leg], lard it here and there with pieces of *prosciutto*, then make a *soffritto* of garlic and onion chopped up very finely. Lay the meat on this together with salt and pepper and spices, a glass of wine, two glasses of water and a very small amount of tomato conserve. Cover the pan and let it cook very gently until the meat is done, remember that there should remain a little sauce to serve with the meat.

Chapter One – Finding Beppina

Bragioline con Salsa (Cutlets with Sauce)

This rather enigmatic recipe with the word *salsa* – sauce – in the title, might mean that one should beat up the eggs and seasonings, then dip the cutlets into the mixture and proceed to fry them, adding the butter and tomato to the pan to make a light sauce.

> Take the meat from the *culaccio*, rump or fillet of beef, and pound it very well. And put two egg yolks and a white of egg, pepper and salt and Parmesan, fry the cutlets and then throw in some tomato and butter.

Bracioline Buonissime (Excellent Chops)

> Take a piece of butter and a tablespoon of white flour [put the butter into a pan, let it melt then stir in the flour], when this mixture has taken on a good colour add two anchovies and seven or eight juniper berries, a piece of lemon peel and the juice of half a lemon and put the chops into this little sauce to cook, adding a little broth or water as you like until they are done.

Bracioline alla Cacciatora (Hunters' Chops according to Beppina)

> Take a clove of garlic, sage, oil, pepper and salt, and the chops. Let them fry a little then add a little tomato and leave them until they are done. Then, take some slices of toasted and lightly buttered bread, place the chops and their sauce over these and serve it up at table.

This recipe is written in a bold copperplate hand. As in most recipes of the period, except when baking is concerned, no quantities or timings are given and the method is sketched in. It is assumed that the cook knows his or her business. Beppina's version of this well-known dish has a much lighter hand with the garlic, and relying on the sage and tomato to exalt the flavour of the pork does not employ the *odori* or the fennel seed used in the more modern recipe on page 245.

Manzo alla Moda (Beef a la Mode)

Cook two unpeeled cloves of garlic in a piece of butter until they take on a good colour. Then take a piece of lean beef, sprinkle it with salt, then let it take on colour in the casserole with the butter, then when it is well sealed add some *conserva* or tomato sauce (which is better) and some broth, then let it cook. Add a spoonful of flour and a glass of Marsala ten minutes before serving.

'Manzo alla Moda' (Beef Stew with Marsala Wine), from Beppina's collection of handwritten recipes.

Chapter One – Finding Beppina

Manzo alla California
(Beppina's Beef California)

This is Beppina's version of a very interesting dish. One might suppose from the name that it originated in the United States, but it is actually a Lombard recipe coming from a large dairy farm situated in a *frazione* of Lesmo near Brianza, the name of the *frazione* is California. It is possible that the area was so called because it had been named by an Italian emigrant to America who had returned to Italy; the dish, however is solidly Lombard and employs the milk products of the farm. Beppina uses cloves and nutmeg to spice the beef but at the end adds milk, not the cream given in Pellegrino Artusi's recipe for *Bue alla California* (see subsequent recipe).

> Take a piece of lean beef, flatten it and prick it, dusting it with salt. In a casserole put one tablespoon of white flour and about 2 oz of butter, when this has taken on a good golden colour put in the meat together with half an onion stuck with cloves if you like them, a pinch of nutmeg and a coffee cup full of vinegar. After three-quarters of an hour add a little broth to help the meat cook and after this a glass of milk, let it cook slowly until the sauce is condensed – an exquisite dish although it might not seem so with vinegar and milk together.

Bue Alla California secondo Artusi
(Artusi's Beef California)

Artusi found the name of this recipe peculiar and in his book made one of his testy remarks about it – 'nearly all culinary terms are strange or ridiculous'.

> Put 1 ½ lb of lean beef or veal onto the fire with butter, half an onion cut into four pieces and a chopped carrot.

Season with salt and pepper. When the meat is a good colour pour in the vinegar, 1 tablespoon if the vinegar is strong 2 if it is weak. [NB vinegar in those days was not the mass-produced product to which we are accustomed today. Many people made their own vinegar from turned wine plus a piece of 'mother'.] After this add a little water and 4 oz of cream. Simmer very slowly for about 3 hours but be careful not to let the sauce dry out. Add a little water from time to time if necessary. When the meat is done slice it, strain the sauce, pour it over the meat and send it to the table.

An interesting book on the genuine food of the region in Lombardy known as the Brianza, which is titled *Vecchia Brianza in cucina*, written by Ottorina Perna Bozzi and published in 1968, gives another version of *Manzo alla California*. This recipe, although sharing its name with Beppina's version and not Artusi's, has more in common with the latter's, in that it suggests the use of cream instead of milk in order to give a richer sauce and more tender meat. The writer goes on to say, however, that the use of milk was the old *Brianzolo* way of preparing the dish and the idea of the addition of cream came from Milan. So Beppina, it seems, both with the name of the dish and with the use of milk in it, had a more genuine country version of the recipe than did Artusi. Ottorina Perna Bozzi, who was born in 1909, and in 2012 was still living in Milan at the age of 103, gives a vivid portrait of the life and food of that area, which inspired both her and Stendhal, whose words she includes in her book.

Manzo alla California secondo Ottorina Perna Bozzi
(Ottorina Perna Bozzi's Beef California)

One kilo of well matured rump of beef
30 g of *pancetta* to lard the meat
30 g butter
1 sliced onion

Chapter One – Finding Beppina

1 tablespoon of white flour
half a glass of vinegar
half a litre of milk or cream and stock

Cook the onion in the butter until it is golden then add the beef dusted with flour and turn it until it has taken on some colour on all sides. Add the vinegar and bring it to a boil until the liquid has boiled away. Add the stock and half of the cream (or three-quarters of the milk) and cover the pan. Lower the heat and cook slowly for three and a half hours.

All of Beppina's meat dishes demonstrate a judicious use of differing herbs and spices, wine and cream, in order to exalt the piece of meat. Most of the recipes involve long slow cooking on top of the stove, which may have something to do with the quality and tenderness of the meat available even to the well-to-do of the period, on the other hand long slow cooking is arguably the best way to ensure that any large piece of meat remains tender.

In the Aretine kitchen, then and now, we do not often find plain unadorned roasts. Today, a boned loin of pork, still known by its ancient name *arista*, is invariably flavoured with garlic, cloves and nutmeg. My friend Cristina prepares a *rosbif* by first dressing it carefully with garlic, black pepper, rosemary and olive oil. Roast veal is normally served arranged in slices upon a platter and sprinkled with a small sauce made of the pan juices mixed with a little wine.

Cappone in Cazzeruola (Casseroled Capon)

Put the capon into a casserole with an onion, two cloves, carrots and celery, add water to half cover the bird. Then cover the pot with paper and the lid. When the liquid is cooked away let the bird take on some colour and then bathe it with a glass of Marsala. Let it cook for a short while longer if needs be.

❈ Beppina and the Kitchens of Arezzo ❈

This is the only recipe in Beppina's collection for cooking a capon. She did not leave any notes upon the intricate preparation of the famous *Cappone in Galantina* a dish which would most probably have appeared on her table at a grand luncheon party, however, in her copy of Artusi there is this majestic recipe:

Cappone in Galantina (A Capon Galantine)

Artusi writes – 'I will describe to you a Capon Galantine made in my household and which was served to ten people for luncheon; it could have been enough for twenty as when all was done it weighed 1 kilo 500 g / 3 lb 6 oz. When skinned and boned the capon weighed 700 g / 1 lb 9 oz. [...] Then it was filled with the following ingredients.

200 g / 7 oz of lean milk-fed veal, 200 g / 7 oz of lean pork, half a young chicken breast, 100 g / 3.5 oz of pork or bacon fat, 80 g / 3 oz of salted tongue, 40 g / 1.5 oz of lean and fat *prosciutto*, 40 g / 1.5 oz of black truffle, 20 g / 0.75 oz of pistachio nuts.

If you do not have pork you can use turkey breast. The truffles must be cut into pieces the size of a hazel nut and the skins of the pistachio nuts removed with hot water. All the rest of the ingredients should be sliced into fillets slightly smaller than the size of a finger and put to one side, salt the meat.

Take a further 100 g / 3.5 oz of pork and 100 g / 3.5 oz of veal and pulverise it in a mortar with 60 g / 2.2 oz of breadcrumbs soaked in stock; add an egg, the skin of the truffle, the trimmings of the tongue and the *prosciutto*, season it with salt and pepper and when everything is ground fine pass it through a sieve.

Now, open out the boned capon skin [which still contains the breast meat] salt it then start to spread it with a layer of the ground meat, then a layer of the pieces of

❋ Chapter One – Finding Beppina ❋

meat, interlaced in their different sorts [a piece of chicken next to a piece of pork etc.], add pieces of truffle here and there and also the pistachios. Continue thus with a layer of meat mixture and then a layer of pieces of meat until you have used up all the ingredients. Take care that you place the fillets of chicken breast at the tail end of the capon as there will already be enough at the breast end. Now, draw the edges of the capon skin together and sew them up. Tie the carcass lengthways with string. Wrap it up tightly in a cloth which you have taken care to rinse to get rid of the smell of washing soap, tie the ends of the cloth firmly and place the capon in water to boil for two and a half hours. After this take the capon out, unwrap it, wash the cloth then wrap the capon again and put the bird under a heavy weight, breast side up or down and keep it in this position for at least two hours until its shape is flattened.

The water in which the capon was boiled can be used for a broth or to make gelatine.

Galantina is an expensive, time consuming dish to make which also requires considerable skill, not least in boning the chicken. It was served at special festive meals, as clearly it is not something that one would contemplate making every week. Today, many people buy their *galantina* from their *pizzicheria di fiducia*, the delicatessen that they trust. Artusi, nothing if not a practical cook, gives meticulous advice as to the desirability of thoroughly rinsing the cloth used to wrap the chicken to avoid the disagreeable smell of soap which would have ruined the delicate flavour of the galantine (see also page 195).

Carne sotto l'aceto (Beppina's Pickled Meat)

Half a kilo of meat, beef, from the *coscia* [thigh] which must be marinated in vinegar for two hours. Before placing the meat in the vinegar, however, you must lard the meat with small pieces of *prosciutto* wrapped around very small amounts of crushed garlic. You then put the meat into a casserole with some bone marrow, a little butter or oil, but a small quantity, better if it is two drops. Let it cook over a slow fire and when it has taken on colour add a little chopped parsley and a little stock if needed. With the parsley you can add chopped capers, anchovies, or grape juice if you like it.

Polpette di Lesso (Meatballs)

The following recipe is written on the back of a domestic fire insurance policy dated 13th March 1894, addressed to a certain Angiolo Franceschi of Bibbiena. The insurance company is La Fonderia Agenzia Generale di Arezzo.

> Take some leftover boiled meat [presumably hashed with a sharp knife] and fry it with an onion and *odori*. Put the chopped *odori* into a pan with a little oil then when this *soffritto* is golden add the meat and a little tomato. After this step mix in a little grated *cacio*, cheese [probably *pecorino* but *cacio* can also be made of cows' milk], and a small amount of breadcrumbs. Form this mixture into balls. Next you must flour them and throw them into a pan of boiling water for five or six minutes. Scoop the balls out of the water then put them into a dish and sprinkle them with grated Parmesan.

This recipe is written in a different hand, possibly that of a member of the Franceschi family. In the repetition of the instruction to fry the meat with the *odori*, you can observe the writer thinking of the method of the recipe and then amplifying the instructions to make them more understandable and precise. In contrast, here is one of Olindo Guerrini's recipes from his posthumous book on the art of using up leftovers, published

Chapter One – Finding Beppina

in 1918, two years after his death. In the fashion of the period, Guerrini writes in an informal manner with much less detail than is expected today in modern cookery books, which are written for those who have not been taught to cook by the example of their family members.

Polpette di Agnello di Olindo Guerrini
(Olindo Guerrini's Meatballs made with Lamb)

For 350 grams of roast lamb take 50 grams of fat bacon, 50 grams of Bolognese Mortadella. Chop the meats together as finely as you can and put them into a bowl with parsley, a little garlic and dried mushrooms (two spoonfuls) which you have plumped up in warm water, and all of these last ingredients chopped up fine too. Add a handful of grated Parmesan and breadcrumbs soaked in milk and squeezed dry. Adjust the salt and finally mix in two beaten eggs. Form the mixture into a great many little balls, if needed, add a little flour if the paste is too wet and on the other hand, another beaten egg if it is too dry and tends to crumble. Dip the balls into beaten egg and then breadcrumbs and fry them.

Clearly and simply put – and very tempting. Guerrini has exalted the humble meatball with Mortadella and the fine flavour of dried *porcini*.

Polpettone alla Casalinga
(Meatloaf according to Beppina)

Take a pound of lean meat and hash it into tiny pieces then add 100 grams of salami, salt, pepper, and *Droga Toscana* [which is usually a mixture of ground cloves, nutmeg and cinnamon although in this instance Beppina suggests adding nutmeg separately]. Grind all together until the meat is reduced to a pulp. Then add an egg, some grated Parmesan and some breadcrumbs and mix all together. Then shape the mixture into a large *polpetto* the size and shape of a *cotechino* [a rich boiling sausage much favoured at New Year's Eve dinners where it is served with lentils which are said to be symbols of prosperity and have the power to ward off poverty; a *cotechino* is usually about ten to twelve inches long with the circumference of about six inches]. Make a *soffritto* of onion, *odori* [carrot, celery, parsley], frizzle this in oil and when the onion is well golden add some tomato sauce, pepper, salt, nutmeg, then put the *polpetto* into the pan and let it cook very slowly *adagio, adagio* for 2 ½ hours. In the meantime cook some zucchini, potatoes and cabbage which you can then arrange around the *polpetto*.

Beppina uses spices here which are typical of Arezzo and it seems she intends that the meat should be fresh. Much preferable to reheating cooked meat, which unless cooked at a heat of 70 degrees centigrade may present a risk of a type of food poisoning, *Clostridium perfringens* to be precise. As I have mentioned, in these old recipes, quantities are not always given, *q.b.* being the rule, *quanto basta*, as much as is sufficient.

Francesco Gaudentio, also a thrifty cook, has recipes for meatballs and meatloaf in his seventeenth-century manual – three of which are given below – and fundamentally they do not greatly differ from those of Guerrini and Beppina.

Carne Battuta per Farne Riempiture (Chopped Meat for Making Fillings)

From this composition you can make *polpette*, meatballs and *piccatiglio* [a dish of minced not chopped meat flavoured with a sauce of vinegar and spices]; or make pies or use for any other type of fillings that you please. In this stuffing you may put beef from a cow, veal, chicken and similar meats as long as they are not dry. To make either a pie filling or mince meat fry the mixture with lard or chopped *ventresca*, belly of pork, until it is half cooked; then allow it to finish cooking in a little broth, which must not be fatty and when it is cooked add some gooseberries or chopped sour grapes and, shortly before serving, a little egg yolk, sour juice and colour.

Carne Battuta per Farne Polpette (Chopped Meat for Making Meatballs)

You may also make meatballs with the above mixture by adding breadcrumbs, un-matured cheese and eggs. Then make the *polpette* in any form that pleases you, pear shaped or sausage shaped, oval, small or large, as you like. When you have done this, chop up some lard and put it in the pan, when it has melted add the *polpette* and let them fry for half an hour, turning them. Add some boiling broth and let them cook through, lastly mix in some egg yolk [beaten], saffron and mace. Serve them up when they are ready, and you may also add some fresh fennel from the fields which will work well.

Polpettone Grosso (Meatloaf)

You may also [use the above mixture] to make a large *polpettone* and cook it in a pan with the same broth. And with this you can give a slice to each person. Otherwise you may cook it in the oven and then cut it into slices over which you may sprinkle some sugar.

Apart from the sugar and *agreste*, juice of sour grapes, the composition of Gaudentio's meatballs does not differ in any great manner from those of Beppina, Artusi or even our present day recipes. Eggs for binding, spices, grated cheese and breadcrumbs figure in them all.

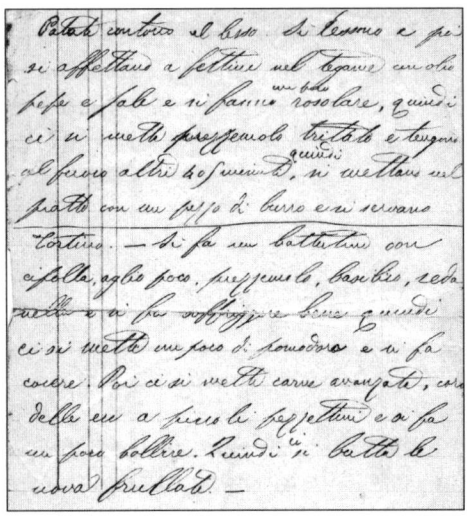

A dish of potatoes and a 'Tortino', from Beppina's collection of handwritten recipes.

Tortino (Beppina's Savoury Pie)

Make a *battuto* with onion, a little garlic, parsley, basil, celery and fry it up well then add a little tomato and let it cook through. Then add little pieces of leftover meat and let them cook thoroughly. At this point add your well beaten eggs.

This seems to be a recipe for a savoury pie. According to my Welsh grandmother's strict rules (and she was an excellent cook), pieces of leftover meat were never to be reheated, however thoroughly, and the inclusion of them in this recipe sounds unappetising. However, if one employs some fresh minced beef or a crumbled Tuscan sausage or two to the *battuto* instead of the leftover meat, it makes a very tasty dish.

✻ Chapter One – Finding Beppina ✻

Uova alle Svedese (Swedish Eggs)

Mash up some anchovies with olive oil and mix this with a little garlic finely chopped up with parsley and some tomato conserve. Put the mixture into a pan and let it simmer. When the anchovies are melted break the eggs into the pan and let them cook through.

Beppina's recipe for 'Frittata Ripiena' (omelette filled with chicken livers and tomato).

Frittata Ripiena (A Filled Omelette)

Take some chopped chicken livers and fry them in a little pan with butter, tomato, pepper and salt. After this, make the *frittata*, spread it with the sauce and roll it up.

Chicken livers have always been a favourite in Arezzo and here Beppina suggests a different way of serving them, as opposed to the usual *crostini* topping which today is the most commonly found use for chicken livers in Tuscany. In this recipe, Beppina once more uses butter instead of the olive oil which is usual today. This recipe makes a very savoury and pretty party dish if the rolled *frittata* is cut into slices and arranged on a dish.

❋ Beppina and the Kitchens of Arezzo ❋

Conserva di Pomodoro (Tomato Conserve)

To make conserve in jars – boil up tomatoes cut up into several pieces for an hour and a quarter. Sieve them afterwards and let the liquid cool then mix the conserve well and pour into the jars adding for every jar of liquid 2.5 g of salt and *sale citrico* [citric acid]. The *sale citrico* must be well dissolved in a glass of the *polpa di pomodoro* then added to the jar mixing it in well.

Nota Bene. The jars should be covered lightly for 5 to 6 days because the conserve ferments easily; after this time add a finger of olive oil as one does with wine and cork the jars well, storing them in a cool place.

Un Piatto di Patate (A Dish of Potatoes)

Boil the potatoes then slice them, put them into a pan with oil, pepper and salt and fry them until they are golden, then add chopped parsley and let them cook for another 40 minutes, then put them onto a plate with a piece of butter and serve them.

It would seem that the potatoes were just parboiled if one takes into account the 40 minutes required to finish the cooking after the parsley was added! Recipes of that period do, however, often stipulate far longer cooking times than we would consider necessary today. This might be because cooking over a wood-fired stove is much slower than over a modern gas or electric stove and requires a different technique.

Minestra di Patate (Beppina's Potato Soup)

Peel some potatoes and put them to boil until tender in some stock. Then [take the potatoes out of the stock with

CHAPTER ONE – FINDING BEPPINA

a slotted spoon and] pass them through a sieve and return them to the same stock. You will need about two potatoes per person. Should the soup be too liquid you can add small pieces of fried bread [croutons]. You can use the same method for Pumpkin Soup.

FAGIOLINI TRIFOLATI
(GREEN BEANS WITH PARMESAN AND EGGS)

Put the green beans in a pan with oil and butter, a little stock or water and salt. When they are cooked, take them off the fire, sprinkle on some grated Parmesan and two beaten eggs. Mix all together well without returning the pan to the heat and serve.

In Beppina's day, it was fashionable at the tables of the middle classes to serve vegetable dishes that were complex in nature. Flans and *sformati* served with various sauces were much appreciated and were a showcase for the skill of the household's cook. In these dishes, the vegetable of choice was first cooked with seasonings and spices then puréed, mixed with béchamel sauce and grated Parmesan, and baked slowly in a *bain marie* in the oven. As Artusi himself says, only the English eat their vegetables with no seasonings at all or at most a small piece of butter, while the people of the South like their vegetables to be honoured. *Sformati* (*forma* is a mould and to *sformare* is to unmould) were served on their own as an entremet or with various boiled meats as an accompaniment. One of the most famous of these dishes, *Sformato di Spinaci con Cibreo*, Spinach Mould with Chicken Liver Sauce, can still be eaten at one of the traditional Arezzo restaurants today, but appearances are deceptive. This particular recipe was put together in the 1950s by the father of a friend who was a celebrated chef of his time. He combined a classic *sformato* with *cibreo*, a sauce of chicken livers which is a genuinely ancient recipe, resulting in a dish of great character.

❋ Beppina and the Kitchens of Arezzo ❋

Budino di fagiolini, di sedani, o di Carciofi
(A Pudding of Green Beans or Celery or Artichokes)

Boil a piece of meat with oil, pepper, salt, onion, garlic and *prosciutto*. Then [par]boil the fresh young beans and when they are sufficiently cooked let them simmer in the broth of the *stracotto* [the meat above]. Next mash the cooked beans up, but, leave a few of them whole to line the mould, being careful to oil the latter well with butter. Having done this take the well pulped and drained beans and mix them with a beaten egg. After [having filled the mould with the mixture], cook it in the *bain marie* until a little crust has formed on the surface; however, take care that the water boils continuously but does not get into the mould.

Flan de Zucchette (Zucchini Flan)

Cook the zucchini cut in half in salted water, drain them then put them through a sieve to make them into a mash, then put them into a pan with a little butter and garlic for a few minutes, add a little spice. After this make a béchamel with 25 g of liquefied butter and 3 tablespoons of white flour, bringing it to a boil with ½ a litre of milk for a quarter of an hour. Then mix the zucchini mixture and the béchamel with some grated Parmesan stirring it all well together. Put the mix into a mould which you have oiled with butter and scattered with breadcrumbs. Cook it in a *bain marie* for 1 ½ hours.

This recipe is a variation on one of Artusi's for *Sformato di Zucchini Passati*, A Mould of Puréed Zucchini (see below). Beppina, however, treats the zucchini in a rather lighter manner. Instead of cooking them in a pan with a *soffritto* of *odori* and olive oil until they are golden, she first simmers the cut-up vegetables in boiling water then finishes them in a pan with a little butter and garlic before puréeing them and adding them to the béchamel.

✳ Chapter One – Finding Beppina ✳

Sformato di Zucchini Passati
(A Mould of Puréed Zucchini)

1 ¼ lb of zucchini, 4 eggs, 3 tablespoons of grated Parmesan cheese.

Make a *battuto* with a quarter of an onion, celery, carrot and parsley. Put it into a pan with oil and when it has taken on colour add the zucchini cut into chunks and seasoned with salt and pepper. When the zucchini are golden add water and cook them until they are tender. Strain off the liquid through a sieve and add the Parmesan and the beaten eggs.

Make a béchamel sauce with 2 oz of butter, 2 spoonfuls of flour and two cups of milk. Mix all the ingredients together and pour the mixture into a circular mould with a hole in the centre. Cook the *sformato* in a *bagno maria*. Tip it out when hot and fill the centre of the mould with a delicate meat stew.

Artusi also gives a good recipe for a *Tortino di Zucchini*, Zucchini Pie.

Cut the zucchini into pieces the size of a nut, brown them in butter and season with salt and pepper. Turn them into a fireproof dish, sprinkle them with Parmesan cheese which you have seasoned with nutmeg and cover them with a thick béchamel sauce. Brown the top lightly and serve as an entrée or with boiled meat or a meat stew.

Here again Artusi provides an element of extra richness by browning the vegetable in oil or butter before covering them with the béchamel. Perhaps Beppina had delicate stomachs to cater for and was inclined towards lighter dishes. Artusi, however, has a nice notion in spicing his *parmigiano*. A bowl of freshly grated Parmesan into which you have stirred a little nutmeg, also freshly grated, is an excellent thing to serve with a cream of pea or zucchini soup.

Salsa (A Sauce)

Take anchovies and a few capers and mash them together in some oil. Then add a little *agreste*, verjuice.

Gelatina Spiritosa (Liqueur Jelly)

One ounce of fish gelatine, a third of which should be red. Two and a half pounds of pure water, four lemons, 8 oz of sugar, *alchérmes* or *rosolio* 10 dl.

Put the fish gelatine and the sugar into the water and boil it until it has reduced by a third. Then take it off the stove and add the juice of the lemons and the *alchérmes*, then stirring all the while pour the liquid into a mould. Place the mould in cold water or ice until the jelly is set. To tip it out, immerse the mould for a moment into hot water.

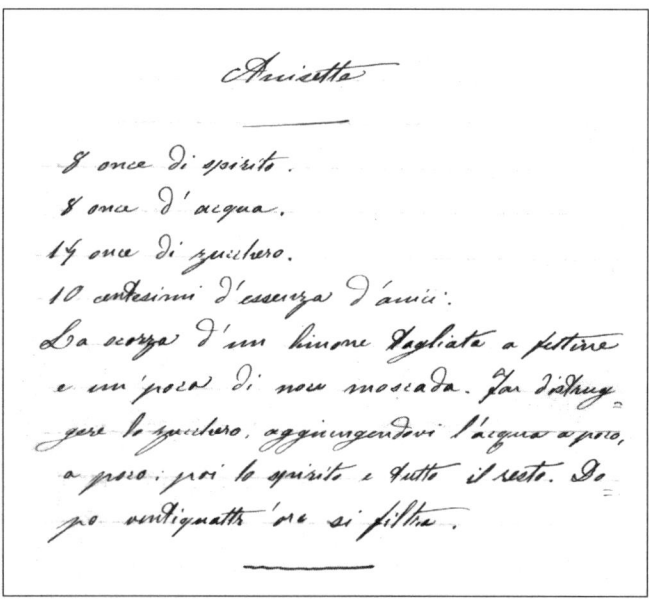

Beppina's recipe for an Anisette Liqueur, to be served with home-made biscuits.

Chapter One – Finding Beppina

Anisette

8 oz of spirit [pure alcohol]
8 oz water
15 oz of sugar
10 *centesimi*'s worth of essence of anise
The peel of one lemon cut into strips and a little nutmeg.

Dissolve the sugar adding the water little by little; then add the spirit and the rest of the ingredients. After 24 hours filter the Anisette.

Here we have another method of measurement – as much essence of anise as could be bought for ten cents! The Anisette was clearly meant to be served to guests with the *Biscottini*, the dainty biscuits made with the recipe below. These biscuits are still enjoyed today in Arezzo and all over Tuscany.

Biscottini

1 lb of flour, 1 lb of almonds, shelled, chopped a little then toasted, 1 lb of sugar. A pinch of bicarbonate of soda, 4 whole eggs and one yolk.

Make a heap of the flour with a dip at the centre, break the eggs into this and mix them gently into the flour with a fork. When this is done add the sugar and the other ingredients and work them together for more than an hour. Eventually on a biscuit tin lightly dusted with flour place the dough [presumably rolled out] which you mark into strips about two fingers wide. Make sure that the dough is supple. Put the biscuits into the oven when you open it the first time after putting the bread in. When the biscuits are cooked break them up along the marked lines then put the separate biscuits into the oven a second time to brown the edges. To make the biscuits shiny whip a white of egg and brush a little on to the dough before putting the biscuits into the oven.

Biscottini (Dainty Biscuits), from Beppina's collection of handwritten recipes.

❋ Chapter One – Finding Beppina ❋

This method of baking is clearly dependent on the experience of the cook and her knowledge of her oven's various and descending heat from the moment when the bread was first placed into it. Pastry is best cooked in a dry heat, that achieved when the damp from the bread dough has been dissipated. Heat was not wasted in European nineteenth-century ovens in whichever country they were, whether they were rural stone ovens built in or against the walls of the houses, or wood or coal fired cast iron ones in town houses. In the Italian countryside, the outside oven was fired once a fortnight to provide sufficient bread for large families until the next baking day. After the bread, meat was cooked in the diminishing heat, then last of all came the drying of figs when they were in season. In England, pastry, puddings and pies were baked in the bread oven's dry and dying heat.

The *cucina economica* was invented during the first half of the 1800s and quickly became of common usage throughout Europe by the end of the century. The following instructions for using such an oven are taken from the Katharina Prato's cookery manual, originally published in Graz, Austria, but translated into Italian in 1901, four years after her death. She had been the widow of a Captain Eduard Pratobevera (hence the pen name Prato), but later married Joseph dei Nobili von Scheiger who was a high official in the Habsburg Empire. Katharina, who in a photograph appears a formidable personage, gathered her recipes on travels throughout the Austro-Hungarian Empire, including northern areas of Italy like the Trentino and Friuli, but, however well placed her friends and associates in diplomatic circles may have been, the book is practical and very thorough. Here is her explanation of how to cook successfully in a wood- or coal-fired kitchen stove; clearly the nature of the beast made the task no automatic, simple matter. After Bastanzetti's introduction of the *cucina economica* into Arezzo in 1890, Beppina may well have had such a stove in her kitchen at around the turn of the century.

✷ Chapter One – Finding Beppina ✷

To roast in the oven or in the small oven of the *focolaio economico* (*Sparherd*).

With experience one learns to know the correct gradations of heat; it is enough to put one's hand for a moment into the oven to judge if the necessary degree of heat has been reached; another method is to place a piece of paper in the oven; if this becomes yellow immediately then the oven is hot enough to bake puff pastry or other types of pastry. If, however, the paper blackens instantly, then the heat is too high for any purpose. In this case one must leave the oven door open and the fire (the source of heat) must be removed. Alternatively you may place some pieces of tile in the oven, allow them to heat through then place whatever is to be cooked on top of them. If the oven's heat is more intense at the bottom than at the top, then place the food on a higher stack of tiles. If the heat is moderate and the paper yellows slowly it is a sign that the oven is suitable for cooking and baking doughs made with yeast or other preparations with fat and eggs. When the oven is of a very low heat and the paper hardly changes its colour, one can bake mixtures made of egg white, which must dry out and stay white [presumably meringues].

In the third edition of her *Cookery and Housekeeping*, published in 1882, Mrs Henry Reeve is even more critical of the household cooking range:

The best grate or hot-plate for cooking purposes has yet to be devised. The old-fashioned open range roasts admirably, but it does everything else very badly. A hot-plate or gas rings, or charcoal fires in a hot-plate must exist in every kitchen where there is to be varied cooking. There must be a boiler for hot water and a baking oven. In France a combination of hot-plate, oven, boiler and

❋ Chapter One – Finding Beppina ❋

open fire is to be seen in the kitchens of all the hotels, presided over in general by the 'Host' who is both landlord and cook, and therefore a judge of the amount of fuel it consumes as well as of the ordinary advantages it offers. This hot-plate is never imbedded in masonry, and is always so placed that the light falls on it, a very important point in frying.

Cooking in Italy, however, was not just confined to domestic ovens! It is said that one of the most delicious Tuscan dishes, *peposo*, was cooked slowly through the night at the kiln doors of potteries in villages surrounding Florence, for example, Impruneta. This meat stew, flavoured with a truly abundant quantity of black peppercorns, was also, it is said, baked at the brick ovens on the site of the Duomo in Florence and was hauled up in a basket to Brunelleschi along with the roof tiles as he supervised the building of the great dome. Whether a culinary myth or not, the very thought of this dish makes the sight of the dome even more enjoyable.

Crostata (A Pastry Tart)

Here we have only the quantities for the pastry, presumably the method was well known to Beppina.

> One pound of flour, half of butter, half of sugar, six egg yolks, one white.

Pan di Caffé (Coffee Pudding)

Take 4 ounces of ground coffee beans and with it make sufficient coffee to fill ten and a half coffee cups [small cups for serving black coffee or espresso]. When the coffee is cold beat eight whole eggs and eight spoons of sugar [stir this mixture into the coffee]. Then butter the mould, pour into it the liquid and cook it in the *bagna maria*.

Torta di Mandorle (Almond Cake)

This charming recipe was clearly written down as it was being dictated. You can almost hear the voice of the speaker as the various steps in the process of making the *Torta* come into her mind.

> Take 450 g of sweet almonds, about 20 or 15 bitter almonds, 450 g of sugar, four eggs. First beat the egg yolks well, then the whites then mix them well together with the almonds. [The almonds must have been crushed although the recipe does not mention this step.] Four ounces of butter [and] for oiling the baking sheet enough to stop the pastry sticking. [Then] Make a little sheet of pastry adding a little egg before rolling it out, a large spoon of sugar and the butter then two glasses of Vin Santo or if you prefer another type of wine like Marsala. [No quantities are given for this part of the recipe.] Then grate the entire peel of one lemon and put a little into the almond paste and a little into the pastry. Spread the pastry over the baking sheet it must be slightly larger than the almond paste which you must spread over the pastry. Inside the *Torta* you can also add some berries to make it pretty, and this is all.

Many of Beppina's dishes are still served in Aretine homes and there is little in her recipes that a present-day cook would find archaic or strange. As I have previously noted, the timings of the recipes are suitable for wood-fired stoves, but in fact many Italians today still choose to use these and they are readily available for purchase. It is probably the case that, as well as writing them down, Beppina passed her recipes on verbally to

Chapter One – Finding Beppina

her daughters, granddaughters and daughters-in-law, as did most Italian women. This is the essential mechanism by which 'traditional' methods of domestic cooking have been transmitted through the centuries. Cookery books became, as we have seen with the example of Pellegrino Artusi, Olindo Guerrini and Giovanni Battista Magi, much more common during the nineteenth century and were directed at middle-class home cooks. The great historic cookery treatises such as Maestro Martino of Como's *Libro de arte coquinaria* (c. 1465), the *Trattato della natura de' cibi et del bere* of Baldassarre Pisanelli (1611), the *Herbario nuovo* of Castore Durante (1585), and Vincenzo Corrado's *Il cuoco galante* (1773), were written by courtiers and professionals who were attached to the households of popes, kings and princes, their instructions are for professional cooks preparing food for the elite.

As we have seen in this chapter, Beppina's style of life and eating was conditioned by her social position, economic status and an Arezzo that was entering a new industrial age. However, Aretine food was in her time – and still remains today – firmly based on a far older tradition springing from the fertile, well-watered land which surrounds the city, a resource that provides both the rural tranquillity and sustenance that have made the region notable for centuries.

✲ Chapter Two ✲

Bishop Tarlati's Soup

> The city of Arezzo is very old, and according to ancient chronicles it was a noble city even before the Romans came to Tuscany. It is situated near the river Arno, which rises in the Casentino over Pratovecchio in a mountain called Falterona; the river Tiber, which flows to Rome, also originates in this mountain. The city of Arezzo is forty miles from Florence, a distance which can be travelled in one day. Its site is strong and well-placed, descending from the hill on which the citadel is located and spreading below onto a plain furnished with many springs of running water. The nearby countryside is flat rather than hilly and possesses more fine land than anywhere else in that region. For there is an abundance of grain, oats and fine game. The town is well-situated and has good air, and it begets men of keen intellect.
>
> Goro Dati, *Istoria di Firenze*

So wrote the Florentine historian, Goro Dati, in the early 1400s. His description is succinct and one can still recognize the present day Aretine landscape in his words.

Today, from the viewpoint of the Medicean wall of 'Il Prato', at the very summit of the hill on which the city of Arezzo was

✳ Beppina and the Kitchens of Arezzo ✳

built, one can overlook the olive groves and vines that still climb up to the Sangallo bastion. Here the townspeople come and watch the evening sky, walk their dogs and enjoy an *aperitivo* bought from the iron bandstand café. Even the ex-citizens are not far away, as to the right there lies the ornate cemetery, which dates from 1667 and was originally built to bury the victims of a plague.

Il Prato ('the meadow') is a good place in which to sit and contemplate the history of Arezzo, a pine-shaded grassy garden between the massive Cathedral and the Fortezza Medicea, a fortress which the Florentines built to better control Arezzo's citizens and which in 2016 was renovated to form a magnificent viewing point for the encircling Aretine landscape. Further down Dati's hill lie the venerable buildings which house the city's ample historical archives. Arezzo, as Dati states, is a very ancient city and its history is complex. The influences and incidents contained within the time span of its existence are immense, and these millennial events have left their marks on the sensibilities of modern Aretines.

Histories are often coloured by the individual writer's political opinions and philosophy – many historians tend to view the past through the lenses of their own spectacles. More than that of any other subject, perhaps culinary history is most beset by imagination, fantasy, folklore, propaganda, and often nationalism, dressed and served up as fact. And why not, one may ask? Food is enjoyable, lighthearted and pleasant; what does it matter if glamorous tales are woven around the history of a particular national dish? We would all choose to present our best face to the world, and fortunate are those who have good reason to be proud of their particular styles of cooking. Yet food and its preparation are a fundamental activity; food preparation and eating is something that links all humans throughout history. 'Tell me what you eat and I will tell you who you are', as Brillat Savarin so perceptively remarked,

Chapter Two – Bishop Tarlati's Soup

although Homer and many other Greek writers had anticipated him by millennia. A lack of sustenance, however, is devastating to society. Starvation, whether the companion of war, the result of weather induced famine, or careless and incompetent government – *carestia* and *miseria*, those words often intoned by long memoried Tuscans – means slow and painful death. The ways in which famine, hunger and abject poverty are coped with and alleviated – or not – are things by which governments are judged. Therefore an objective history of sustenance, and the lack thereof, is to be desired.

In times of plenty, one has to consider various needs and expectations when it comes to sustenance; there is the comfortable food that we eat in the intimacy of our homes, and the more elaborate food that we might offer to guests and prepare for personal celebrations. There is also the sort of food presented at official events, whether provincial, governmental, or international. In this last instance especially, the very best face must be presented to the world. In Italy, the dishes served when heads of state gather are sometimes discussed on television news programmes, and the chefs interviewed.

As we have seen in the previous chapter, the traditional recipes of Arezzo have three main categories: those recipes which emanate from the lives of rural workers; those from the urban poor; and those from the tables of the well-to-do. Amongst the latter are to be found dishes that have both historical and literary roots which on occasion provide even a political dimension to food. As an illustration of the part that food can play in the presentation of the past, the following account concerning the *Giostra del Saracino* ('The Saracen Joust'), and Bishop Tarlati's Soup, shows how in Arezzo food history, politics and pride in the city have, in the near past, been most elaborately expressed.

From the Prato, on the first Sunday in September, one of two such days in the year, one can hear in the distance drums and trumpets and a roaring crowd; the *Giostra del Saracino* is taking place in the Piazza Grande. The flags of the four quarters of the city hang from windows and lamp posts, stalls sell scarves and banners; this festival is cherished as much as the league matches played by the city's football team in their dark wine-coloured jerseys.

If one tries to delve back and disentangle the roots of the *Giostra*, an annual series of jousts far removed from a simple folkloric celebration got up for the entertainment of tourists, they appear to date from the 1200s, as there are documents in the city archives from that period which mention the Aretine taste for jousting. But apart from this vague hint, there is no hard evidence of a specific event at that early period. However, in the Statute of the *Comune* of Arezzo, written in 1327, we find the following description of a race (not a joust), to be held in honour of the Patron Saint of Arezzo:

On the festivities of the Blessed Donato, Martyr, Guiding Light, Bishop and Patron of the City of Arezzo

In honour and reverence of the Blessed Donato, Martyr, Lord and Patron of the City of Arezzo, it is decided that in the City of Arezzo, on the day of the aforesaid festivity, a race must be run for a length of rich cloth and a hawk, according to the following rule, and that is, on the day of the pre-mentioned festival, which is on the 7th of August, the *Podestà* [mayor] must order a length of cloth and a young hawk to be placed at the foot of the stairs of the *Comune* which face the Street of the Pelliceria, in order that the men can, if they so wish, ride their horses, and those amongst the riders who are ahead and arrive first at the place where the cloth is hung, will receive it, and the second who arrives will receive the hawk; the third will receive a young female pig, the fourth, a duck and a string of garlic. All these things must be mounted in that

Chapter Two – Bishop Tarlati's Soup

place on a wooden lance, except the hawk. [Presumably the duck and the pig have been slaughtered and only the hawk is still living, which latter as an aid to hunting, is only of value if alive.]

There is a gap in the records until 1535, when we have documentary evidence that a joust took place on the 6th of August. Again in 1536 and 1556 there are records of two events which were arranged to entertain the Grand Dukes Alessandro and Cosimo Medici when these illustrious gentlemen visited the city. The choice of a Saracen as a target probably initially reflected the Crusades; he was a mythic figure, a worthy adversary, a classic 'bogeyman' with which to frighten children. Later, many Aretines from noble families belonged to the Order of St Stephen, and spent their time fighting piratical Arab ships which continually disturbed the trading vessels of both Venetian and Genoese merchants. These battles again served to put flesh on a set of mythic bones.

Eventually, the joust faded and was merely played out with a stuffed dummy which was attacked by the citizens with sticks and rustic javelins. This doubtless riotous event was suppressed by Napoleon during his occupation of Tuscany. The joust was to reappear for public amusement only in 1904, when a single event was organised to celebrate the six hundredth anniversary of the birth of Petrarch.

The present *Giostra*, a much grander revival in which splendidly accoutred horsemen tilt at the revolving Saracen, who is called Buratto, King of the Indies, dates from 1931. Conte Pier Lodovico Occhini who was *podestà* of Arezzo from 1931 to 1939, was, it is said, a great *urbanista*, a man passionately interested in his city's architectural panorama and who presided over a great deal of new building work, in the way of large blocks of apartments designed in pure 1930s style and also a grand cattle market on the outskirts of the town. He too devoted much energy to the revival of the fourteenth-century glories of Arezzo. To name but a few of his projects, the house of Petrarch was completely transformed, and much Ghibelline swallow-tail crenellation was added to the town hall, and some of the city walls and gateways were also restored in a more elaborate manner. It was in this same spirit that Occhini presided over the revival of the *Giostra del Saracino*, and the Piazza Grande, where the joust was to take place, was transformed into a fitting setting for such an event. The large *palazzi* were restored, their towers rebuilt to near their original heights, and the whole place was re-paved in red brick and fitted out in the mediaeval style.

The merit of all these alterations is still the source of discussion in Arezzo. Some think that they obscure the true ancient nature of Arezzo and the real inheritance of the city. This wish to recreate the era when Arezzo was at the height of its power and led by its greatest citizen, Bishop Tarlati (see below), is, however, typical of the climate of the Fascist period when Mussolini himself put the resources of the state behind massive archaeological projects, and the restoration of Italy's ancient and mediaeval past. He it was who ordered every Italian city to build up any ancient tower that had survived from antiquity and furnish it with bells with which to summon the citizenry on occasions for celebrations. By means of invoking their country's history, the Fascist organisation sought to enthuse and involve Italians in their ambitions for a glorious future for Italy and its planned Empire.

The history of Arezzo too goes some way to explain the desire for a re-evocation of a period when the city was prosperous and successful. In 1384, near the end of Arezzo's 'golden' fourteenth century, the city was bought by Florence and subjugated for centuries. At the close of 1385 all of the Aretine *contado* – the land of its four great valleys, their castles, great houses and fortresses – came under the control of Florentine officials. Much of the city's original mediaeval architecture was brutally

Chapter Two – Bishop Tarlati's Soup

razed to the ground and ruthlessly replaced by the Florentines, in order to make the city easier to control and defend. The ancient cathedral of San Donato at La Pionta outside the city walls was completely destroyed. A hundred and sixty-eight years on, during the later phases of these works of fortification, the Etruscan bronze sculpture of a Chimera, a potent symbol of Arezzo, was unearthed and promptly removed – some say sold – to Florence, where it yet remains. This was a humiliation that rankled, and it is a wound that some *Aretini* still feel deeply, especially those of the quarter of the Porta del Foro, because it was here, beside the town gate, formally called the Porta San Lorentino, that the Chimera was discovered on the 15th of November 1553. Today the quarter's purple-crimson flag bears an image of the mythical beast.

The *Giostra* has, for the sake of the activity itself, become a vital expression of *Aretinità*, the very identity of Arezzo. It is more popular and vigorous than ever, and arouses a deep and genuine emotion among the inhabitants of the various quarters of the city, who cheer their own champions and hurl insults at those of the other quarters with passionate abandon. Historically, the knights who took part in the mediaeval joust were all from the noble families of Arezzo, however, in the 1930s the city was divided into its various quarters by the city authorities and the riders were chosen from among the inhabitants of each *rione*. The target, Buratto the King of the Indies, which revolves when struck by a rider's lance, can give as good as he gets, as attached to his outspread arms there are chains and metal balls which swing around and can unseat a knight too slow to dodge the flailing metal. Judges dressed in mediaeval costume decide the score of each rider by means of an intricate system of rules, and by examining the position of the lance marks on Buratto's targeted chest. The winners, carrying their prize – a golden lance – parade immediately to the Cathedral, where thanksgiving prayers are said, often drowned out by the triumphant shouts of the horsemen and the raucous cheers of their followers. Later a feast, *La Cena della Vittoria*, is held for the riders, officials and the people of the victorious *rione*. It is cooked in the kitchens of the offices of the various quarters where, as tradition dictates, vast quantities of pasta are prepared in giant pans.

Around the year 1931, when, as we have seen above, Arezzo was in the throes of the great renovations in the style of the earlier 1300s, it was reported that a scholar, who happened to be searching in the city archives for documents to aid in the revival of the *Giostra del Saracino*, accidentally came across an ancient recipe that was to become known as *zuppa Tarlati*, Bishop Tarlati's Soup. A timely find if one considers how food is a major expression of culture, and how suitable this grand recipe would have been to serve to the upper echelons at a *Giostra* feast.

The famous chicken soup is known as one of the historic dishes of Arezzo. It has been written that the recipe originated in a noble household of Anghiari, in the Province of Arezzo, before the dawn of the twelfth century, and that it then progressed by way of a last will and testament to the Prior of Camaldoli, from whence it was handed down from one Bishop of Arezzo to the next. In 1312, the great warrior bishop Guido Tarlati was enthroned in Arezzo and naturally, because of his position, one is led to think that the precious recipe came into his possession. Tarlati is probably the most celebrated of Arezzo's citizens. His strength and acute sense of politics made the city powerful and independent in the early 1300s – his reign is seen by many as being the acme of Arezzo's history. At this period, the Papacy resided in Avignon, where Clement V, a Frenchman, had installed it, and his successor, Pope John XXII, had made it into a byword for magnificence, aided no doubt by the many Italian cardinals who resided there. Now the able and ambitious Tarlati, by way of making allies out of Arezzo's old enemies such as Florence and Siena, and strengthening the city walls, felt able to challenge the Pope; raiding the Papal States and even

Chapter Two – Bishop Tarlati's Soup

sequestrating the ample funds of the Franciscans. As a result many a Papal ambassador was sent from Avignon in an attempt to instil decorum and obedience into the rebellious bishop. It has been suggested that the famous soup was prepared for these Papal messengers and having enjoyed his dinner one of them took the recipe back to Avignon in his diplomatic baggage. Now once in France its flavour was much appreciated, but naturally the French cooks decided to gild the Tuscan lily, to elaborate on the original dish and so transform it into *Zuppa all'Avignonese*. The soup's fame spread to the royal court, where it was further improved to become *Crème de Poulet à la Reine*.

Now if this chronicle is true – and it must be said that the whereabouts of the recipe found in *circa* 1931 are obscure – it would mean that the putative influence of Italy upon the cuisine of France started more than two hundred years before the marriage of Catherine de Medici to Henry II in 1533. It is often proposed that, at this date, the French court cooks were influenced by their Italian counterparts, and that French cooking was thereby radically changed – a theory that is still held by many, but which has been discarded by modern food historians. It is now considered that Catherine de Medici, when she became an adult, had more influence on the lavish entertainments that accompanied courtly banquets rather than the food that was served at them.

These romantic, sometimes grandiloquent stories of queens and courts and bishops – however beguiling – often stray from the path of exactitude to linger on the side of imagination, and the creators of these culinary myths are, unsurprisingly, often more concerned with national pride and patriotism. A prime example of this being the story of the Turkish invasion of Vienna leading to the invention of the croissant, a flavoursome device by which the Viennese were able to eat the crescent – the symbol of their enemy! Another more modern example might be the changing of the name of the Italian version of the humble

English trifle from *zuppa inglese* to *zuppa impero*, this during the period of the Ethiopian Campaign, which commenced in 1935. However, the new name did not stick, and the pudding is still listed on countless Trattoria and restaurant menus in Italy as *zuppa inglese*.

What we do know about possible recipes extant in the 1300s, which might serve to narrow the field a little, is that in Livorno in 1899 a scholar by the name of Ludovico Frati published *Libro di cucina del secolo XIV* (A Fourteenth-Century Cookery Book). The volume includes a discussion of research done by two other scholars, Salomone Morpurgo and Olindo Guerrini, on the same subject, and a comparison between certain recipes given in three extant codices: Codex Riccardiano (Florence), Codex Bologna and Codex Casanatense (Rome). All three codices contain versions differing slightly in length and wording of what is most probably the same text. In his book, Frati gives the Codex Casanatense in its entirety. One of the above-mentioned scholars, Olindo Guerrini, who was chief librarian at the University of Bologna, a food historian, author of a cookery book and, as we have seen (see page 46), a great friend of Pellegrino Artusi, dated the earliest fragments of the text to the second half of the 1300s. Bishop Tarlati died in 1327, so at least we are in the right century. Judging by variations in the language used, the three texts were written or copied by a Sienese, a Florentine and a Venetian. Recipe number VI in the Codex Casanatense is for a *Brodo de Polastri* (Chicken Broth). Could this be our soup?

Brodo di Polastri (Chicken Broth)

> If you want to make a chicken broth, take some chickens and boil them up, take peeled almonds and crush them and mix them into the broth, add rose water and verjuice and mix all together. Then take cinnamon, ginger and cloves half crushed and half chopped and put these into the broth and boil all together. When you send it to the

✻ Chapter Two – Bishop Tarlati's Soup ✻

table put the chickens into the broth and make sure that they are good and hot. When you serve it sprinkle some sugar into the soup plates and it will be a good dish.

Zuppa Tarlati does, however, have more things in common with the recipe for the well-known *Bramagere, Blancmanger, Biancomangiare* which is recipe number V in the Codex Casanatense and involves boiling a chicken until the flesh falls off the bones, grinding the flesh into a paste and then mixing it with sugar, ground almonds, rice and spices. The chief purpose and attraction of this dish was that it should be as white as possible, hence its name, *Blancmanger*. A dish fit for royalty – and also for the sick, due to the then considered healing properties of sugar and chicken – it has, however, had a long and intricate history of its own that is difficult to pin down. It was widely known in the fourteenth and fifteenth centuries all over Europe, and it is possible but not provable that the recipe was influenced by mediaeval Arab cuisine.

Probably the most we can say about our elusive soup is that in Tuscany, in the second half of the 1300s, there were written recipes that bore some resemblance to what has been known in Arezzo since the 1930s as *zuppa Tarlati* – the recipe that came to light when the great revival of the *Giostra del Saracino* took place in that decade.

It is a good recipe in all its forms, simple or luxurious, whether the soup really does have a distinguished and complicated history, or whether, as Signora Mazzoni – who, together with her family, owns a splendid *trattoria* and *alimentari* in Arezzo serving beautifully prepared traditional dishes – says, 'Here in Tuscany we have always eaten a lot of chicken and therefore make a lot of chicken soup.' And here we have a perfect illustration of our two sorts of dishes: the simple chicken soup that we would eat at home, made with chicken breast, broth, carrots chopped fine and simmered in butter and served with slices of fried bread (below), followed by the complicated dish with the historic pedigree that we would serve when we wish to impress.

Zuppa di Pollo all'Aretina
(Aretine Chicken Soup in its simplest form)

One plump chicken, one carrot, two ribs of celery, broth as needed, one white onion, a small bunch of parsley, 100 g / 4 oz of unsalted butter, three or four sage leaves, salt.

Wash the chicken and put it whole into a large pot half full of cold broth with one rib of celery and a little salt. Bring gently to the boil and simmer slowly until the meat falls off the carcass.

Take the chicken out of the pot and remove all the meat from the bones being careful to discard all the bits of gristle and cartilage. Tear the chicken into bite size pieces, put the breast meat aside in a little of the liquid to keep it moist and tender. Strain the pan full of broth and let it cool, skim off any fat.

Chop the carrot, celery, onion and parsley together finely. In a clean saucepan melt 50 g / 2 oz of the butter and in it simmer the *battuto* (latter ingredients) until the onion is golden but not brown. Add all the pieces of chicken to the golden *battuto*, stir them around and let them take on the flavours of the vegetables. After a few minutes add the broth and simmer gently together for fifteen minutes. Adjust the salt to your taste.

To be called a *zuppa* in Tuscany, the soup has to be served ladled over a slice of toasted or fried bread. In this case, melt the rest of the butter in a small pan, add the sage leaves and fry slices of stale Tuscan bread until they are golden on both sides. Place one slice of fried bread in the bottom of each bowl then ladle on the hot chicken soup.

Chapter Two – Bishop Tarlati's Soup

Zuppa Tarlati

The recipes for this celebrated Aretine soup differ in their detail, but all of them require the chicken to be twice cooked.

> One chicken of about 1 kilo / 2 lb 2 oz in weight, one onion, five or six cloves, a rib of celery. Enough decent stock, possibly veal stock, to almost cover the chicken in its pot. One large or two small carrots, a small onion, one rib of celery, two small cloves of garlic, 50 g / 2 oz of unsalted butter, half a glass of dry white wine.

> Peel the onion and stud it with the cloves, place this and the stick of celery in the cavity of the chicken. Put the bird in a large pan and add cold stock to almost cover. Bring to the boil gently and then let the bird simmer until the flesh is near falling off the bones. When the chicken is done, remove it from the broth, drain it well and take off the flesh, making sure that all bones and pieces of cartilage are dispensed with. Tear the white meat into strips and put them aside in a little stock to keep them from hardening. Chop the rest of the meat finely into a mush and reserve.*
> Strain the broth well, then set it aside.
>   Take the carrots, the small onion, the celery rib and garlic and chop them very finely together. Melt the butter in a pan and add the *soffritto*, the chopped vegetables. Let them cook through in the butter but do not let them brown or burn. Drain and dry the reserved pieces of chicken breast and turn them in the pan so that they take on the flavours of the vegetables. Next raise the heat and add the half glass of white wine. Let it sizzle and evaporate but again do not let the ingredients become brown as this would spoil the appearance of the soup.
>   Finally, put some of the broth into a clean pan, heat it and add the mushed chicken,** stir it in then add the contents of the pan of chicken breast and finely chopped vegetables.

Stir and let the *zupp*a simmer for about fifteen minutes adding some more stock if the consistency is too thick.

Zuppa di Pollo all'Avignonese

This is our famous Aretino soup gilded by the French cooks at the Papal court at Avignon. Follow the previous recipe but with these additions. The asterisks (*) in the recipe above indicate where the recipe changes.

> * When chopping the chicken into a mush go a step further, put the meat into a mortar and grind it with the pestle until it is reduced to a fine paste. At this point you may also thicken the soup with a roux made from a little flour and butter and some of the stock. This will serve to improve the texture of the soup.

> ** At the last minute before serving add a glass of cream and stir it carefully into the hot but not boiling soup. Just before serving sprinkle on a very little grated nutmeg. Delicious.

As we have seen in this story of Bishop Tarlati's soup, people at times wish to present themselves in a particular light and genuine, sustaining food, redolent of a culture based on the land, can be manipulated into an expression of much more ambitious visions of society. What then can we take from the Arezzo of the 1300s which expresses a practical cultural inheritance, and is witness to the necessity for simple survival? In 1327 the population of Arezzo numbered some 10,000 souls and hunger was commonplace. The city elders thought it wise to decree, in what is known as the Statute of 1327, that all landowners within the walls of the city should make kitchen gardens to provide sustenance in case of siege or famine, and in those gardens they should raise poultry and

Chapter Two – Bishop Tarlati's Soup

pigs. Today, a casual passerby might catch a glimpse of one of Arezzo's secrets, behind the usually closed outer doors and the encircling high walls of the houses of the *centro storico* there still lie many hidden ancient gardens, the finest of which are protected by law from being turned to other uses. Recently, in the gardens of the Via del Orto, the street of the garden, a householder kept a fine cockerel which would crow mightily at a hint of dawn. So assiduous was the bird in his duties that the neighbours complained and eventually the bird was removed. The Priors of 1327 would not have approved!

'Here is November' - a time for turnip gathering, from a thirteenth-century relief in the doorway of Santa Maria della Pieve, Arezzo.

Apart from times of war, famine and pestilence from which Arezzo has suffered through the ages, the indispensable fount of support to the city has always been its surrounding fertile landscape, together with those who toiled in the fields and vineyards. The magnificent main doorway of Arezzo's Romanesque *pieve* (church) celebrates this fact with its immaculately preserved depictions of the activities of each month of the farming year. Here, we see real food grown for sustenance by stocky farmers sowing and harvesting fat turnips and cutting abundant sheaves of corn. Here, too, we see both faces of food coming together – the everyday celebrated as the special.

And to thoroughly illustrate the extreme importance with which both the health and just sustenance of the citizens and the cleanliness of their city were regarded, there is no better source than the Statute of the *Comune* of Arezzo of 1327, the year in which Bishop Tarlati died. The Statute controlled most aspects of the life of the City, and in a wise manner. Here below are some of the rules for the conduct of butchers.

Book 4: 76: Punishments for butchers who disobey the rules of the Statute

All butchers who provide meat to be sold are bound to swear to and observe the rule that they will not kill, singe or skin any beast outside their premises, but will carry out all these aforesaid activities inside, they will not throw away or pour into the earth the blood of animals, and will not throw anything putrid into the street, nor knowingly take spoilt meat or the meat from deceased animals, and sell it, for themselves or for others, in the City of Arezzo within its encircling walls. He who contravenes these rules will be fined ten lire, and anyone can denounce such contraventions, their statements must be taken seriously, and they must be paid half of the fine.

If someone asks a butcher what type of meats he is selling, he must, without lying, inform the enquirer truthfully on the pain of forty *soldi* for each person and on every occasion. No butcher may kill or sell in his shop the flesh of a sow or a *porcastra* a young female wild boar except at the beginning of the Feast of St Andrew (30th November) until the following Friday; however they cannot and must not keep that meat on the same counter as the meat of a male pig, but must keep them divided and separate on the pain of a fine of three *lire*. Anyone can make a denunciation and expect half the

Chapter Two – Bishop Tarlati's Soup

fine. The same rule must be observed for the flesh of bucks (male goats), rams and ewes, which must be kept separate. They must not fill any carcass with air whether from their breath or any other sort, nor introduce any sort of fat into the testicles or in any other part of the animal, under the pain of one hundred *soldi* for every offence.

No butcher, then, must keep meat for more than one day, for the period between the Easter Resurrection and the Feast of St. Michael in the month of September (the 29th), under the pain of twenty *soldi* for each person for every offence. Every butcher must sell each type of meat by weight, except that of kid, lamb, bull and cow. The *podestà* and the tax official must enquire once a week at each butcher's shop about these aforesaid matters to see that the rules have been observed. No butcher, then, must skin donkeys, mules or horses or dogs, and he who disobeys cannot slaughter and must be fined twenty *soldi* for every offence. The butchers must also separate the meat of bucks (he goats) and sheep so that they can be distinguished from the meat of wethers (castrated male lambs/sheep) under the pain of twenty *soldi* for each one on every occasion. The governors or a governor of the butchers are bound by and must possess a copy of this present chapter and have it read to the butchers, on the pain of one hundred *soldi*. These same butchers then, in their dwellings, must not throw away nor clear out anything that will create dirt or an offensive smell for their neighbours, nor must they throw bones or horns onto the street. No butcher nor anyone else must hang the skins of beasts in the streets or the squares nor on the walls of the streets on the pain of twenty *soldi* for every offence, and whoever can make the accusation may receive half the fine. Each and every butcher who exercises the skill must have a balance which can weigh one ounce at the minimum, with which they can sell fresh and salted meat, and it must be of iron or other metal, not made of stone, and stamped with the sign of the *Comune*, and it must be a twelve ounce balance, and with this they may sell in good faith without any fraud, under the pain of a fine of one hundred *soldi* for every person on every occasion. Then, no butcher may keep in the City of Arezzo, in the surrounding hamlets and suburbs, sows, goats, rams or wethers and pigs, except for a pig or pigs which are solely for his own consumption, and he may not keep sheep for that latter purpose. However, butchers must be allowed, with a licence from the *podestà*, to keep, for each butcher that sells meat, up to twelve head of cattle which must be butchered and sold according to their quality and the conditions of the time, and the cattle of every butcher must be pastured separately from, not together with, the cattle of others, under the pain of a fine of forty *soldi* for each one and every time; and the tax men must be allowed to count the beasts out of and into the gates of the city. Any or all of these same butchers cannot and must not in any way keep at the same time on the same counter a pig and a sow, or their flesh, a wether and a sheep, or their flesh, under the pain of forty *soldi* for each one and every time. Whoever on the same day kills and sells a wether, cannot on the same day kill or sell the flesh of a sheep, under the same penalty. The *podestà*'s officials of the offices of the streets and of the laws, must have jurisdiction and authority to enquire into, to proceed and to punish with the force of his office all and every rule contained in this chapter and to have them observed in an inviolable way on every point.

The Statute gives an extraordinarily vivid insight into the lives of the citizens of Arezzo in mediaeval times, and shows the *Comune*'s efforts to protect the citizenry from petty fraud.

Returning to Il Prato, at the summit of Arezzo, from the Medicean ramparts the view eastward reveals some of Arezzo's greatest treasures, soft green hillsides dotted with noble villas.

❋ Chapter Two – Bishop Tarlati's Soup ❋

The architecture tends to the most graceful of the seventeenth and eighteenth centuries, gentle, elegant and reached by tiny lanes that wander through fertile fields, olive groves and vineyards. It is from these hills that, over the centuries, some of the best Aretino oil and wine has come.

On these south-facing hillsides, very close to the walls of Arezzo – at the end of the aqueduct inspired by Vasari to provide the city with fresh water – lies some of the property of the Conti Borghini Baldovinetti de' Bacci Venuti, an old and noble family with roots in Florence and Arezzo. The Fattoria di San Fabiano forms part of this most elegant of estates, complete with villas and palaces at least one of which dates back to the fourteenth century. In 1370, Francesco de' Bacci, an Aretine ancestor of the family, sold a vineyard on the hillside in order to pay Piero della Francesco for painting another of Arezzo's great treasures: the frescoes describing the Legend of the True Cross which exalt the Bacci family chapel in the Church of San Francesco at the heart of Arezzo. Through the generations wine has always been made on the family estates – and today even more so, with well in excess of 300,000 bottles produced each year. As well as organic wines, these include bottles in the two highest wine categories, the Denominazione di Origine Controllata (DOC) – wine that has been certified and produced in a specific region – and Denominazione di Origine Controllata e Garantita (DOCG), which means the strictest wine regulations have to be followed. In addition they also make a Chianti, Vin Santo di Caratello, whose Trebbiano and Malvasia Toscano grapes are treated in the traditional manner, hand-gathered into baskets then laid on canes in the attics of the Fattoria where they lie undisturbed while the grapes mature and their flavour develops. The wizened grapes are pressed before the Christmas festivities and the resulting juice is fermented in small wooden barrels for a period of four years. The strong dessert wine is made to be served, as is the Tuscan custom, with *cantuccini* and other sweet dry biscuits. On the highest slopes of the Borghini Baldovinetti lands there are venerable olive groves whose fruit provides an oil of subtlety and excellence.

In the example of the Fattoria di San Fabiano we can see how long-lived and deeply ingrained the culture of winemaking and olive pressing is to the people of Arezzo, this land called *Oenetria* by the ancient Greeks. However, it is not necessary to be the possessor of fine vineyards to make wine. Around the city in modest plots of land owned by regular people there are vines lovingly tended, and wine is made in small vats to be enjoyed around the year at home. Olive groves, too, are not the prerogative of the privileged. Our neighbours, normal *Aretini da sempre*, make their own superb oil, of which they are justly proud.

It is this intense and long-lived culinary and oenological culture that has supported and sustained the Aretines through the centuries, and which today many of them energetically defend. The illustration below (courtesy of Sir John Soane's Museum, London) is a good example of the historic Tuscan appreciation of wine. It is a design by the school of Vasari artist Teofilo Torri (Arezzo, 1554–1623) for an elegant wine table fountain to be made in silver, and then, most probably, intended to be used for celebratory banquets. Around the neck of the rearing horse there is a collar inscribed with the word 'Arezzo', and the saddle appears to be a cartouche decorated with the Medici coat of arms. This suggests that the wine fountain may have been commissioned by one of the Medicean *capitani*, the commanders of Arezzo, along with a member of the Aretine aristocracy. Torri's drawing, with its Baroque style, must date between 1600 – the beginning of the Baroque style in Italy – and 1623, the year of Torri's death. The work is, however, a rare item of evidence to an agreement made between the Aretines and the Florentines in 1511. Since 1384 Arezzo had suffered a long period of fierce domination by Florence, and the imposition of the Florentine symbol of a lily instead of the Aretine rearing horse, which in the 1300s had been identified with the Republic of Arezzo. In the agreement,

Chapter Two – Bishop Tarlati's Soup

the image of a rearing horse was accepted as the coat of arms of the city and the *Comune.* It is a fundamental symbol that has remained throughout the years, and is still a source of pride and identity. The remaining mystery, however, is whether the silver fountain was ever made.

Design for a decorative silver wine fountain by the Aretine artist Teofilo Torri, c. 1600–1623.

After the *vendemmia* (grape harvest) of 2004, when passing a large palazzo near the *Comune* of Arezzo, through the doors that opened onto the street I saw an old man carefully hanging magnificent bunches of grapes from the rafters of the storeroom. He had selected perfect specimens and was preparing to make Vin Santo di Caratello in the traditional way. Here was an Aretino absorbed in making this increasingly rare, genuine dessert wine. After pressing, the must would be poured into small casks and left for extended periods to complete the vinification process. Latterly, much Vin Santo on sale is made by fortifying regular wine. He, however, like Beppina, preferred the real thing. He was a true epicure, an ordinary Aretino intent on living well, in harmony with nature.

❊ Beppina and the Kitchens of Arezzo ❊

The villas surrounding the city belong to important Aretine families, and many are still lived in by their historic owners. One, the Villa degli Orti, now fittingly houses a convent, as in the 1700s it was the home of several nuns among the Redi family, one of whom, Margherita, was declared a saint by Pope Pius XI in 1934. Miraculously, the villa has not been subjected to modern improvements, and retains its original lineaments in a graceful but worn way. In front of the elegant house there is a massive walled garden, in which all kinds of vegetables and herbs were grown. In the manner of great country houses of the seventeenth and eighteenth centuries, the produce of the garden, vineyards and olive groves was taken to the family's town house in the Via de Redi for their sustenance, and some was taken by cart to Florence, where other members of the Redi family resided. The surplus was then sold to Arezzo's citizens. Indeed, as we have seen in a previous chapter, landowners like Pellegrino Artusi continued this wise practice in later centuries, when the good produce of his farms was brought from the Marche to be prepared in his Florentine kitchen. To reiterate, the ties between the city and the countryside have, of necessity, always been strong, as the city relies on that which the country provides.

The Redi family's most famous member was Francesco Redi, who was born in Arezzo on the 18th of February 1626, the same year in which Peter Minuit bought the entire island of Manhattan from native Indian chiefs, Francis Bacon died, and the façade of St Peter's in Rome was finished. A statue of Redi stands in a niche, one of a row of similar sculptures, facing the Uffizi Gallery in Florence. He is depicted as being tall and elegant, the perfect seventeenth-century gentleman. Francesco Redi, son of a physician, was one of those Aretines endowed with 'a keen intellect'. Educated at the University of Pisa in medicine and science, he then became court physician to the Grand Duke Ferdinand II (as was Redi's father before him) and then to Cosimo III. In the 1600s the Medici court

Chapter Two – Bishop Tarlati's Soup

was still rich, magnificent, and very indulgent. Fortunes were spent on masques, pageants and banquets but the good-natured Ferdinand was also fascinated by the work of scientists like Galileo. The Accademia del Cimento, which latter word signifies venturesome testing or proving, was formed expressly to continue the Galilean scientific tradition. It met at the Pitti Palace, and during the ten years of its existence this group of Italy's greatest scientists – along with some from other European countries – accomplished much in the way of new scientific experimentation, discovery and invention. They forsook the old arts of alchemy in favour of investigations into optics, and such things as the study of geology, which was to eventually contradict the Biblical account and prove the enormous antiquity of planet Earth. Redi, who was a leading member of the academy, was an able biologist, his most important experiment being a refutation of the theory of spontaneous generation. He proved, by observation, that maggots did not issue by themselves from rotting meat but were the produce of flies. To come to this conclusion he placed raw meat in glass jars, sealing some and leaving others open to the air and insects. The meat in the sealed jars remained free of maggots but that which was fly-blown soon developed larvae.

Redi was also a linguist, a member of the Accademia della Crusca, a society devoted to the pure Tuscan language. Its name and emblem, a bolting sieve, signifies a wish to separate the wheat from the chaff in distinguishing the good usage of language from the dross of the impure. Redi, an enthusiastic collector of rare manuscripts, was a poet too, writing amongst other works a large collection of love poetry; but most importantly for our purposes he was an epicure. Although his extreme slimness caused his friends to tease him, he had the reputation of having exquisite taste and sensibility for excellent food and wine. His dithyrambic poem *Bacco in Toscana* (*Bacchus in Tuscany*) is considered to be the greatest Italian example of that form of writing. Written for an extravagant courtly entertainment, and going through many changes in its composition, the poem describes the gods Bacchus and Ariadne, which latter is silent for most of the verses, as they consider and taste the wines of Italy. At the end of the poem they are both drunk, but have decided that the king of wines is that of Montepulciano, a decision with which, today, many would concur. The lively verses devoted to wine describe such pleasures as that of chilled wine in ice-encrusted bottles, kept in elegant coolers, Redi exquisitely expressing the cracking, splintering noises made by the melting ice. He also, while extolling the greatest wines of Italy, praises the wines of Arezzo, including those emanating from his own vineyards:

My lips are purified,
submerged in a gilded goblet of wine from the good vines which
flame in Sansovino,
or that brilliant red which makes an Aretine proud grown in
Tregozzano and between the stones of Ciggiano.

Perhaps a wine more pétillante, sharp and pungent if you should
want would be that of Albano or Vaiano, glowing pale, or that
which reddens in the gardens of Redi.

Title page of the first edition (1685) of Francesco Redi's poem 'Bacco in Toscana'.

✳ Chapter Two – Bishop Tarlati's Soup ✳

Whilst exalting the good wines of Italy, Redi pokes fun at the drinks of the barbarous North. Bacchus proclaims that those who drink English cider will soon find themselves in their graves, and a similar fate awaited beer drinkers too. Jokingly, Bacchus also scorns the newly fashionable exotic beverages which were becoming de rigueur at the Florentine court at the time – tea, coffee and of course chocolate.

Redi's predilections were not, however, solely confined to wine. He had the reputation of having an exquisite taste and sensibility for excellent food. In a period when travel was opening up to the adventurous, and strange and new items of food and novel medicaments arrived in Florence in the trunks of intrepid voyagers, he was ever in search of new flavours, medicines and ingredients, and as a scientist and physician he eagerly tested these new elements in order to understand their properties. The further away the novel ingredient came from the more it was appreciated and marvelled at by the *cognoscenti*, such as he, of the period.

Redi was intrigued when he learnt that the Chinese had a taste for birds' nests, which made them in his eyes as adventurous in their gustatory pleasures as the most modern of Florentines. In his collection of writings, *Esperienze intorno a diverse cose naturale* (Experiences of various natural things), dated 1671, Redi writes to his friend Father Athanasius Kircher, of the Company of Jesus, that 'although their own distant ancestors used birds' nests in some of their medicines, he had never heard or read of anyone eating them'. However, he continues 'there are birds not so very different from swallows which build their nests in the cliffs on the shores of Coccincina, these little nests are of a whitish colour and of a material not dissimilar to fish glue. These nests when pulled from the cliffs are sold at a huge price and used to enhance the flavour of food, and without this strange ingredient, which is actually very palatable when handled by a master cook, the resulting dishes would be considered of little nobility or worth. One of the ways to use the nests is to soak them in a good capon or veal broth until they have become slippery and swollen; then they are cooked in the broth with a little butter and various sorts of spices.'

Redi discusses one of these novel spices with Kircher and it would appear that between them we have one of the first mentions of star anise in the West:

> From China comes a certain seed which they call Chinese fennel, saying that it cures many ailments, but I find that it is little more effective than our native fennel seed, than aniseed, wild carrot (*Daucus carota*), or cumin...Recently it is to be found on sale in Florence and as you know from your book (*China illustrata*, 1667) it is formed like a star with eight rays and is of a leonine, a reddish blonde colour. Each ray encloses a smooth and shiny brown seed and inside one finds a tiny heart which does not have much flavour, neither the heart nor its shell; but the rays of the star which enfold the seeds have a flavour not much different from our sweet fennel, not very pungent with a hint of aniseed. I have not yet found out what sort of plant the seeds come from.

Redi goes on to discuss the strange properties of sassafras: according to Olao Vormio, who had a collection of curious natural phenomena, and Francesco Ximenez, a Spanish monk who studied and wrote about the plants of Mexico, when a piece of sassafras wood was soaked in sea water for eight days the water became sweet and good to drink. Redi himself experimented with sassafras wood, but came to the conclusion that the sea water which Ximenez used must have been very different from Mediterranean water, as for however long Redi soaked the wood he did not achieve the desired result.

Another novelty which appealed to Redi was a substance

Chapter Two – Bishop Tarlati's Soup

known as *puju* (possibly from a member of the *Piperaceae* family, a succulent native to tropical America, now rampant in the Philippines), which had the reputation of making men immortal, while ginseng, although not potent enough to provide immortality, was, Redi believed, certainly of great use in keeping one healthy, happy and free from illness.

Francesco Redi.

Since the early 1600s when chocolate from the New World first came to Italy by way of Spain, the Medici had been more than anxious to discover all they could of this new wonder, so that they too could trade in it and enjoy its astonishing properties. The Granducal aim, especially of Cosimo III, was to produce a chocolate to rival and surpass the perfection of that made according to the recipe of the Spanish King.

Redi's positions as court physician to Cosimo III, and then in 1666 as Superintendent of the Granducal Spezieria and Fonderia (a workshop or laboratory where spices and scents were mixed and melded together and variously perfumed chocolate was manufactured), were central to the love story between the Tuscan court and chocolate. Redi's talents were

❋ Beppina and the Kitchens of Arezzo ❋

precisely what was needed to feed the fashion for ever more exquisitely flavoured drinking and eating chocolate, a mania for which became more pronounced in the second half of the seventeenth century. Moreover, Cosimo III had a passion for rare and exotic plants from all over the world, and the more perfumed they were the more he loved them. Cosimo created gardens in which to grow these plants, and his gardeners excelled in the art of grafting, so forming strange and wonderful trees that bore many diverse fruits, an art useful to Redi in his search for ever more esoteric sensations. While in charge of the Spezieria, Redi – helped by a key artisan, Vincenzo Sandrini – was much engaged in making chocolate and experimenting to make it even more delicate and of many different flavours. Redi added the perfumes of various flowers, then of citrus fruits, mixing the chocolate with fresh lemon peel, the peel of sweet Portuguese oranges, and that of the bitter orange, the Bigerade, similar to those now named Seville. Then he used the bergamot orange, probably a hybrid of bitter oranges and the Palestine sweet lime, which are now bred for the perfumed oil contained in the peel. Redi also experimented with spices and vanilla, amber and ambergris.

At that period, when what one might term the first really scientific experiments were made by the Accademia del Cimento, Redi, together with friends such as Lorenzo Magalotti, were fascinated by taste and smell, the stranger and more exotic the better. Indeed, Magalotti, having what French perfumers would call 'a nose', created perfumes in his studio which his footman would then spray all over his master's rooms. Redi, too, was an *odorista*, someone who had a pronounced liking for and an ability to distinguish between both scents and flavours.

As is well known, the physical relationship between taste and smell is extremely close and complicated. In Italian the word *odore* means smell or scent, but its plural, *odori*, can also signify

Chapter Two – Bishop Tarlati's Soup

that sacred collection of scented vegetables – carrot, onion and celery plus herbs and garlic – that chopped fine form the basis of flavour for all manner of Italian sauces and meat dishes. In 1611, in his *Trattato della natura de' cibi et del bere*, Baldassarre Pisanelli described parsley, just one component often included in the *odori*, in the following manner.

> Parsley in ancient times was called the *Apio degli horti* and was used, as it still is in nearly all dishes where an odiferous and flavourful condiment is needed, and it really seems as if this herb is preferred above all others in that it is included in sauces, soups, in ragouts, small stews in a way that makes it seem impossible to cook without parsley.

Francesco Gaudentio, a near contemporary of Redi, in his *Il panunto toscano* (which is dated 1705 but which describes his methods and experience in the kitchen over the last quarter of the seventeenth century), goes into much detail about herbs and spices, and describes the making of what we now know as the preparatory step of chopping up *odori*, making a *battuto* to form the basis of a dish. For example:

> To cook a Hare. If the hare is old you can stew it or cook it in broth as I have described for wild boar, but if it is young then cook it like this. Take a little fat (from the belly of the pig) and chop it up together with little onions and perfumed herbs and put it to *soffriggere* [fry gently] with a little salt, pepper and cloves, when you have cooked this for half an hour with the hare, turning it often, add a little wine and an hour before serving add a little cooked must and spices as you prefer.

Gaudentio uses both terms *battuto* and *soffritto*, meaning chopped ingredients and fried chopped ingredients, which are basic to Italian recipes. The method of this recipe is almost identical to that of modern dishes which we enjoy today.

❈ Beppina and the Kitchens of Arezzo ❈

Redi famously remarked that the Spanish were the first to make a chocolate of perfection, but that during his time in the Tuscan court he and his colleagues had managed to add a certain *je ne sais quoi*, an indefinable '*squisita gentilezza*' to the precious substance. An 'exquisite delicacy' might be one translation of the words, but underlying this meaning there is also a connotation of something that has the perfection of its kind, a perfect example of the genuine nature of a substance. Here, one is again reminded of the old Aretine opinion of the essence of good food. Something of genuine and excellent quality, good enough to stand up for itself without unnecessary adornment.

In the Florence of the late 1600s chocolate was largely consumed by the Granducal family and the courtiers surrounding them. According to an account written in 1688 by the Major Domo of the Grand Duchess Vittoria della Rovere, wife of Cosimo III, and a friend of Francesco Redi, the chocolate was taken hot, almost boiling, sipped slowly from little maiolica or silver cups placed on small saucers. Cups were also imported from China and were made of fine porcelain. To enhance the elegance of chocolate drinking, Redi and his friends thought it necessary to have two small round napkins which were placed beneath the cups. The Florentine napkins, *pezzuoli*, as they were called, were used to wipe the lips clean of the dark stain of the liquid chocolate.

Chocolate was also eaten with great enthusiasm. It was made in the form of round flat *pasticche* (pastilles), *bogli* (larger pieces weighing probably from 20 to 30 grams), as well as in small drops and broken pieces. It was often given by those who were fortunate enough to have access to it, to people to whom favours might be owed. Redi was most generous to acquaintances in his gifts of chocolate and drinking cups, especially to his family in Arezzo with whom he was in constant communication.

In 1688, Gian Gastone – who was destined to be the last Medici ruler of the Grand Duchy – visited Arezzo. As he was to be

Chapter Two – Bishop Tarlati's Soup

entertained by Redi's brother Giovanni Battista, Redi hastily sent his brother six beautiful lidded porcelain chocolate cups decorated with silver filigree, and a quantity of tablets of the finest Spanish chocolate. He wrote to tell him that it was only necessary to place the cups, with the chocolate heaped around them, on a shallow silver vessel in order to have a suitable gift for a brother of the most refined courtier of the Pitti Palace to present to the Grand Duke. In a letter to Redi, Giovanni Battista described a supper he gave in their family home at Arezzo for some illustrious guests at this same time, and it is tempting to think that it was Gian Gastone himself who graced the dinner. There were four *portate*, or courses, each comprised of many different savoury dishes. The first service contained cold antipasti, the second, hot antipasti, the third, boiled dishes and the fourth was made up of various roasted meats. There is, however, no mention of chocolate, nor indeed dessert.

1. *Servito freddo per antipasto* (Cold dishes for antipasto):
Schiena e salciccia (haunch of beef and sausages), *Salsicciotti* (various salami), *Limoni tagliati* (lemon quarters), *Pasticcio freddo* (cold pie), *Paste di due sorte* (two sorts of pastry), *Cappone freddo* (cold capon).

2. *Antipasti caldi* (Hot antipasti):
Polpette (meatballs), *Cervelli* (brains), *Frittura bianca* (fried sweetbreads or white meats), *Trippa* (tripe), *Coradelle* [*coratella*] (the offal – lungs, liver and spleen of a small animal e.g. a sheep), *Lombi* (loin), *Uccelli* (small birds, field fare).

3. *Allesso* (Boiled dishes):
Allattato (suckling pig), *Suppette con prugnoli* (soup with prugnoli mushrooms – *Calocybe gambosa*), *Tartufi e coradelle* (truffled offal), *Capponi* (capons), *Pasticcio caldo* (hot pie), *Piccioni* (pigeons), *Lepre coperta con cardi e sedani* (hare covered with cardoons and celery), *Mostarda, Zampi di vitella* (mustard-flavoured fruit preserve, shin of veal).

4. *Pollo d'India* (turkey), *Lepre Marinato* (marinated hare), *Piccioni Grossi Nr 12* (twelve large pigeons), *Starne* (female grey partridges), *Quarti di Cordesco Arrosto* (roast quarters of summer lamb), *Cicotti alla Lucchese* (small pieces of lean meat? cooked in the Lucchese manner), *Quarti di cordesco stufati* (stewed quarters of summer lamb), *Uccelli* (small birds), *Pasticci* (pies).

Interestingly, as we shall see towards the end of this chapter, there are recipes known in Arezzo at exactly this period which describe the cooking method for some of the dishes very similar to those served at Giovanni Battista Redi's ample feast. (See *Cappone coperto*, for example, page 139 below.)

And here is a menu enjoyed recently in Arezzo for a New Year's Eve celebration. The dishes, prepared by our friend Cristina, also contain echoes of the Redi feast.

Crostini di fegatini, piccolissimi raffinatissimi,
olive farciti

Capelletti in brodo di capone

Sformato di gobbi
Sformato di cavolo

Capon en gelée
Galantina

Cardi e carciofi
Mostarda
Sottaceto sott'olio
Funghi porcini sott'olio

Vitello arrosto con cipollini in agrodolce
Rape tenera freschi, in padella
Piccioni arrosti delicati servito con crostini fatto con loro interiori.

On another occasion Redi sent his sister Maria Diomira, who was a nun at the Dominican Convent of Santa Maria Novella at

Chapter Two – Bishop Tarlati's Soup

Arezzo, two chocolate cups which she could use in her Spezieria, or Apothecary, at the convent. At that time, in the Galenic tradition, spices, foods (including chocolate), herbs and medicines were all dispensed together, with no particular reflection as to what was strictly a medicament and what was an item of food.

Redi's greatest gift to the Medici family was his famous recipe for jasmine scented chocolate, which really did rival the recipe of the King of Spain. So important was the chocolate to the Tuscan court that its method of manufacture was designated a state secret. Although Redi never wrote down the recipe, he did reveal it verbally to a trusted friend, Antonio Vallisnieri, in 1668, but it was only in 1712, well after the Redi's death, that his friend published it.

The Granduca of Tuscany's recipe for jasmine-scented chocolate, created by Francesco Redi of Arezzo

> Take 10 *libbre* (lbs) of cacao beans, dry them, clean them and crumble them roughly. Fresh jasmine blossoms sufficient for the quantity of cacao. In a container place layer upon layer of first cacao then the flowers and leave it to infuse for 24 hours. At this point tip out the cacao and flowers then repeat the process adding yet more fresh jasmine. Repeat every 24 hours for ten or 12 days.
> Then take 8 *libbre* of good dry white sugar, three ounces of perfect vanilla, six ounces of perfect cinnamon, two *scrupoli* of ambergris [a *scrupolo* is an ancient measurement equal to a 24th part of an ounce], and according to the best practice make the chocolate. Make sure that the stone on which the chocolate is worked is not too hot and that not more than four or five *libbre* are worked at the same time, because if the stone becomes too hot then the flavour will be lost.

The important difference in this recipe to other scented

chocolate made at the period was that the jasmine flavour was not added to the cacao by means of adding jasmine-scented liquid or drops of scented oil – it was infusion in jasmine blooms which gave the chocolate its *'squisita gentilezza'*. A secret long kept and much coveted.

A passion for chocolate similar to that of Redi's is still to be found in Arezzo in the shape of Vestri Cioccolato. On the outskirts of the city Danielo Vestri has the most elegant of chocolate shops, selling his own products in exquisitely designed boxes. However, the shop, which is attached to a good coffee bar, is mainly open for the sale of chocolate only at key times of the year – Christmas, New Year, and Easter, when it is crowded with eager customers. Clearly the hot summer months are not the most suitable for such a delicate product. In tune with Francesco Redi is the fact that Vestri's main selling point is in Florence! The cocoa used to make his chocolate comes from a plantation in the Dominican Republic, which Vestri bought in 2002. Recently, with input from the Universities of Pisa and Siena, he has been experimenting with a dark chocolate that may be of benefit to people suffering from cardiac problems. This Toscolato – Tuscan chocolate – is variously flavoured with pure olive oil, chestnut flour and most delicious of all, traditional, strongly perfumed Panaia apples, a rare mountain species from the Casentino. One of Vestri's other specialities is *Cioccolato del Granduca di Toscano al Gelsomina ingentilito all'arancia*. His version of Francesco Redi's precious chocolate perfumed with jasmine. Vestri however has 'tamed' the flavour with orange to please modern tastes. However, some years ago he did reproduce Redi's original recipe without the addition of any modern ingredients, some of which have the effect of making chocolate silky. Interestingly Redi's recipe resulted in a chocolate with a dry and powdery consistency.

Although Redi lived most of his life at the Medici court, he intended to retire to the Villa degli Orti, one of the two country

Chapter Two – Bishop Tarlati's Soup

villas owned by his family in the hinterlands of Arezzo. Sadly his wish was never to be granted, he died in Pisa on the 1st of March 1697. Francesco Redi was embalmed in Pisa after a post-mortem revealed, among other things, just how many kidney stones were contained in his right kidney. Something that, with his penchant for cutting things up to see exactly how they functioned, might have interested him greatly. He was then transported to Arezzo where he lay in state in the Cathedral, and, as he requested in his will, was buried in the Church of San Francesco.

Unfortunately in 1812 French bureaucracy, which came in the wake of Napoleon's invading armies, in collaboration with an Aretino called Giuseppe Massetani, had a less pious idea of what use the venerable church might be put to. It was decided that San Francesco should be deconsecrated and turned into a theatre, to be named in honour of Napoleon. A somewhat backhanded compliment, as the theatre was intended to be the venue for comedians and farces! Happily this plan was thwarted by the timely intervention of a member of a leading Aretine family, the de Giudici, who politely pointed out that in creating the theatre the frescoes of Piero della Francesca would be destroyed. However, the noble de Giudici's intercession came too late for Redi. It was said that his body had been exhumed on the orders of his family, after hearing about the plans for the deconsecration of the church, and from that point on its location seems uncertain. Arguments have taken place between local historians, particularly in the 1920s and onwards, about where Redi's body actually lies. There was a theory that his corpse had been secretly moved to the 'Escuriale Etrusco', a family burial place at the Villa di Piscinale, situated half an hour's walk away from the Porta San Clemente. In the 1920s the burial ground was excavated, but to no avail, researchers simply found the well-preserved bodies of three of Redi's sisters, who had all been nuns. An elegant monument to Redi is to be found in the Duomo, but it is also said that searches there for his bones were fruitless.

❋ Beppina and the Kitchens of Arezzo ❋

After this account of the life and gustatory predilections of such a cultured and privileged Aretine as Francesco Redi one might well inquire as to what the less well-placed citizens of Tuscan Arezzo were eating every day in the seventeenth century. In other words, those who weren't courtiers or accustomed to luxurious banquets, but who lived simpler lives in the city. Possibly the best answer to the question is to be found in a bound manuscript kept in the Arezzo City Library: *Il panunto toscano,* which was compiled by Francesco Gaudentio. This manuscript, the cover of which bears the date 1705, relates Gaudentio's experiences as a cook and shares his recipes. His career partly covers the same period as Redi's. Gaudentio was born in Florence in 1648, and in 1670, at the age of 22, he became a novice in the Jesuit Order. In fact Gaudentio did not become a priest, but served as a layman who aided the works of the Order. He acted as a gatekeeper, a steward and predominantly as a cook, moving from city to city with the Jesuits as they expanded their presence in Italy. He arrived in Arezzo in 1686 and for two years served as cook to the large new Jesuit College of Sant'Ignazio which was, of course, named after Ignatius of Loyola, the founder of the Order.

Gaudentio speaks in a simple, direct way about food that is both economical and good to eat. His title page announces that in his book the reader could find an easy way of modern cooking at little expense. One can almost hear his voice as he expresses his thoughts, occasionally contradicting himself as he thinks of another instance in which an ingredient might be used. He humbly states in his short introduction that his recipes are not intended for skilled cooks, but for those of his brothers who had no knowledge of making food and yet would like some instruction in the art. He adds that if the reader did not have any of the spices he mentions in his recipe it was of little consequence, and the dish might be cooked as well without. A notion that Pietro Aretino would have agreed with:

☀ Chapter Two – Bishop Tarlati's Soup ☀

Letter 598 Book V
To Perroto and al Salla
February, in Venice, 1550

…It is very true that in my opinion the pretentiousness of artifice spoils the vivacity of nature, and using these new mixtures of condiments steals the innate flavour from diverse meats which simplicity conserves…

Gaudentio's job was to make ends meet and provide nourishment for the hungry young scholars at the College – and in later years suitable food for the elderly and sick of the Order. Indeed, there is a separate section in his writings devoted to invalid food, a preoccupation that, as we have seen in the previous chapter, was still of as great an import in the nineteenth century as it had been in the 1600s. Below is a translation of Gaudentio's earnest advice on the use of herbs:

Ways of using all sorts of flavoursome herbs, also garlic and onions.

You can use garlic in all the foods that I have indicated, wherever you use it, it will do well; but be careful to use it in small quantities except in the case of legumes; in other dishes chop it finely and add it at the beginning of cooking. The same rule applies to onions except in the case of stews where you may put them in whole, but in other instances, chop them up. Parsley must be chopped fine and used in small quantities and added only when the dish is half cooked. Note that if you use parsley when boiling meats, leave it whole and add it when the meat is halfway cooked and if the parsley has some roots attached it will be much better. I cannot give you a universal rule because in some dishes it [parsley] is added initially, in others in the middle of cooking and yet others when the dish is ready. You can, however, manage if you follow my hints and use your own judgement. If by chance you have to keep parsley for some time put it into a ceramic pot, cover it well and keep it in a cool place and you will be able to use the herb when you have need.

As to marjoram. This is a herb which must be collected when young and tender, make it into little bunches, leave it to hang in the shade, in this way you can dry it and then use it for legumes or stews, particularly those of lamb and *castrato*, castrated ram. You can do the same thing with *persa* [another variety of marjoram]. It has smaller stalks and an ashy colour but use only a small quantity as it has a pungent flavour. Equally you can make the same use of hyssop, oregano, basil, wild thyme, which you must dry in the shade; note that all these herbs should not be ground in a pestle and mortar but crumbled with the fingers, taking care when you employ them that they are wholesome and dry. *Puleggio*, penny-royal [a type of mint], this is a perfumed plant that lives on damp ground. Collect it when it is young and tender, dry it as the herbs mentioned above and it is good in diverse dishes particularly legumes. *Santoreggio*, savoury, grows in summer in the garden and in certain localities, in the fields. You must collect it when it is fresh and new. Dry it in the way I have indicated and use it with legumes particularly lentils. *Menta romana*, roman mint, you can only use when fresh but use it in the dishes that I mention especially with tripe. *Mentuccia*, field mint, can be used to cook *funghi* and other foods cooked in a similar way. Sage, fresh or dry can be used in all the foods that I indicate, particularly in items pickled in vinegar, *fegatelli*, liver, and birds, field fare. *Ravano acuto*, horse radish, this root must be grated and scattered over boiled meat like a sauce and will give a good flavour. As to rosemary, again you can serve it either fresh or dry in all the dishes I have noted, especially in pickled fish, roasted pork loin, chops. With these last mentioned herbs be careful to put them into the

✻ Chapter Two – Bishop Tarlati's Soup ✻

dish late in its cooking otherwise some of them may make the food bitter. As for the *pomi d'oro*, tomato, you can use it as a condiment in meat stews.

This last throwaway comment is remarkable in that Gaudentio seems to demonstrate that tomatoes were being grown and appearing on the tables of the less exalted population during the last quarter of the seventeenth century. His words also remind us of Antonio Latini's *Cassuola alla spagnuola*, a rich meat stew flavoured with tomatoes, one of three recipes for the *pomi d'oro* published in Latini's *Lo scalco alla moderna* (Naples, 1694).

Gaudentio's simple recipe given below precedes the luxurious examples found in Vincenzo Corrado's *Il cuoco galante* (The Gallant Chef), first published in 1773, but appears after Castor Durante's testy description of the tomato in his *Herbario nuovo*, published in 1585, though the latter's dismissive words (below) can hardly be termed a recipe:

> Like the aubergine, eat the tomato with pepper, salt and oil, though it gives but little and bad nourishment. (*Come le melanzane mangiansi il pomodoro, con pepe, sale e olio, ma danno poco e cattivo nutrimento.*)

Corrado's recipe, one of thirteen, for *Pomodoro alla salsa di tartufi*, is more elaborate and goes as follows:

> Tomatoes filled with anchovies, green herbs and truffles, all well pounded together and dressed with oil and lemon juice, then floured, fried in oil and served with a truffle sauce are of the finest of dishes. (*Sono ottimi i pomodori ripieni d'aciughe, erbette, e tartufi, tutto ben pesto e condito d'olio, e sugo di limone, infarinati, fritti con olio, e serviti con salsa di tartufi.*)

Here is Francesco Gaudentio's way of cooking tomatoes – simple and good:

This fruit is almost similar to the apple, it is grown in the garden and one cooks them in the following way. Take the tomatoes, cut them into pieces and put them in a pan with oil, pepper, salt, chopped garlic and *mentuccia* [wild mint]. Let them fry, turning them often and if you like add some soft breadcrumbs, and *cucuzze lunche* [pumpkin slices] is enjoyable too.'

Gaudentio also lists his condiments and spices with as great a care and common sense.

Ways of using salt and all sorts of spices.
Salt is the most common of all condiments and it is necessary in all foods but used in proportion and in the right amount. Otherwise it is unpleasant and noxious when its quantity is excessive. So to avoid this disorder take care to begin with less than the required quantity and after the dish has cooked for some time, taste it and if there is not sufficient add a little more. But if at the beginning you add all the salt you think you require, it may be that when the dish is ready that you will find it too salty.

Of mace, *fior di noce moscata,* you may use it in delicate soups like a *brodetto,* in things cooked in the *bain marie,* in *suscello,* a pork-flavoured soup, and in any other dish in which you include eggs. It is necessary to grind it finely. When you want to use some put a little in a bronze mortar and crush it well with the pestle then steep it thoroughly in some cold water. You can use the same method with saffron, make sure it is well ground and add it to the other ingredients such as eggs. Of both saffron and mace use a small quantity except in the case of [flavouring?]oil. Of sweet cinnamon sticks, you may add a small piece in various sorts of boiled dishes, roasts and pies. Of the powder you can mix it with sugar in broths, white soup and similar dishes. And of the quantity with which you

Chapter Two – Bishop Tarlati's Soup

intend to season a dish, reserve and add a quarter of it just before sending the dish to table. Cloves and clove-scented cinnamon you can use to stud various types of roasts and pies. And if you use them ground be careful not to grind them too finely or the food will become bitter and add them always at the beginning. Do the same with pepper but crush it roughly so that it does not become a powder because in that case it will be noxious to the health and to the taste; if you crush a little saffron together with the pepper, it will do very well, use it on foods like broccoli, cauliflower, *baccalà* and similar things. With peppers one puts them to dry in the air and when they become red crush them a little in a mortar and use them in stews, *spezzatello, guazzetti* and similar dishes. To serve ten people you only need a quantity the size of a nut, because as they are very sharp [hot] more would make the dish unpleasant. When the peppers are fresh put them into vinegar and serve them as they are, raw. Nutmeg is not crushed but grated with a small cheese grater or shave them with a knife because if you crush them in a mortar they will make the food bitter, be careful, however, not to add too little. Elderflowers are to be collected before they begin to drop and put into a low oven to dry and they will serve to make *pizze* as I have indicated. You may use cumin seed with wild dove and pigeon and in stews, but only use a small quantity as in the case of anise, for they are both very strong. Wild fennel is conserved as follows. When it has flowered collect the flowers with diligence and spread them out on paper in a warm place until they are dry, you may then keep them in a box and use them in those dishes that I have suggested. You may treat wild fennel grains [seeds] in the same way and you can use them on some fried foods, fish baked in the oven, chops and similar things. *Pitartima* [coriander seed], should be broken up a little but not ground; take care that it is not old and it should be crushed only when you are ready to use it as it loses its flavour rapidly. With ginger you must crush it finely like sweet cinnamon and you may use it in those sauces of boiling oil and vinegar served over fish as I mention above.

And with all these things be careful to use them in small quantities so that one flavour is not stronger than another nor do they dominate the flavour of the main ingredient of the dish.

Gaudentio's wise words ring true today, here we are reading the thoughts of a well-practiced cook possessed of great sense and sensitivity and a love of food.

At the time during which Gaudentio lived and cooked in Arezzo much of the terrain surrounding the city was *palude*, wetland, and the bogs, streams and river teemed with fresh water fish, frogs and eels (see pages 239–40). Here was nourishment for the taking. Gaudentio has several recipes for *Tinca* – or *Tinga* as he spells it. Tench, bony and tasting of mud, still made a good meal when treated correctly. He advises that if the fish was small and reddish it was best to clean it well, bone it, dip it into flour and cook as other types of fish, in other words fry it. If, however, the fish was large and black in colour then it was better to fill a pan with one part vinegar, two parts wine, three parts water, bring it to a vigorous boil then throw in the fish, when it was half cooked it was time to add chopped parsley, pepper and oil then when the fish was done to serve it up with slices of bread (possibly toasted) in each dish. Gaudentio, by adding vinegar and wine to the water, ameliorated the muddy taste of the fish.

To grill tench Gaudentio advises the following:

> Take a large tench, scale it and wash it well, drain it and dry it well. Next, flour it and sprinkle it with oil and vinegar in which you have mixed *pitartima*, which is

Chapter Two – Bishop Tarlati's Soup

Maestro Martino of Como's term for coriander, crushed fennel seeds and salt. Put the fish on the grill turning it and basting it frequently with a branch of rosemary or thyme [dipped into the perfumed oil and vinegar mixture]. Cook it thus and take it to the table with a little *agro* [*agreste*, unfermented juice of unripe grapes, used in the place of vinegar], on top.

Another simple and appetising recipe using ingredients easily to hand, fish fresh from the river, which at that time flowed through Arezzo, and herbs. One can imagine Gaudentio beside the great *camino* of the kitchen in the vast Jesuit College busily basting his fish with branches of rosemary or thyme. Today, tench is still eaten grilled, scented with rosemary and irrigated with olive oil.

As a thrifty and practical cook, Gaudentio made the best use of offal and fresh blood from slaughtered pigs. His recipe for *Sanguinaccio* is remarkably like that used today in the country around Arezzo:

Per Fare li Sanguinacci secondo Gaudentio (How to make Gaudentio's Black Pudding)

As soon as you have collected the pig's blood stir it, otherwise it will quickly coagulate. Afterwards sieve it, add salt and spices, particularly pepper, grated breadcrumbs, a little [grated] sweet [unmatured] cheese and a little sharp [mature] cheese, the seeds of field fennel well crushed, *uva passata*, dried grapes [sultanas], pine kernels and fat cut into cubes. If you do not need to keep the sausage a long time you can also add a little milk. Afterwards take the pig's intestine, turn it inside out and wash it several times in hot water and wine, rubbing it with *merancolo*, a type of citrus fruit. In this way the disagreeable smell of the skin will be lost. Put the mixture of blood and spices into the *budello* [intestine] and cook it in boiling water for a quarter of an hour with a little salt. Be careful not to fill the skin entirely as it might burst and when you want to serve it send it to the table cut into slices grilled, roasted or fried in a pan.

Similarly you can make a cake in a flat pan which you must first oil well, then you may cook it either in the oven or on a tripod with embers under and on top of it. You may add a little onion fried gently in lard which you include where you have only used dried grapes. You may also make a *frittata* with the *sanguinaccio*.

In contrast here is a description of the making of *Sanguinaccio* taken from *The Tuscan Year*, my book which describes the life and ways of cooking of my neighbour Silvana Cerotti who lives in the Province of Arezzo:

> ...the pigs's blood is made into *sanguinaccio*, a blood pudding flavoured with pine kernels, currants, candied fruit, cinnamon and nutmeg and thickened with breadcrumbs...The method is as follows. First you must sieve the blood. Then simmer the breadcrumbs in stock for ten minutes, drain them and squeeze them dry. In a bowl mix the blood and the breadcrumbs together. Add the fruit and pine kernels, a pinch of salt and a good sprinkling of all the spices, cinnamon, coriander, nutmeg, white pepper and salt. When the pudding is thoroughly mixed stuff it into a well-cleaned skin. Tie each end but leave a little empty space so that the contents will have room to swell in the cooking and in that way you will prevent the skin from bursting. Place the sausage into a pan of cold water, bring to the boil and boil gently for thirty minutes. When you are ready to serve the dish cut the cold pudding into thick slices and fry them in a pan with a little butter. This is an interesting and very old recipe which combines sweet and savoury elements.

❊ Chapter Two – Bishop Tarlati's Soup ❊

Sanguinaccio has several different names. *Biroldo* is a common name for the version of the pudding which is boiled in a skin like a sausage. *Burischio, migliaccio* or *mueccia*, the later a dialect name used in Silvana's native hamlet, are the names for the pudding that is cooked solely in a flat pan or *tegame*…which is a mixture of the pig's blood, grated *pecorino*, lemon peel, a small amount of breadcrumbs, nutmeg, a little sugar, salt and wine. Silvana puts this mixture into a *tegame* and cooks it over the open fire. She covers the pan with an old tin lid and on top of the lid heaps hot embers, this has the effect of cooking the top of the pudding until it is quite crisp.

The old country people made another interesting dish with *sanguinaccio*, a *frittata di sanguinaccio*. This consists of fried slices of the pudding with beaten egg poured around them in a hot pan to make the *frittata* or Italian omelette.

I would add now that Silvana places her pan on a three-legged trivet over embers drawn away from the main fire, just as did Francesco Gaudentio.

Sanguinaccio in all its forms cooked by Gaudentio and my neighbour Silvana Cerotti are essentially the same; same ingredients, same method. This recipe clearly demonstrates the firm ties between the Tuscan Aretine kitchens of 1686 and 1986 – and beyond.

However, having described Gaudentio's methods of cooking for the students and teachers in the Jesuit College one must return again to the ample banquet provided by Francesco Redi's brother for the Florentine grandees who came to Arezzo to dine in 1668. Here, in the list of foods served on that occasion, are some of Gaudentio's dishes! Are we in the presence of a host equipped with the true Aretine virtues of modesty, parsimony and good sense, or were the Jesuits more inclined to comfortable living than one might be led to think?

※ Beppina and the Kitchens of Arezzo ※

Perhaps the answer is that, like all good cooks, Gaudentio had a modicum of elegant dishes in his repertoire.

Here is Gaudentio's recipe for making *mostarda*, which condiment featured in the third service of Giovanni Battista Redi's banquet, along with a selection of boiled dishes. This *mostarda* is not a classic mustard as we know it today but a fruit preserve, which was mixed with softened mustard seed before serving. Versions of *mostarda* are still a popular condiment in some parts of Italy today, particularly in Modena and Cremona. Gaudentio's instructions are clear and simple and his culinary abilities shine through in his succinct description of how one can tell when jam is sufficiently cooked.

Per far la Mostarda
(To make Mostarda, with Fruit, Spices and Mustard Seed)

> Take the best quality, well-ripened black grapes and as soon as you have removed the pips put the grapes into a preserving pan with a small quantity of well-ripened quinces cut into quarters, some apples of the bright red variety (*melappioni*), some pears and peaches, all cut up and cleaned but not peeled, but with their cores and stones removed. Let these things boil over a bright fire and as soon as the quince and apples are cooked pass the pulp through a fine sieve before it cools. If you let the pulp cool it will be very difficult to sieve. When you have emptied the preserving pan of its contents wash the pan well, then replace the sieved pulp and let it cook over a gentle fire stirring all the while so that it does not stick. I cannot tell you the time it will take to cook as it depends on the quantity. But to know when it is done put a little onto a plate and watch to see that it does not exude water but remains dense, because when you send it to the table you must mix it with cooked must (*mostocotto*). If you have

Chapter Two – Bishop Tarlati's Soup

aromatics like citron, orange, or lemon peel or similar, chop them up finely and add them after you have sieved the pulp, and an hour before the preserve is done you may add all the spices that you please as all will serve well. When the 'jam' is cooked keep it in a glazed terracotta jar and when you want to add the mustard seed let it first soak in water for twelve hours in a warm place. Be careful to add the mustard in proportion to the quantity of jam every time you want to serve some up at table.

Another dish presented in the third service was *Lepre coperta con cardi e sedani* (Hare covered with cardoons and celery). Gaudentio gives a recipe for a similar dish, but he uses a capon not a hare in his written version:

Cappone coperto (Covered Capon)

After having cooked the capon in water with a little salt put into the [resulting] broth a little ground *fior di noce moscato* [which may signify good quality nutmeg or possibly mace, which has the finer flavour as the expression *'fior'* then signified the finest example of a substance, as it does today], crushed almonds and egg yolk beaten into the broth. Then put the capon onto a serving dish and cover it with small slices of bread without the crust, then bathe them with the hot broth containing the egg yolks and spices, make sure the bread is well soaked and afterwards cover it with well-cleaned cardoons which you kept in cold water then cooked in a fat broth. Send it hot to the table.

The handsome parchment bound manuscript of Gaudentio's *Il panunto toscano* 'written in Rome in the year of our Lord 1705' lies today in a department of Arezzo City Library. The manuscript in its original state was not published. However, it was transcribed into modern Italian and commented on by Guido Gianni, a citizen of Arezzo who wrote exceedingly well about his passion – the traditional food of his city. According to the Library's notes regarding Gaudentio's original work, it is not certain as to when it came to be in their possession. The great Aretine bibliophile and archaeologist Gian Francesco Gammurini (1835–1923), whose books form an important part of the Library's collection did not comment on the provenance of the Gaudentio manuscript. Library notes, however, state that it is possible the manuscript's contents were the result of Gaudentio's experience working in the kitchen of the Jesuit College in Arezzo between 1686 and 1688.

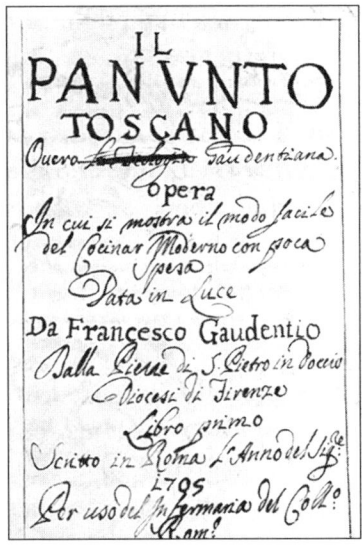

Title page of Il panunto toscano. *The ms is dated 1705, but it was compiled from notes written decades earlier.*

So, the manuscript volume of *Il panunto toscano* is tied to Arezzo by its presence there today in the city's library. However, there is also another curious connection to the city. Page 439 is the last page written by Gaudentio, but on the last three blank pages of the volume are notes written by a certain Lorenzo Baldi and they list some household expenses made by him and his assistant, Giovanni Sallei. Amongst various purchases are those of sultanas, pine kernels and nutmeg. Baldi and Sallei were the Factor and Vice Factor of the Fattoria of Piscinale. This grand villa was, alongside the Villa degli Orti, the property of Francesco Redi and his family. The accounts are, however, addressed to the Signore Cavaliere Ignazio Maria Redi, Francesco Redi's nephew. Now how does it come about that a manuscript presumably written in Rome and dated 1705 comes

Chapter Two – Bishop Tarlati's Soup

to be annotated by members of the Redi household in Arezzo? It is an interesting possibility that the Redi family had some association with Francesco Gaudentio. As we have seen above, two of the dishes served at Giovanni Battista Redi's feast for his distinguished Florentine guests appear in the manuscript. Could Gaudentio have had a hand in preparing this feast? And as we have also seen, records say that Gian Gastone did make a visit to Arezzo in November 1688 and was to be entertained by Giovanni Battista Redi. Giovanni Battista had anxiously written to his brother asking advice about suitable gifts for such important guests – maybe he also sought the help of the more than competent cook Francesco Gaudentio?

The magnificent bound manuscript of *Il panunto toscano* could conceivably be the fine copy of the working notes of Francesco Gaudentio and was sent by him from Rome to his benefactors the Redi family in Arezzo.

Francesco Gaudentio lived to be an old man. He died in 1733 in Rome at the age of 85, still cooking for the Jesuits. At the end of his foreword to *Il panunto toscano* – the simplest and perhaps best of Tuscan dishes, bread toasted over an open fire and spread with olive oil – he wrote the words '*Vivi Felice*', so wishing his readers happy lives.

The Emblem of Arezzo.

❋ Chapter Three ❋

The Land and the City

Spread on the slopes of a gentle hill in eastern Tuscany the ancient city of Arezzo was shrewdly placed at the confluence of four great valleys. The fertile plain which touches the city to the north is where the River Arno running down the narrow Casentino valley curves back on itself and via the Valdarno finds its way to Florence. To the south of the city the low-lying Val di Chiana with its graceful Leopoldina farmhouses widens out and, skirting mediaeval Lucignano and Cortona, descends to the north western tip of Lake Trasimeno. The Via Libbia climbs north east through the Alpe della Luna to join the countryside of the Aretine Valtiberina, passing on its way Anghiari and from there reaching that outpost of Tuscany, Borgo Sansepolcro. And to the east of the city a road traversing the wooded valley of the river Cerfone passes the town of Monterchi and eventually, reaches the Tiber in Umbria at Città di Castello.

This admirable landscape encircling Arezzo, a mixture of softly curved hillsides, steep wooded ravines and fertile plain, has sustained the city for millennia, providing the food sold in that precious link between town and country, the city market.

Arezzo market has been a moveable feast, over the years it has gradually slipped down from the ancient centre on the crown of

✳ Beppina and the Kitchens of Arezzo ✳

The market in the Piazza Grande in the mid-nineteenth century.

the hill to the edge of the city. For hundreds of years it was held high in the venerable Piazza Grande, in times past called the Piazza Vasari in homage to the imposing Vasari arcade which edges one side of the open space. Opposite the Vasari arcade is a fountain in which the pigeons splash and arrange themselves like birds on a Byzantine mosaic. Its abundant waters came from a spring in Poggio di Poti three kilometres outside the city. To bring the water such a distance and to such a height was no small undertaking. However, thanks to the inspiration of Vasari, after much investigation and study, between 1594 and 1603, the Florentine engineer Raffaello di Zanobi di Pagno managed by way of an aqueduct and a tunnel which pierced the city walls to furnish the city with 'copious and salubrious water'.

Through the centuries the market was a focus for the city's necessary relationship with the surrounding countryside. During the deeply unpopular Napoleonic occupation the city had famously been wracked by both plague and a series of famines. The *Maire* of Arezzo, as the *Sindaco* was called at that

Chapter Three – The Land and the City

time, being mindful of the famines that had afflicted Tuscany and which had caused the citizens to riot, was very concerned to ensure that the supply of food to the citizenry was adequate and constant. Bakers were instructed that they must on no account go out of business without informing the *Maire* of that fact. To make sure that enough grain entered the city a second weekly market was ordained. And to assess the quantities of grain provided, in 1813, the French metric system of weights and measures was introduced into Italy.

In the nineteenth century and up until 1968 the Piazza Vasari's old fountain was the place where the vegetable sellers washed their produce and arranged it in elaborate decorative displays for the *Aretini* to buy each day. The piazza was also where the sellers of live chickens and rabbits offered their wares, and doubtless it was here that Beppina's cook came to choose fresh vegetables and plump birds for dinner. It was in this piazza too that the *contadini* coming into Arezzo left their wooden carts. There is an *enoteca* – a wine shop – called La Torre di Gnicche, just off the Piazza Grande, and besides excellent wines it sells good traditional food, exceptional local cheeses, *prosciutto* and salami. They also provide comfortably domestic dishes like their delicious *Polpettone*, a dish for which Beppina too has left us a recipe.

The *enoteca* is named after 'Gnicche', the nickname of one of the great nineteenth-century characters of Arezzo. He was a brigand, but also a popular rascal who was loved and feared by country people in equal measure. Gnicche, whose real name was Federico Bobini, was born in the Borgo di Santa Croce in 1845. Although police records state that his official profession was building and house painting he was in fact a thief, a bandit and eventually a ferocious murderer. However, he was also a charming villain who despised work and loved inns, dancing, gambling and card games. One of his favourite pastimes was to dance in the evenings on the Prato, the park created next to the Duomo for the enjoyment of the *Aretini*. A story is still told

✳ Beppina and the Kitchens of Arezzo ✳

about Gnicche who one evening was overcome by his desire to dance, but as the police were on the lookout for him he decided on an interesting solution. He stopped a woman who was walking in a side street and demanded that she give him her clothes. Dressed in her attire he spent the rest of the night thus disguised, dancing to his heart's content. There is still a humorous saying in Arezzo: '*Sei peggio di Gnicche*' – You're worse than Gnicche!

The handsome Gnicche wore elegant clothes and was a dedicated womaniser, he had several mistresses at the same time, all of whom were jealous of each other. His fame became even greater after he was arrested and incarcerated in the jail which was at the top of what is now the Corso Italia. Today, the building houses the municipal library. From there, he, along with some fellow prisoners, made a daring escape and remained free until Tuesday, 14th March 1871, when he was caught by the *carabinieri*. And here we find a down-to-earth connection with the culture of sustenance at that period. Gnicche was hiding in a farm in Tegoleto, a small village outside Arezzo. The police were combing the countryside for sight of him and whilst they were walking through the fields near Tegoleto one of them noticed an unusual scent, that of meat frying. Poor country people ate meat rarely and then only on a Sunday or a Feast Day. So, with suspicions aroused by the aroma, one of the officers entered a nearby house and found an old man cooking a large pan full of liver. This, the perspicacious officer thought, was far too abundant and expensive a dish for an Aretino *contadino* family to eat on a Tuesday in March. Country families would not have indulged themselves in that manner and on the usually single occasion in winter when the pig was killed and its flesh preserved in the form of *prosciutto* and salami to last around the year, the liver, as we will see below, was made into *fegatelli* which were often kept in jars under lard to be enjoyed in due course of time. The officer, now even more suspicious at the sight of the feast being prepared, left, and he and his

Chapter Three – The Land and the City

fellows hid in a stable and kept watch. First the old man then his wife and daughter tried to slip out of the house but they were all stopped as the police were convinced that the family would try and warn Gnicche whom they surmised was hiding in the barn. And so it was that after a little time had passed Gnicche suddenly appeared brandishing his rifle and handgun. The officer aimed his gun and wounded him and after a very fierce struggle, in which Gnicche bit his assailants hard, he and his fellows manacled the young man. They dragged him down the road and, still struggling, Gnicche jumped into a ditch. It was here that he was shot and later died in the police station at Badia al Pino. He was but twenty-six years of age.

The shooting of the brigand Gnicche.

After his death, which was announced with a placard hung on the *colonnaccia*, a stone column on which civic notices to the public were customarily placed, he became an instant legend and was celebrated in narrative poems and songs. The gentleman brigand was seen as a Robin Hood figure by the country people, who felt that their lives were too hard and their poverty was too great and they needed a hero from their own class in society. His death notice was the last placard to be hung on the column which, since the 1930s, has stood in the Piazza Vasari very near the *enoteca*.

❋ Beppina and the Kitchens of Arezzo ❋

In the late nineteenth century the square was considered to be a working class place, whilst the Piazza San Francesco, at that time called the Piazza Umberto I, with its fashionable Caffé dei Costanti and the nearby Teatro Petrarca, was where the *borghesia* of Arezzo met and left their carriages. Because of the removal of the food market in 1968, today, the Piazza Grande is the least frequented space for daily commerce in Arezzo. It only comes into its full glory at the time of the *Giostra* and the monthly antique market which took the place of the food market, but it is not an area where numerous citizens habitually go in the evening to promenade, although it is a place to eat – two of the grandest and most appreciated restaurants in Arezzo edge the square under the Vasari arcade: Le Logge and La Lancia d'Oro. La Bottega di Gnicche, with its view of the piazza, is the perfect place for an *aperitivo*.

The surplus water which issued from the fountain in the Piazza Grande was sent downhill to the Piazza San Agostino, where it filled the horse troughs. Ultimately, it was used to wash the horses, but according to an account written in 1838, in its course between the two *piazze* the water was channelled through mills where its power was used to grind grain. Several of these mills were to be found in the old city, as befitted Arezzo's status as a large agricultural centre. The waters of Arezzo's river, the Castro, which were covered in 1868 to prevent flooding, pass under the Piazza San Agostino and were used to supply the public washing place where many women came to do their laundry until the 1940s.

The Piazza San Agostino, once called the Piazza Paniere, the piazza of the baskets, was where in the nineteenth and early twentieth centuries, grain, chestnuts, olive oil, wine, river fish, eels and live frogs were sold – it was the liveliest of the city's markets and much loved. It was the chief focus of the September Fair, during which the piazza was filled with massive wooden wine barrels, boxes and crates for carrying

Chapter Three – The Land and the City

grapes, wooden implements, cane baskets as its old name would suggest, even rolling pins and wooden spoons. The custom was that gallant young country men would buy a spoon and then try and slap the bottoms of girls who caught their eye. I have been told that if you did not receive a slap with a spoon at least once during the fair it was a great disappointment. The September Fair is still held in the piazza as was Arezzo's large weekly market from 1968 until a few years ago. A covered fish market survived until recently and every morning there are clothing stalls and plant and fruit sellers and occasionally a farmers' market selling biological produce, artisan candles and hand knitted socks; it is now one of Arezzo's four small daily markets. Near the piazza on a corner of the main shopping street, the Corso Italia, is the place where country people are permitted to bring whatever items they have to sell. It is here that in their seasons you can find baskets of *funghi*, egg yellow *giallini*, chanterelles, or strongly perfumed *porcini*, bunches of thin green wild asparagus from the woods tied into neat bundles with osiers, chestnuts, walnuts, apples, pears, rosemary and fronds of scented fennel replete with their flowers, wild iris, and at Christmas time bunches of holly and mistletoe: good things that have been carefully collected by country women and old men in battered hats and laid out without ceremony on a piece of sacking or a wooden box for the *cognoscenti* of Arezzo to buy.

The Piazza San Agostino, nearby streets and an area outside the walls where livestock was sold, served well until congestion and labyrinthine new traffic systems forced the Saturday market ever further from the *centro storico*. However, the longer walk outside the city walls is still worth the effort in the search for fresh food. The present market stretches for about a mile down the Viale Giotto, a wide road edged with modern buildings and shaded with umbrella pines that leads southwards out of the city. Here, one can observe how present day Aretines go about the ancient business of going to market to look, compare prices and buy.

✳ Beppina and the Kitchens of Arezzo ✳

In 2009, due to the efforts of the *Coldiretti* movement a farmers' market was instituted and it takes place on Wednesday mornings in the street where the traditional Saturday market now takes place. On Wednesday mornings it is therefore possible to buy fresh fruit, vegetables and *pecorino* cheese directly from the farmers themselves.

On the last Saturday before Christmas the market stalls are crowded with people examining sweaters, and sorting through boots and shoes. Black satin skirts and sequinned tops suitable for parties hang from one stall, next to it they are selling pink and green blankets and tablecloths big enough for twelve with matching napkins, all decorated with holly. Arezzo's traditional white curtains – these, however, embroidered in China – hang from a huge awning that covers the merchandise, and large shepherd-sized umbrellas opened and stood upside down hold piles of brightly striped kitchen towels. Further along, a youngish woman accompanied by her father exclaims over china ornaments, perhaps her mother will receive a demure figurine of a lady in crinoline to grace her sideboard, or maybe a large fruit bowl painted with scarlet cherries.

Three stout women choose a roasting dish large enough for the fattest bird, from a stall selling saucepans of all dimensions, huge preserving pans with lids, enamel mugs for heating milk, deep sided pans for tossing pasta in its sauce, and tall cake moulds for *ciambellone,* the high rising sponge cakes that some still make in spite of the variety of *panettone* and *pandoro* on sale in *pasticcierie* and supermarkets. Here too are simple pasta machines to roll out the dough for *tagliatelle* and an Aretino favourite, *pappardelle.* In general this stall sells everything of metal for use in the kitchen. They have knives, choppers and *mezzalune* – curved two handled blades for chopping ingredients such as celery, carrot and onion, herbs and garlic to make the indispensable *battuto,* the perfumed basis for sauces, stews and soups. Boxes on the front of the stall contain forks and table knives with serrated blades and cheap

Chapter Three – The Land and the City

plastic handles, and there are sets of sieves, long handled spoons, pronged forks and funnels. *Passatutta* (moulis) are sold in thin card boxes, they are still favoured for puréeing vegetables like cauliflower or artichokes to add to a béchamel and beaten eggs, all to be poured into a mould and baked in a moderate oven to produce the classic *sformato* much beloved of Beppina and present day Aretines.

On the flower stalls there are mobs of cyclamens, pink, white and fuchsia, stately lilies, poinsettias – *stelle di natale*, but oddly few Christmas trees. Perhaps they were bought earlier in the month, many people begin their decorating after the 8th of December, the Feast of the Immaculate Conception, on the other hand the Christmas tree is a relative newcomer to Tuscany.

Stalls, each to their own trade, are piled with silvery cardoons, crusty white triangles of dried *stoccafissa* and *baccalà*, time- and Church-sanctioned foods for the meatless Christmas Eve meal. The fish stall from Grossetto displays shellfish, *orata* (gilt-headed bream), piles of prawns and writhing eels contained in plastic boxes, another seasonal delicacy. And long before our Christmas festivities came into being, in the Rome of the third century AD, as one of the diners relates in Book III of *The Deipnosophists* by Athenaeus of Naucratis, a goodly fish dinner was not to be disdained.

> First, I spied oysters, wrapped in seaweed, in the shop of an Old Man of the Sea, and sea-urchins too. I grabbed them; for they are the prelude to a daintily ordered dinner. Next, I came upon some little fish, all trembling for fear of what was to happen to them. But I bade them have no fears so far as I was concerned, promising that I wouldn't harm a single one, and bought a large greyfish. Then I took an electric ray-fish, being mindful that when a lady lays tender fingers upon it she must not suffer any hurt

from its thorny touch. For the frying-pan I got some wrasse, sole, shrimp, jack hake, gudgeon, perch, and seabream, and made the dish gayer than a peacock.

There are queues at the cheese stalls which sell local *pecorino nostrano* and *grana* from Reggio Emilia. Hoarse-voiced men intone prices in euros and *centesimi* precise to the last cent to thrifty housewives still nostalgic for the old currency. They handle with ease the great drums of hard, well-aged and flavoured cheese, made in Italy since ancient Roman times, cutting and splitting the forms with iron tools. A stall selling *insaccati* (cured meats and salami) is, in lieu of paper chains, garlanded with strings of sausages both rosy Tuscan and bright red ones flavoured with *peperoncino*. The fruit stalls have mountains of clementines and Tarocco oranges from Sicily, the pavements beneath them are covered with drifts of their bright green leaves and the air is full of the sharp scent of crushed citrus. A middle-aged man walks away from a stall carrying two huge bags of clementines. I have noticed that it is the men who come to the market to buy fruit just as men drive out to vinyards to buy wine together, the latter is not an activity to which women are invited.

I pass through the long street edged with massive pines whose roots have lifted and distorted the pavements, and walk to the far reaches of the market where the farmers sell their produce from handcarts and often a single basket. Old men who come to chat to their mates and make a few extra euros by selling what they can spare from their gardens, a little salad, some onions, chestnuts from the woods, *insalata di campo* from the meadows and, in their season, wild asparagus. I buy a bunch of garlic heads tied with raffia and a few very fresh eggs, all that one old man has left in his twig basket. Returning home I buy lemons from Sorrento and sprigs of scarlet *peperoncino*.

The best stalls in the market are those run by the old farmers

Chapter Three – The Land and the City

who have plots of land outside the city. They pick the produce themselves, load it on to elderly vans and set their stalls up at the very end of the market past the vendors of clothes and shoes and kitchen ware. There are professional market gardeners too who come from places like Cortona whose produce is also good but they do not have the charm of the old men who have been selling sweet carrots, dark Tuscan cabbage, onions and herbs since the market was held in the *centro storico*. As time passes, however, the old men become fewer and some have sold their fields to the industrial market gardeners who now dominate the trade whether in produce or flowers.

On a March day I buy violet artichokes from an aged farmer who tells me how good they are for my health, then to prove his point launches into a long tale of the legendary Arezzo physician who owned land next to his. The doctor lived to the age of ninety-six, had twelve children and was a vegetarian, his advice to my friend was to keep away from the medical profession and their potions until it was the absolute last resort and injections were particularly to be avoided. 'He called me an idiot,' the old man continued, 'when I thought of selling my land. The earth is what we stand on, the doctor told me, only a fool would sell the piece he owns.' I agree with this sentiment and buy a bunch of freshly picked carrots from him, their stalks and leaves un-wilted, their flesh still dusted with grit, he has a basket of wild field salad too, picked that morning, scarce this year due to last summer's over-fierce heat and scanty rainfall. Next to the salad are bundles of *rape* (turnip greens) and a few branches of bay, indispensable ingredient for flavouring *fegatelli*, pieces of liver wrapped in caul and scented with fennel and bay. *Aretini* favour using dried fennel blossoms, which more resemble pollen, rather than the stronger flavoured seed which is used in Florence, and *fegatelli* baked in the oven or braised in a pan are a much enjoyed delicacy in the city. This is not an easy dish to cook, much depends on timing. Too little time gives liver that is bloody, too much and the liver becomes hard, neither of which states make good eating. Fifty to sixty minutes in a medium oven is about right. Piercing the liver with a sharp skewer and seeing whether the juices emerging are pink or golden is the way to judge their fitness for the plate. The Aretines have been eating *fegatelli* for centuries, there is a succinct recipe in *Il panunto toscano* by Francesco Gaudentio who as we have seen (see page 128) came in 1686 to Arezzo as cook to the newly opened school and Church of Saint Ignatius.

> **To make pig's liver *fegatelli* or other sorts except for that of beef.**
> Take the liver and cut it into pieces of about two ounces in weight put them into a pan with the same mixture which I told you to use for fried liver (two or three cloves of crushed garlic, wild fennel seed, dried marjoram), all well crushed; mix some salt into the pan and leave it aside for half an hour then take some pig's caul which you have softened in warm water and if you do not have any to hand you can use any other sort. Roll each piece of liver in a piece of caul putting in a slice of fresh fat and a piece of rosemary or fennel, or otherwise tie them with string and put them onto a skewer made with a branch of bay: let them cook over a lively fire, cut into one and if it has lost its blood, well then, they are ready.

Gaudentio, an experienced and practical cook, includes here essential advice, modern recipes often neglect to tell you to soften the caul in warm water, which makes it easier to wrap around the liver.

However, even earlier in the Mediterranean's rich culinary history we again find Athenaeus' *The Deipnosophists*, in this instance discussing, with humour and scholarship, pieces of liver wrapped in caul.

> The next dish to be brought in was fried liver wrapped

CHAPTER THREE – THE LAND AND THE CITY

in 'fold-over', the so-called *epiplus*, which Philetaerus in Tereus calls *epiploon*. After gazing upon it Cynulcus said, 'Tell us, learned Ulpian, whether liver thus encased is mentioned anywhere.' He answered, 'Show us first in what author *epiplus* is used for the fatty caul.' Thereupon Myrtilus took up their challenge and said: 'The word **epiplus** for caul' occurs in *The Bacchants* of Epicharmus: 'The leader he hid in a caul'; also in his *Envoys*: 'round the loin and the caul.' So, too, Ion of Chios in his *Sojournings II*: 'hiding it in the caul'.

'You are reserving the caul, my dear Ulpian, against the time when you shall be wrapped in it and consumed, and so rid us all of your questionings. But it is only fair that you should cite testimony about liver dressed in this way, since you said a while ago, when we were discussing ears and feet, that Alexis mentions it in *Crateias* or *The Apothecary*. The entire passage is valuable as illustrating a number of things, and since your memory at present is not equal to it, I will recite it at length myself.'

'Then came some meats – feet, snouts, and swines' ears, and liver wrapped in caul; for it is ashamed of its own livid colour. No professional cook shall come near these, or even look upon them. He will rue it, let me tell you. Rather, I shall myself act as steward, so cleverly, so smoothly, and elegantly (yes, I shall make the dish myself), that I shall cause the feasters now and then to push their teeth into their plates for very joy. The preparation and composition of all these foods I am ready to disclose, proclaim, and teach for nothing if anybody wishes to learn.'

The Deipnosophists, Athenaeus of Naucratis, Book III.

But one cannot speak of *fegatelli* without remembering a verse of the Tuscan Luigi Pulci in his comic masterpiece about the giant Morgante where the giant's greedy friend Margutte recites a gastronomic version of the Creed.

❊ Beppina and the Kitchens of Arezzo ❊

Canto Eighteen, 116
I believe in the tart and in the tartlet:
one is the mother and the other is her son;
but our real holy father is the *fegatello*

Cantare Decimottavo, 116
e credo nella torta e nel tortello:
l'una e la madre e l'altro e il suo figliuolo;
e 'l vero paternostro e il fegatello
Il Morgante maggiore, 1483

Next to the talkative old farmer there is the man who keeps the organic produce stall. He grows lentils and beans, onions and garlic, herbs of all sorts and all grown to the strictest standards. All over the stall there are painstakingly written placards typed out on an old typewriter, which explain his philosophy and the healthy virtues of his wares. His garlic heads look on the small side but he explains that one tiny clove has more flavour and power in it than a whole head of supermarket garlic. I have my doubts but buy some anyway, later I find that he was quite right in his judgement, the garlic has abundant fire and flavour.

The stalls that sell the best cheese always have queues of people patiently waiting their turn; their cheese is good and so are the prices. I watch two men who return each week and are always laughing and joking with their customers. They are serving a very old woman who is carrying a cloth shopping bag. They cut her a large piece of *pecorino*, it is firm and creamy of flesh and about seventy days in age. She protests that it is too much, they laugh and tell her how good it is, then they add a chunk of Parmesan to the scale despite her protests. With a flourish they wrap it all up and charge her much less than the cheese is worth. When my turn comes I buy *pecorino* too from the same form and when I get home I find that they have also added a piece of a longer-seasoned cheese at no charge, to let me taste the quality. Naturally, I will return.

Chapter Three – The Land and the City

Three-quarters of the way down the market street the stalls expand into two rows, left to the food sellers, on the right, more cloth merchants. Just next to the large stall that sells picks and shovels, copper bowls and ornate iron letter boxes, the Evangelical Christians have their stall; a tiny one, neatly stacked with bibles and tracts. It is manned by one or two gloomy looking men who stare disapprovingly at the crowd. I sense that they do not enjoy the exuberance of market days, and suspect that perhaps they view this duty as some sort of penance for past misdemeanours or sins of omission. Their silence and very stance dissuades one from looking too closely, their presence seems totally alien amongst the bustling good-humoured crowd. The Evangelicals make a strong contrast to the Catholic priest that I have just seen giving the Easter blessing in a *profumeria* in the Corso Italia. Dressed in a deep violet cassock covered with a sparklingly white lace surplice, wearing his black *berrétta* at a discreet angle, he sprinkled a little holy water and blessed the shop and its owners before processing on to the next store. Arezzo is divided into parishes and their priest will visit each house that requests a blessing during Holy Week. In the country, as I have written elsewhere, my neighbours the Cerotti family prepare a bowl of new-laid eggs for the priest to bless during his visit and cook him a magnificent lunch. In contrast, my city neighbour tells the story of the parish priest, one who was famously held in great affection by his flock, who came to his apartment one Easter. Gianpaulo is not a practising Catholic but, he says, 'this priest was a friend so I invited him in and offered him some Vin Santo to fortify him in his labours. As I turned my back to pour him out a drink I noticed in the mirror that he was hastily sprinkling holy water and blessing the house whilst I was not looking. I poured the wine slowly until I saw that he had finished, then I turned around.' Both honours satisfied! It seems to me that the Evangelicals have a hard row to hoe in this most subtle of lands.

Right at the very end of the market are the *vivaiüsti* who come

Beppina and the Kitchens of Arezzo

in lorries carefully stacked with young olive trees and bundles of vine shoots, herbs and flowering shrubs. The vine shoots are laid out on the ground in piles, they are about 60 cm long, the short roots splay out at the end and the woody stem is liberally coated with burgundy-coloured wax. To plant vines successfully it is necessary to dig them a deep hole and plant at least 50 cm of the woody stem below the soil. The roots are trimmed with secateurs before the vine is planted.

This year I buy two very young but tall olive trees from a stall right at the end of the market; whilst carrying them carefully towards the car a small country man rushes up to me and caresses the foliage and gives me a lesson in pruning. I can see his fingers are itching to get his hands on a pair of clippers to trim my trees before I ruin them. He is carrying a large bag full of a remarkable amount of herring and *baccalà*, he explains that he has to rush home to put the fish in the fridge before he can return to get his young olive trees of which he needs six. We part with a cordial handshake.

❋ Chapter Four ❋

Sustenance

Arezzo owes much of its intimate character to its position in the middle of a fertile landscape. The small shops of the *Quartieri* are filled with the good produce of the Casentino, the valley of the shepherds that it is said once provided the ancient Romans with cheese; it has been said that the valley's name comes from the Latin *casus*, cheese. However it is more likely that the name derives from the Latin term for closed, *clusus*. This as the valley is narrow and confined and was not easy of access. Game, truffles, freshwater fish and of course *pecorino* cheese are delivered from its hillsides. From the Val di Chiana comes the excellent meat of the huge white Chianina cattle, and the quiet white wine, Bianco Vergine del Val di Chiana which at its best tastes of honey. The Aretine hillsides provide Chianti and magnificent green olive oil, which in Tuscany has a reputation for being of a particularly intense flavour.

From the Cathedral and the Medicean fortress the old city spreads out in a semi-circle, it is divided into quarters each with their own colours and devices: Porta Crucifero, Porta Sant' Andrea, Porta Santo Spirito and Porta del Foro. Churches, squares, narrow lanes, some of which have never been paved, and broad streets that date from the nineteenth century punctuate and rib the old city, still contained in large part by the venerable walls. You may walk from Arezzo's highest point to the lower bastion walls in a matter of ten or so minutes, the *centro storico* still remains an intimate space. Citizens play out their lives on this beguiling stage and in spite of the ever-increasing industrialisation of European life many seek a harmonious balance between modernity and tradition, life in the city and that of the surrounding countryside.

This is a city that has grown throughout the ages, each civilisation and generation leaving their mark, from the Etruscan core to the Roman vision of a city, from mediaeval solidity through the brittle vitality of the Renaissance and on to the grace of the Habsburg-Lorraine era (known in Italy as the Habsburg-Lorena). Then, as we have seen, after the Unification of Italy, came the solemn architecture of the later nineteenth century. Each period added new forms, buildings and decorations to the city. On the hills to the east reached by narrow lanes that wind through olive groves and vineyards there lie the ancestral villas of the leading families of Arezzo's past. Today, from north to south the industrial zones of the present time embrace the old city, the adjuncts of contemporary life. Only a slender stem of green which accompanies the historic water bearing Vasari arches still connects the city to its surrounding countryside and this too was threatened by a plan to build a new church and its accompanying offices, a plan which during 2014–15 was the cause of dispute between the citizens of Arezzo and the city's Bishop. Fortunately the voices of the defenders of Arezzo's beauteous *paesaggio* were heard.

Today, walking down through the city along the radiating streets, one passes easily from one epoch of architecture to the next. And now on the surface the city surges with activity; Arezzo is not yet an open-air museum, it has a large young population and a vigorous modern life of its own that does not solely depend upon tourism for sustenance. Arezzo is the capital of its own Province and as such is a magnet for the

Chapter Four – Sustenance

inhabitants of the surrounding countryside who come to the city for its market, its shops and entertainment. In reverse, the citizens of Arezzo still have strong ties to the countryside and base much of their diet on the good produce the land provides. Besides thriving wholesale businesses which Arezzo's geographic position and proximity to the A1, Italy's main artery, encourages, it is the working of gold that makes the city prosperous. Arezzo is the largest producer of gold chain in the world; not that you would easily divine that fact, the gold working factories and those which make machinery for the trade, are discreetly hidden in the neat industrial zones on the outskirts of the old city.

The *Aretini* besides being resilient and industrious are also sensual people, they appreciate gold and coral, subtle colour and fine texture. Aretines, as the city's diverse shops display, appreciate oriental carpets, paintings, rich fabrics, porcelain, indeed all manner of antiques and not merely because these things represent wealth but also because of their intrinsic beauty. For millennia the Aretines have been craftsmen, and, as archaeologists such as Mortimer Wheeler found, their wares travelled wide:

> This little book first took shape on a hot May morning in 1945, when an Indian student of mine emerged excitedly from a deep trench beside the Bay of Bengal waving a large slice of a red dish in his hand. Removal of the slimy sea-mud revealed the dish as a signed work of a potter whose kilns flourished nearly 2,000 years ago and 5,000 miles away, on the outskirts of Arezzo in Tuscany. Were drama admissible to the archaeological scene, I should have been tempted to describe the moment as dramatic. In that moment the pages of the historians and the geographers leapt to life; the long, acquisitive arm of imperial Rome became an actuality.
> Mortimer Wheeler, *Rome beyond the Imperial Frontiers*

✳ Beppina and the Kitchens of Arezzo ✳

Wheeler's student had found a piece of Aretine *terra sigillata* ware, which was the first to be designed for the ancient Roman table.

A grape picker on a piece of ancient Roman Aretine ware c. 1st century AD.

The memories of Tuscan Arezzo are encapsulated in the city's lovingly preserved architecture and they can be perceived as clearly as one hears the chimes of the church clocks that mark out the passing of the hours. The street where I live high up in the historic centre of Arezzo runs along the line of the ancient Etruscan walls of the city; in fact there is Etruscan stonework in the cellars which has been dated to 400 BC. The first dwelling on the site was built shortly after 1150 AD upon this massive foundation and the remains of two early mediaeval towers, but no one knows who owned or lived in that building. From documents preserved in the municipal archives one can see that the house enters into the city records in 1443 as the property of one Cristofano di Ristoro di Mauro, a baker, but there are no traces left of his ovens. Between then and 1493 it passed into the possession of the noble family of the Ricoveri and three hundred years later into the hands of the Bishops of Arezzo. Our wine is kept cool amidst stones that are in the region of two thousand four hundred years old, the vast cellars shelter too an ancient olive press and for that matter the baskets of vegetables,

☀ Chapter Four – Sustenance ☀

bicycles and discarded furniture that belong to everyone who inhabits the various floors of the palazzo.

The street is a narrow one edged with buildings of diverse ages, some of them belong to the Church, some to the *Comune*, the council, others to medical practitioners which is a venerable tradition; just as there is a street in Arezzo where many of the shops sell knives and hunting equipment and which was the street of the armourers, our street has always been inhabited by physicians for whose presence during and also after the Renaissance, Arezzo was renowned. Our sitting room was once the studio of the much consulted doctor, Lorentino Presciani, who was born in Arezzo in 1721; perhaps not an entirely easeful notion, considering the type of remedies available in his day and the probable sufferings of his patients. I imagine a portly Aretino merchant being bled with leeches while the distinguished physician looks on and makes notes for his collection of consultations. In his portrait, Presciani is shown seated beneath what is now our window with its stone window seat, there is a quill pen in his hand and books all around him. His face has a kindly expression and it seems that kind he was, as although he was often called upon to attend the ruling Habsburg-Lorraine family who in 1737 succeeded the last of the Medici Dukes, he also initiated medical services for the poor of the city.

Presciani died on the 13th of May 1799 at the age of seventy-eight, whilst the people of Cortona, co-instigators along with the Aretines of the Viva Maria uprising, were engaged in fierce skirmishes with Polish soldiers, who on their way from Rome to Venice were acting as a police force on behalf of Napoleon. In spite of what the film starring Brigitte Bardot and Jeanne Moreau would intimate, the Viva Maria rebellion actually took place in the Province of Arezzo, not Mexico.

Arezzo had been taken under the control of a small French

force in 1799, and unlikely though it may seem, a wooden tree of Liberty sporting the French flag was erected in the Piazza Vasari; the angry and very religious *Aretini* were exhorted to embrace the new age of Revolution, a concept that they naturally met with suspicion and hostility. The majority of the citizens took exception to the greedy foreigners who commandeered their mules, urinated in the streets and harassed the women.

During the previous years the province had suffered badly from continuous famines and an earthquake and the people were already enraged and discontented; feelings which had only been softened by the timely occurrence of a miracle. In 1796 an image of the Madonna in a cellar near the Porta San Clemente was seen to have suddenly become shining white and radiant, with tears coursing down her cheeks.

One month after the arrival of the French a carriage was seen entering Arezzo; in it were a coachman and an old woman waving the Habsburg flag. Swiftly the rumour spread that the Madonna del Conforto and San Donato the patron saint of the city had come to the aid of the citizens. Encouraged by this divine sign of approval the citizens and the country people armed themselves with whatever they could and started the Viva Maria rebellion which erupted too in other nearby cities. The French were routed and sent on their way. It is to be hoped that Dr Presciani lived long enough to know that the Aretines sent the foreign troops packing, at least for a while.

However, after the initial defeat Napoleon's troops returned the following year and this time stayed until 1814. They exacted a savage revenge upon the Aretines, ransacking the churches, emptying the coffers and then going on to reorganise the public finances, sending the proceeds back to Paris. They did, however, have some positive effects upon the life of Arezzo. The Caffè dei Costanti is the most historically important café in

✳ Chapter Four – Sustenance ✳

Arezzo, and is the legacy of Napoleon's intrusion into Arezzo. The Academy of the Costanti was formed on the 28th of July 1804 and was installed in a set of rooms near the great Church of San Francesco with its sublime frescoes created by Piero della Francesca. The Academy was an enterprise in which its members held shares and it was originally mainly patronised not exclusively by the nobility but by the rising middle classes and the professional people of the city who held Jacobin opinions. Debates and political discussions were held there as well as social events. Citizens, men and women, which latter was a very modern idea, were permitted to enter the rooms on the understanding that they were to be correctly dressed, men wearing boots and coats. There were some, however, who were denied entrance, those who followed vile professions and wives who had separated from their husbands. Within a few years the Academy enlarged and in 1808 the familiar Caffé dei Costanti was inaugurated on the ground floor, a venue which still today delights the citizens. The beautiful painted rooms of the Academy above the Caffé were used until the 1970s to hold meetings, balls and entertainments and were and still are known as *Le Stanze*.

Another pleasant legacy left by Napoleon is *'gattò'* – *gâteau* – a cake that has since those times figured large in celebratory feasts in the Aretine countryside. Made from sponge cake and cream and Alkermes, *gattò* is still to be found in the city and delicious examples of it were sold in the Caffé dei Costanti.

There is a curious intimacy about living in an ancient building in a small *centro storico*. The spaces that surround us have been formed through millennia, the rooms changed to suit the needs and whims of countless generations, windows opened and closed in the fabric of the walls, doors enlarged and diminished. The plaster of ancient vaults bears the finger prints of anonymous builders who each led lives filled with individual minutiae. Diverse families have lived here. I sit on the same

❋ Beppina and the Kitchens of Arezzo ❋

window seat where five hundred years ago another woman surely sat and gazed into the garden below at her herbs and vegetables and where Dr Presciani too wrote in the sunlight; and in time, others will take our places.

At the end of our street is a narrow road which climbs from the lower town right up to the Piazza del Duomo and the town hall; Pietro Aretino, writer, satirist, courtier, author of witty erotica and sometimes blackmailing letters, *buongustaio*, and scourge not only of princes but also of filthy kitchens was born here in 1492, at about the same time that our palazzo was enlarged into near its present form and Christopher Columbus was about to discover America for the Europeans. Aretino was destined to pass much of his life in Rome and Venice but in his letters wrote magnificently about food and in so doing demonstrated his nostalgia and longing for the flavour and simplicity of Aretine cuisine.

Around five hundred years earlier, the monk Guido d'Arezzo, who invented musical notation, was also born in a house on this same street. He is commemorated by a large statue erected in 1882 in the eponymous Piazza Guido Monaco and also with a Philharmonic Society again named for him. On the other hand, in a guidebook written in the late 1880s, the author conceals Aretino under the name of Pietro Bacci. There is reason to suppose that Aretino's father might have been of the noble Bacci family and not a humble cobbler, but the writer goes on to describe the divine Pietro as a satiric poet and a '*cittadino depravatissimo*'! As Aretino himself writes:

> Take care that Aretino be your friend,
> for he's a bad enemy to wrong.
> His words alone the Pope's high fame could rend,
> so may God guard us all from such a tongue.

Even today Pietro Aretino tends to be discussed rather in the *sotto voce* manner in which one might talk about some reprobate

❋ Chapter Four — Sustenance ❋

uncle, which is odd, as it is said that the *Aretini* are proud of their ability to be outspoken. However, the works of Piero della Francesco, Vasari, Signorelli and Cimabue, in which Arezzo is also rich, are obviously far easier to present to visitors than a collection of even the wittiest of writings. But it would seem that if the local press is to be believed the voluptuous legacy of Aretino and other earlier masters is as deeply ingrained in the Aretine consciousness as their love of art and music. These days, writing in Aretino's scurrilous tradition, local newspapers from time to time have fun with the scandalous behaviour of various townsfolk, real and perhaps apocryphal, as names are never mentioned. One might remember at this point that in the Vicolo del Orto, near the Cathedral, there is the well that Boccaccio mentions in his *Decameron,* in the Fourth story of the Seventh day, the account of the jealous Tofano and his quick-witted and unfaithful wife Monna Ghita. Perhaps it is the cautionary tale of the indiscreet Tofano intent on the unnecessary broadcasting of his wife's infidelities to the town that partly nurtured the secrecy for which the *Aretini* are famed.

Il Vernacoliere, a monthly paper published in Livorno which is written in dialect, is much appreciated in Arezzo. It is both comic and bawdy and anti-authoritarian and springs from a Tuscany that for centuries was under the control of the Medici and then the House of Habsburg-Lorraine whose domination produced a healthy disrespect for the powerful in the population. Another literary device reminiscent of Pietro Aretino's pasquinades, his anonymously presented diatribes against those in power who displeased him, are the poems that on occasion appear plastered onto walls and lamp posts in Arezzo, well-written verses, making pointed politically orientated comments upon city affairs. Aretino's appeared in the Rome of the 1500s hung onto a battered ancient Roman statue whose nickname was Pasquino, the statue standing at a corner of the Palazzo Orsini. The pasquinades of the 1500s were used by members of the Curia as a weapon against powerful citizens, cardinals and

❋ Beppina and the Kitchens of Arezzo ❋

popes. Today's Aretine pasquinades follow in the tradition of the anonymous anti-clerical poems sold in Arezzo's market in the nineteenth century which joyously described the peccadilloes of certain members of the priesthood and high society.

Aretino who wrote as voluptuously about food as he did about sex, amongst many banquets he described, gives in his *Dialogues*, the 'lives of nuns, wives and courtesans', an enticing menu of a meal enjoyed – 'the delicate parts of a chicken, a whole fat capon, olives, red apples, cheese relishes, quince jelly and sugar plums to sweeten the breath'. Such a meal contrasts well with his blasts of scorn about the 'foul repasts' he suffered when a servant in Rome: '…the dinner bell, that ambassador of starvation', beckoned them to a table 'covered with more stains than a painter's apron'. 'For meat we have some ancient scrap of beef…[and] ox milk cheese so hard and dry that it brings on a colic that would kill a statue'. While 'the stench of a prison is less unpleasant than the stink of a servants' hall, the former comes from prisoners and the latter from the dying'. Aretino was, however, born in Arezzo and along with a sharp Aretine tongue was, if not quite an adherent of those eminent Tuscan virtues of simplicity and parsimony, certainly appreciative of them when it came to daily sustenance. In a letter written in Venice in 1538 to a sculptor friend, *Messer* Simon Bianco, who was born in Loro Ciuffenna, in the Province of Arezzo, Aretino offers advice on obtaining and enjoying simple food:

> In the morning rise and happily practising your art enjoy the wait for two chops or a little *frittata* or *la carbonata*, some fried salt pork to call you to your feet […] buy a portion of fish, some eggs brought by the villagers […], never return to your lodgings without some radishes in your hand and some field salad in your handkerchief, and sing as you go.

Aretino also quotes Socrates, saying: 'Eat to live – don't live to

Chapter Four – Sustenance

eat' (*Mangiate per vivere e non vivete per mangiare*), advice which was probably favourably received by Bianco, who as well as having a reputation for parsimony was also pitifully poor.

Aretino's use of the words *frittatina* and *la carbonata* are interesting. He is trying to tempt Bianco to eat by conjuring up an appetising scent, one that we might also think of as being an ideal call to breakfast – eggs and bacon. The famous Roman dish *Spaghetti alla carbonara* which has attached to it many stories as to its origins such as charcoal burners carrying eggs to the forest, hungry carters arriving in the city and US and British soldiers introducing army issue bacon into Rome after the war, might simply encapsulate the antiquated Italian word *carbonata* for today's *rigatino* or *pancetta*, a prime ingredient in the recipe.

As I have mentioned above, the scandalous adventures of the *Aretini* usually remain discreetly anonymous and although outspoken the citizens tend to confine their observations to those topics that reside in the public domain; about their own affairs and private lives the Aretines are believed to be intensely reserved. It is also said the citizens are extremely discreet about their food, indeed it has been written by a distinguished Aretino writer that 'it is the occupation of the mad' to try and write about the cuisine of the Aretines, so reluctant are they to discuss what they eat at home. This ingrained and exquisite discretion is perhaps not unexpected as it is also said that the citizens have astonishingly attenuated memories and bear the legacy of the silence imposed by centuries of subjugation and harsh taxation firstly under the hated Florentines who owned their city and repressed them vigorously from the towering walls of the Sangallo fortress and secondly by the French. History and literature it seems, have influenced the people of Arezzo in decided and surprising ways which affect their outlook on life. The *Aretini* are tenacious and energetic, secretive and at the same time outspoken, their distinguished and often turbulent

✺ Beppina and the Kitchens of Arezzo ✺

past has endowed them with wit, a robust sense of humour, piety and caution. Similarly the Aretines at table display both gusto and frugality, quick to feast in times of plenty they have, however, learned the millennial lessons of war and famine. Sustenance is a serious thing; in Tuscany, bread is not to be taken lightly and never wasted. As small children have often been told: 'When you go to Heaven, before they let you in, Saint Peter will send you to pick up each crumb of bread that you wasted.'

So, bearing in mind hints of the secretive tendencies of the Aretines when it comes to discussing their food, how can we best discover what it is that the citizens prefer to eat for daily nourishment and even the occasional feast?

Near the summit of the venerable road that leads from the Church of San Francesco to the Duomo, close to the house of Pietro Aretino, there is a small grocery store. It is owned by Quinto and Fiorella (Dina) Peruzzi who have made it their living for nearly 30 years. Their shop is neither large, smart nor modern but this small room filled to bursting with the items of sustenance used every day in every Aretine household is like a tough heart, pumping energy to its customers. It is stores like this that best demonstrate what the elusive *Aretini* really eat. They sell a myriad items, from *acqua minerale* to *zucchero*, plus stamps for legal documents, handy for those who have business in the nearby town hall and magistrates' court. It is here that I buy our daily bread and much besides.

Filling a Gothic stone doorway, the shop's façade is a legacy of the thirties, on a dark red cornice there is a government licence, their permission to retail groceries and tobacco, salt and stamps. Here there is no attempt to entice customers with elegant typography and fancy displays, this *alimentari* is necessary.

In summer the glass door is held open but one passes through

Chapter Four – Sustenance

a curtain of plastic ribbons, which discourage insects from gathering in the aromatic interior of the shop. It is dark and usually full of people more or less patiently waiting their turn. This morning there are a few elderly housewives who are here to buy precisely enough fresh bread for a day, tomorrow the bread will be fresh again, so why buy more? Alongside the colours of the association of grocers to which the Peruzzi belong there is a poster in the shop window that advertises bread baked in a wood-fired oven. There is a rumour circulating that EU regulations have banned the cooking of food like pizza and bread in ovens fuelled by wood but up to now these particular regulations seem to have got mislaid on the way from Brussels to Arezzo. The bread that the Peruzzi sell is all good but probably best are the loaves baked in a wood-fired oven and those made with stoneground flour that is milled in the Casentino valley. This flour produces a loaf which is still classed as white bread but the crumb is of a light gold colour. Today, as it was for centuries, good bread is the staple of Tuscan food and as hard as they have tried industrial food companies have not succeeded in changing the Tuscans' taste for traditionally baked loaves with firm texture and unmistakable flavour.

> …in the vicinity of Arezzo…a magnificent plain unfolds. No field could be neater than this one, nowhere even a clod of earth, everything is as finely ground as if it were sifted. Wheat thrives very well here, apparently finding all the conditions appropriate to its nature.
>
> Goethe, *Italian Journey*

At the Peruzzi's you can order specialities in advance and they will deliver if you live in the vicinity. Shopping there is often interrupted by a phone call from a housebound customer with an intricate list, or someone will drop in an order written in sprawling copperplate which Dina will painstakingly make up and Quinto will deliver on the pillion of his motor scooter. He

❊ Beppina and the Kitchens of Arezzo ❊

will also offer to deliver the package of six bottles of mineral water that I am going to buy. One of the women in the queue wants 150 grams of one of the essential, much loved foodstuffs of Italy, some *prosciutto nostrano*, good and salty and home cured, the *prosciutto dolce* from Parma is too mild for her taste. Strange to relate we are standing not far from the remains of the city's Etruscan wall and Dina is carving slices from a large salted ham: the Etruscans too preserved ham either by salting or smoking and became rich from exporting the meat to the appreciative Greeks. Another woman in the queue wants *mortadella* for her sister who is not well, just the gentle food to tempt an invalid and then a small piece of *pecorino stagionato*, hard sheep's cheese that has been kept until it is strong and piquant, and she does not want *pecorino* rendered insipid with additions of cows' milk, thank you, only sheep's milk will produce the intense and particular flavour she requires. A talkative woman who works at the town hall buys enough fresh *tagliatelle* for her family for Sunday lunch and the precise quantity of *sugo* to go with it. The shop is full of customers, young men eating *panini* filled with salami and cheese, a woman buying sugar to make jam with fruit from her walled garden. The old man and his companion, here from the country on an errand at the town hall, are drinking wine. A nun from the nursing home in a nearby piazza buys a very large quantity of yoghurt, perhaps for her residents' breakfast. The crowded shop appears to me as an example of the 'preciousness of the transient', a fleeting few minutes of time in the long history of Arezzo.

Behind the glass of the counter are bowls of pasta sauces made by Dina and her daughter who runs a bar that sells light lunches further down the street. The sauces are simple but made from the best ingredients, there is naturally a meat sauce, *sugo*, a plain tomato sauce and a *Pesto alla genovese* made from basil, *pecorino* and pine kernels. There is also a large bowl of *panzanella*. Boccaccio in his writings mentioned a certain *'pan lavato'*, literally washed bread, which like all good Tuscans

❋ Chapter Four – Sustenance ❋

the *Aretini* still eat. The celebrated salad is made with soaked Tuscan bread squeezed dry and crumbled with the fingers, mixed with pieces of cucumber, onion and tomato, perfumed with basil leaves and irrigated with olive oil. A recipe which is remarkably similar to the one extolled in verse written by the painter 'Bronzino' (1503–72) in the 1500s.

> He who would like to walk above the stars
> of sweet harmony (a quick trip to heaven) should moisten
> bread with oil and vinegar and eat it until his belly bursts.
> A salad of onion cut up
> with purslane and cucumber
> surpasses any other of life's pleasures,
> consider then if one were to add basil and rocket!

> *Ma chi vuol trapassar sopra le stelle*
> *di melodia v'aggiunga olio e aceto*
> *e 'ntinga il pane e mangia a tirapelle.*
> *Un 'insalata di cipolla trita*
> *colla porcellanetta e citrioli*
> *vince ogni altro piacer di questa vita*
> *considerate poi se aggiungessi basilico e ruchetta.*

Next to the *panzanella* sits a dish of chicken liver paste, this is indispensable for a Tuscan Sunday lunch, spread on slices of bread to make the much loved *crostini di fegatini*, the difference being here in Arezzo the mixture contains *milza*, spleen, which has a rich, meaty and very particular flavour much appreciated by the *Aretini*. Sometimes there is a plate of spiced *polpette* made from minced *vitello* in much the same way that Beppina's recipe suggests or a dish piled with tender pieces of chicken breast cooked with sage and butter. Another favourite is Dina's *galantina*. This consists of the pounded white meat from a boned chicken mixed with veal, delicate spices and studded with sliced boiled eggs and green pistachios. The mixture is then stuffed back into the chicken skin and the whole simmered in stock.

❋ Beppina and the Kitchens of Arezzo ❋

Galantina is a delicacy that is much appreciated in Arezzo and often favoured for luncheons of a certain tone. There are recipes in the houses of the *alta borghesia* which have been closely guarded since the early 1800s; it is one of the dishes thought to have been introduced into Tuscany with Napoleon's invading armies. *Galantina* is expensive and time consuming to make but only the exigencies of war time and domestic trouble have occasionally altered its substance.

Three workmen come into the shop, they are there to buy their lunches and cigarettes. Beside the kilo loaves of Tuscan bread which are still made without salt and justly contain no ingredients other than yeast, flour and water, the couple sell *filone*, narrow loaves of 500 grams in weight, *ciabatta*, a flat bread named after old slippers because of its rough flat form, and *panini*, bread rolls made of different doughs and in various shapes. Part of the shop's trade consists of the selling of *panini* to workmen, office workers and, on the first Saturday/Sunday of every month, antique dealers who trade in the Arezzo antique fair, the largest of its kind in Europe which unfolds in the upper reaches of the old town.

These *panini* are far from being mass-produced sandwiches wrapped in packets and kept in refrigerated cabinets which render the food unpleasantly cold to eat. Dina splits a roll and removes some of the crumb to make a space for an abundant filling, or if required, by clutching the kilo loaf to her aproned bosom and wielding a long sharp bread knife, she cuts two thick slices of firm bread; sometimes a labourer, feeling at home, will ask for the crusty heel of the loaf to chew. One workman chooses the succulent tuna in its large round can and wants it spiked with a spoonful of capers; the other wants the fiery Neapolitan salami bright red from the *peperoncino*, he could have chosen a more traditional Arezzo sausage, *finocchiona*, a soft salami made from pork, perfumed with fennel seeds. Then there are the dishes of *sott'olio* to be considered, gherkins, carrots, tiny

❋ Chapter Four – Sustenance ❋

onions, fat artichokes, mouth-watering when stuffed into fresh bread which absorbs the olive oil in which they are preserved. Dina weighs the fillings for these most individual of sandwiches, presses them into the bread, wraps them in brown paper and carrying a two litre bottle of wine the workmen take them off into the nearby park where they will enjoy them in the shade of the trees from which they will have a view of the olive groves and the vines that still grow up to the north eastern walls of Arezzo. These customers are Dina's favourites – it is clear from the loving way she makes up the sandwiches that her vocation is to feed people.

The wine that the Peruzzi sell is ranged on the highest of the shelves that run around three walls of the room. It is a modest selection which includes some of the better chiantis, a few well-known white wines from the north, some *spumante* customary at the end of a festive meal, Vin Santo of various qualities, but their most easily reached bottles, one shelf down, contain good quiet local wine. It comes from the Cantina dei Vini Tipici dell'Aretino, a co-operative association founded in 1970 which makes and sells wine made from grapes grown exclusively in the Province of Arezzo. The five hundred or so farmers who are members of the association harvest their own grapes then transport them to the Cantina where they are weighed, and the farmers are paid accordingly. Although the Cantina produces a range of wines, the Peruzzi stock their Bianco Vergine del Val di Chiana D.O.C. and their Chianti D.O.C.G. These wines are simply presented and unpretentious, which is something to be grateful for in these days of fancy labels often covering poor wine. The Cantina which lies on the outskirts of Arezzo is open to everyone, from owners of *trattorie* who come with *demigiani* to be filled from an apparatus like a petrol pump to individuals who have come for their wine in labelled *bordolese* 75 cl. bottles or flasks of 1.5 litres.

It has been suggested by Brussels that a tax on wine should

❋ Beppina and the Kitchens of Arezzo ❋

be levied in wine-producing countries in the same manner as it is, for example, in Britain or Denmark, the proceeds of this tax, however, to be paid to the EU. Naturally this notion was received about as well as the ban on wood fires for baking. In Italy it is as normal to drink wine as it is in Britain to drink tea. On average Italians drink 54 litres of wine per capita, a year. Wine is an indispensable part of what northerners call the 'Mediterranean diet', a traditional and healthy way of eating that provably helps to prevent the heart disease that afflicts countries outside the wine-producing regions. A dubious notion then to risk turning a normal daily beverage into a luxury and so distort an ancient way of life.

Quinto and Dina like many other small shopkeepers are the unsung heroes of Italian life. They work long hours for profits that tend to decrease every year in face of the competition from the supermarkets on the outskirts of the town. They are cheerful, knowledgeable and passionate about the quality of the food that they sell and it is people like them who are the keepers of the traditional character of Italian daily nourishment. Dina, a small woman with busy fingers and bright brown hair which matches her eyes, doubts the quality of supermarket food reasoning that if the contents of a bottle of a fizzy drink cost less than the plastic container, then naturally the drink can be neither wholesome nor pleasant. She knows from her own experience how long it takes to raise a chicken for the table and that the very young birds that are sold cheaply in the supermarkets are probably fed with dubious foodstuffs and must be forced along with hormones that are more than likely to be damaging to the consumer. The couple see the cult of the supermarket as part of a powerful and impersonal business world that is changing the Italian way of life. It is also, of course, changing and threatening their livelihood.

Dina says that she enjoys each day working in her shop as if it were the first. She and her husband do their very best to please

✵ Chapter Four – Sustenance ✵

their customers and she likes the personal contact she has with them. She knows everyone in the neighbourhood and usually has time for a word. To her the supermarket is unfriendly. 'You push your trolley around, pile it up, then your head held down, pay the bill without exchanging greetings with the cashier, who ten to one you will not know.' 'This,' she says, 'is not a good or healthy aspect of modern life and contributes to loneliness and alienation.'

The shop's customers are often neighbours whom the couple have known from childhood, they probably shared the same school bench. Then there are the people who work in the *Comune* building – the town hall which lies at the top of the street and the magistrates' court which is around the corner. Priests who officiate at the Duomo wander in and pass the time of day. There are also the workmen who mend the paved streets, fix the electric supplies and clean the street, they often come for a glass of wine and will eat their sandwiches and talk. Some of the customers are old, have lived in the neighbouring streets all their lives and many of these do not have cars to get to the supermarket so rely on the Peruzzi for their daily nourishment. Perhaps their children shop for them once a week but Italians traditionally are in the habit of buying a little of this and a handful of that every day in order that their slice of *arista* is freshly cut, moist and tender; and their bread, a few ounces, is cut from a newly baked loaf. Custom is served for the old and the young as Dina provides fish in the form of *Baccalà al Aretino* accompanied by *ceci*, which everyone eats on Christmas Eve and many on Fridays. You can rely on finding other festive foods there too, like scented breads studded with *prosciutto* and *panina*, a soft spiced loaf rich with sultanas, both sold in the period of *Carnevale* before the arrival of Lent. They have carnival *cenci* too, deep-fried sweet pastry sprinkled with icing sugar. And every day the customers exchange fresh news, commiserate on the unseasonable weather and complain about the hole in the street that the *aquedotto* people have not yet filled in: the companionable chatter of the friendly inhabitants of a small town.

When my turn comes to be served there is a brisk conversation going on about the merits of flavoured pasta, the couple have a new display of cellophane packets filled with *conchiglie, farfalle* and *tagliatelle* made with the addition of squid ink, spinach or tomato, giving pink shells, green butterflies and black ribbons. They look pretty but they create a problem, what sauce to use with them – garlic, oil and parsley, suggests one woman, *frutti di mare* says another. I think they all really prefer the ordinary plain variety of pasta which by not competing with the sauce complements it.

Apart from the mineral water, a piece of *pecorino* studded with black truffle whose scent is intoxicating and a small piece of *pecorino del fosso*, the same sheep's cheese but in this case one that has been kept deep in a storage pit and has a corresponding depth of flavour, I want some of Dina's Tuscan sausages. They are still made in the old-fashioned way from ground pork, salt, black pepper and garlic juice. The supermarket versions are now loaded with all manner of additives, included on the doubtless well-meant instructions of Brussels, intended for hygienic industrially produced products for mass sale in such outlets; these sausages have a longer shelf life as they do not darken in the space of three or four days. The use of sucrose and dextrose is, however, inexplicable, considering the increasing prevalence of obesity in the population. Naturally these supermarket sausages do not have the same texture or flavour as the real thing and do not cook up in the same way once in the pan. One of the traditional delicacies of the artisan Tuscan butcher is a raw Tuscan sausage crumbled and spread onto a piece of local bread; this may seem to fly in the face of all received wisdom but the meat is regarded as safe to eat as the trusted butcher vouches for the pig and its impeccable state of health. Until recently, the officials of the Arezzo *Comune* made it

❋ CHAPTER FOUR – SUSTENANCE ❋

their business to ensure that domestically kept and slaughtered pigs were fit for human consumption. Displayed prominently in November on the city walls, posters signed by the Mayor required that the lites of all home killed swine were taken to city laboratories where they were examined for signs of disease or parasites.

I have sometimes overheard women in Arezzo supermarkets where they do not know the butcher, discussing the sausages and saying amongst themselves that it is better not to buy them as *'chi sa'*, who knows what *porcheria*, piggish mess, has gone into them. They do not intend a pun nor do they intend to buy such items, but they do belong to an older age group who are aware of the properties of a good sausage.

So when my neighbour Liliana comes into the shop with her list, what dishes does she intend to cook for her family? Liliana and her husband live on the ground floor of our palazzo. Their historic apartment contains the original kitchen of the house which is dominated by an enormous stone fireplace. The couple also have a house in the countryside and land where they grow olives and an abundance of fruit and vegetables. Roberto is a member of the *Coldiretti* in the Province of Arezzo, a group of farmers who pride themselves on the excellence and naturalness of their various crops. In their vast cellar alongside an ancient olive press and a forge they store produce from their *orto* – like strings of home-grown onions, garlic, baskets of potatoes. Copious amounts of their own olive oil fill stainless steel canisters which protect the oil from its enemies, light, heat, oxygen and odours, all of which can alter and damage the colour and flavour of the precious substance.

On this particular day, Liliana too is buying sausages to make one of the most traditional dishes of the Aretino area, *pulezze con le salsicce*. The word *pulezze* comes from the Latin *pullulare* which means to germinate or sprout and the plant in question is turnip, *rapa,* part of the *Brassica* family. The original wild plant *Brassica campestris* was one of the first to be cultivated and that about four thousand years ago. By ancient Roman times it had been selectively developed into several varieties of turnip. *Napu*s was the more delicate white turnip and *rapa* a coarser, round variety. The green shoots of the *rapa, Brassica subsp. rapa silvestris* var. *esculenta*, which are more appreciated today than the turnip itself are known as *cima di rapa* or *broccoletti di rapa* and they have a very particular almost asparagus-like taste with slightly bitter overtones, and the younger the shoots are the more delicate the flavour. In and around Arezzo in February and March, and also in the autumn when the tender new shoots of the plants appear in the kitchen garden, they are gathered and tied into bundles and enjoyed whether served with pasta or as a vegetable. As we have seen, in the arch of the principal doorway of the Romanesque Pieve di Santa Maria in the centre of Arezzo there is an exquisitely lively sculptured frieze depicting the agricultural activities of each month of the year. For the month of November a farmer is pulling up fat round turnips with dark green leaves the seeds of which would have been sown in the summer. The sculptured frieze is in a magnificent state of preservation, probably largely due to the solid brick wall that wisely was built around it to protect it from damage during the Second World War. It is an irony that during the closing phases of that war, when food was scarce and the population were near starving, *pulezze*, without benefit of oil and certainly without sausages and *pancetta,* was – accompanied by bread made from chestnut flour, maize and potato – what kept most Aretines alive.

In peacetime *pulezze con le salsicce* was a nourishing dish made for the farm workers who toiled in the fields from dawn to dusk and did not have time to return to the farm for their midday meal. The women would gather the shoots, very often of wild edible greens, and cook them in boiling water until tender, then drain them thoroughly, pressing all excess moisture away. In a large

✻ Chapter Four – Sustenance ✻

flat pan they would cook cloves of garlic in a little oil then add the sausages, being careful to prick them to let the fat run and turn them until they were evenly golden on all sides. When the sausages were near done they added the *pulezze* stirring the pan until the greenery was well mixed, then leaving it to cook over a low flame they waited until all the flavours of the garlicky oil were soaked up. This dish was carried to the fields where the men were ploughing and was eaten with saltless bread, wine or *mezzo vino*. When there were no more fresh sausages left after the winter killing of the pig the shoots would be prepared with thick slices of *pancetta, rigatino*, as it is known in Arezzo, the word deriving from *righe*, stripes, meaning the narrow red and white striped flesh of pork belly; *pancetta*, from *pancia*, belly, is the more commonly used term.

Liliana will make a similar meal using the Peruzzi's sausages and turnip shoots that Roberto has brought fresh from their country kitchen garden. She might also make another very ancient dish with them preparing the greens in the same way then folding them into a quantity of *orecchiette*, pasta made in the form of tiny ears, one of the oldest ways of forming home-made pasta. *Orecchiette* are now made semi-industrially and naturally you can buy them at the Peruzzi's store.

Alternatively the sausages can be used to enrich a dish of spaghetti with a sauce of the pale green ridged variety of zucchini, sliced and cooked in olive oil spiked with *peperoncino* until they are *disfatto* or almost disintegrated. When the pasta and sauce is mixed then add some fried pieces of the crumbled Tuscan sausage to the dish tossing it all around before serving; all that is then needed is a little freshly grated Parmesan.

Another characteristic and satisfying dish to be made with Tuscan sausages is *Salsicce alla Montanara*. This is a whole meal served in one pot and consists of finely chopped *odori*, that is celery, carrot, garlic and a little onion, better yet, shallot, cooked in a spoonful or so of olive oil until the mixture softens and is then spiced with a crumbled dried hot red pepper. At this point add chopped tomato and let the sauce simmer in its large pan. In a separate pan brown your sausages until they are golden on all sides, drain them well and add them to the sauce and let them simmer away until they are cooked. Fifteen minutes before serving add cooked white beans, either *cannelloni* or *fagiolini di spagna*, butter beans, and let them soak up the flavour of the sauce. Sprinkle with chopped parsley and serve very hot.

These dishes made in one pot are part of the heritage of Aretino cooking which is firmly rooted in the frugality of Tuscan country dwellers. When made in the traditional way nothing is wasted; the fat that emerges from the sausages as they cook serves to irrigate and flavour the tomatoes or greens that are added to the dish. Today, when much of the population of Europe could be said to be overfed, with the benefit of low cholesterol levels in mind many might, as suggested above, prefer to cook the sausages separately and drain them well of their excess fat but these dishes were born in the countryside where energy giving food was essential for the farm workers and meat was a luxury; to waste the fat was unthinkable.

Roberto's knowledge of the land and wild foods provides another dish which country dwellers traditionally enjoyed and which also emphasises the relationship that Arezzo's citizens have with the land. In February Roberto collects *carline*, *Carlina acaulis*, a spiny wild thistle which bears some resemblance to the artichoke but which is not of the same family. *Carline* best grow on dry flinty ground on hillsides and mountains. Their roots were used by herbalists as their properties are diuretic, sudorific and aid digestion. *Carline* can be cooked in several satisfactory ways. Simply boiled they can be served cold with lemon juice and olive oil, alternatively they can be coated in beaten egg and dipped in flour and fried or better still baked in the oven with

Chapter Four – Sustenance

béchamel and abundant grated Parmesan. They are also superb softened in butter with a little shallot then simmered in a light stock and finally put through a blender with thin cream to make an exceedingly delicate soup. *Carline* have a subtle, smoky and rare flavour. All these dishes can also be made with cardoons which although tedious to prepare have an exquisite flavour that makes the intensity of the labour worth while.

In late November when the olives from their grove are pressed, Liliana and her family make a ceremony of tasting and judging the flavour of the new oil. They enjoy the simplest and best of suppers, saltless Tuscan bread bought at the Peruzzi's, toasted over their majestic open fireplace, rubbed with garlic and sprinkled with the new oil; the recipe which Francesco Gaudentio honoured in naming his book, *Il panunto toscano*. Gaudentio's own fireplace lies a few hundred yards away down the hill in the church of Sant'Ignazio, now a Convitto Nazionale.

Sometimes Liliana will make *crostini al cavolo nero*, which is an old Aretino favourite although eaten in other parts of Tuscany. The black cabbage *Brassica encephala*, is a typical Aretino vegetable and has long extremely dark green plume-like leaves. To make the *crostini*, small cabbage plants are used and like celery they are tastier if they have been touched by frost. The greens are cooked whole in boiling salted water and when done are scooped up without being drained unduly and laid on slices of thick toasted Tuscan bread rubbed with raw garlic, then the best olive oil is dribbled onto the *crostini* and salt and ground black pepper added to taste. This makes a substantial first course, the water still clinging to the cabbage moistens the robust bread and the heat from the vegetable makes the scent of the oil sing. Clearly it would profit no one if the oil is inferior and the bread of less than Tuscan quality; the structure of the bread has to be solid enough to stand up to being bathed in liquid without disintegrating into pap. *Cavolo nero* is also used by the *Aretini* in *zuppa di verdure* and

✳ Beppina and the Kitchens of Arezzo ✳

minestrone and its dark colour contrasts well in these golden soups. In Beppina's day when, as we have seen, the numerous poor existed on a restricted diet, in the absence of citrus fruit, it was from vegetables like cabbage that they obtained the necessary but at that period unidentified Vitamin C.

The oldest Aretino dishes are simple and comfortably domestic, they demonstrate frugality if not parsimony, they employ produce from the *orto*, the kitchen garden, the pig sty and the poultry house. These very traditional and rural dishes have sustained town and country dwellers for generations in times of peace and plenty and, reduced in ingredients and quantity, during times of conflict. As many today remember, war affected Arezzo dramatically, fear and starvation were the order of the day. Those living in the city famously are said to have survived on boiled *rape*, which they collected themselves, seasoned with salt if they were lucky, however by 1944 pepper was not to be found and salt difficult to obtain, some even desperately scraping the whitewash from damp, salt-encrusted walls to use as a substitute. Every crust of bread, however stale, was used, dampened with water and maybe a little of that rarity, oil, mixed with scraps of vegetables, to make an impoverished *'pansanella'*. But the bread in the city was of the worst kind, made from grain mixed with maize, bran, ground chestnuts and worse, it was damp, mouldy and often underbaked, which latter made the loaf heavier and more expensive to buy. In the countryside, as ever, the farmers and labourers fared marginally better, their bread baked in their own ovens was more palatable and slightly more abundant. Many a *prosciutto*, then but a memory in the city, was hidden in the woods to be eked out in secret. The penalty for selling goods on the 'black market' was death.

The few modern buildings that are to be found in the upper *centro storico* of Arezzo are a result of the advancing Front when in 1943 and 1944 allied planes dropped bombs across the greater city, destroying the railway and factories, besides much housing

Chapter Four – Sustenance

and in the oldest part of the town some historic buildings and the mediaeval paintings within them; part of the eighteenth-century cemetery was also destroyed. The city was liberated on 16th of July 1944 by the Partisans who were based in the surrounding hills together with the allied troops. On that day there were barely one hundred people left in the city, the bulk of the population having taken to the countryside. Three thousand one hundred and ten inhabitants of the Province of Arezzo were killed during the war. The retreating German army committed hideous massacres in towns and villages in the Province. At quiet crossroads and beside country roadsides, many sad monuments stand witness to Nazi and Fascist savagery. One of the most cruel of these killings took place at San Polo in the Province of Arezzo on the 14th of July 1944 just two days before the Liberation, the Partisan victims were beaten, buried alive and then blown up by means of dynamite. Forty-seven other villagers were forced to dig three mass graves; they were then brutally murdered and thrown into the pits. Another of the many massacres occurred at Civitella in the Val di Chiana, where 244 citizens of all ages were savagely executed. It was only in 2006 that the last living perpetrator of the San Polo massacre was recommended for prosecution in the court at La Spezia, he, however, died of old age before justice could be done.

In 1984 the Province of Arezzo was awarded the gold medal for valour by the then President of the Republic, Sandro Pertini.

After the War, immense work was undertaken by the *Aretini* to rebuild their lives and the heavily damaged city; the ancient architecture was restored where it was possible and replaced where it was not. The enmity between the vanquished Fascist Party sympathisers and the supporters of the Partisans was eventually subsumed into a general effort to enable a normal life to flourish. Just who espoused which side in the years between 1922 and 1945 is a topic not often discussed with a stranger but memories are long and citizens of a certain age all know.

❋ Beppina and the Kitchens of Arezzo ❋

After thirty years and more of service to our little community, our gallant general store reached its last day, on New Year's Eve 2004, at 8.30 pm. They succumbed to the modern world as Quinto terms it, and their door closed for ever as they became another casualty of industrialisation and globalisation. Dina was upset, they are not closing because they are tired of the work she says, it is because the majority of people have changed their habits. Now everyone goes weekly to the supermarkets on the outskirts of the town and their small store cannot compete with the prices of the giants. For several months I have noticed that the shop is less crowded and she says whereas they once served a hundred or one hundred and twenty customers in a day, recently it has been forty and those spending just a few euros on a piece of fresh bread or some small forgotten item. They no longer fully sustain but merely support.

We walked down the street towards the shop to say goodbye. There were two old ladies there both buying household goods like bleach and washing powder, heavy things which Quinto will deliver to their apartments in the street. I wonder what they will do tomorrow, there are no more food stores at the very top of the old town, the last fruit and vegetable seller closed up two years ago. Another regular customer, an elegant old man who wears an astrakhan cap and speaks very clear English is buying freshly cooked lentils for his dinner this evening. He has a car and shops in the lower town, but, I suspect, he too is dismayed at the closing of our *alimentari*.

We wish Quinto and Dina a happy retirement, greatly deserved after all their years of extremely hard work. Dina cries, she says she has spent *'una vita'* within those stone walls and cannot imagine what her life will be like now. I suspect that they will not be able to resist helping their daughter in her bar, the Borgo San Piero, further down the hill where she provides good, nourishing lunches and exquisite pastries. As we leave the shop a group of young people come in; they ask if

Chapter Four — Sustenance

it is possible to have some *panini* made for them and the couple busy themselves slicing the bread and *prosciutto*, Dina's last customers are her favourites, she has always enjoyed feeding hungry people.

Several months after the closure of their shop we meet Quinto in the street; he looks ten years younger and is clearly enjoying his semi-retirement. He works on some land he owns outside the city and enjoys growing vegetables and raising hens and rabbits; he is supplying his daughter with fresh produce which she serves to her customers. Dina helps her on busy days. They are both free of the worry and hard work of being shopkeepers but still have their lifelong pleasure of helping to feed people.

However, they were also among the casualties of our era where supermarket chains largely control food supplies to the population. How can individuals compete with the prices of the giant supermarkets and still make a living? Writing in 2014, in Arezzo as in other Italian cities it was becoming a rarity to find a simple greengrocers. In that business where spoilage due to the nature of the produce is the main problem, it had become uneconomic to operate. Many greengroceries in Arezzo which have faithfully served their customers, rising in the early hours to go to the wholesale market to obtain *primizie*, the first examples of a new season's produce, have now closed. The few that have survived either have their own market gardens and so are able to produce their own vegetables and fresh salads without a middleman, or they have diversified from the traditional shop, licensed to purvey a single strand of foodstuff: becoming, in essence, mini-markets, which stock a small amount of fresh meat, bread, groceries, perhaps household necessities, alongside their fruit and vegetables. These stores are a success, as a friend who works amongst Arezzo's historic archives explains. She is able to leave her work, go to her local store which is a few yards from her house and buy everything she needs for her family's evening meal. Simple and convenient,

❋ Beppina and the Kitchens of Arezzo ❋

this does not require a car trip and the products sold in this type of shop tend to be local. The olive oil and wine on the shelves are produced on the hillsides surrounding the city, the cheese too comes from the province. Good food, locally produced! And in 2020 these remaining extended greengrocers are ever more popular. La Primizia in the Via Garibaldi is a superb example, one of the jewels of Arezzo. Here, the Santi family provide the best and freshest of local fruits and vegetables to their eager clients, plus excellent cheeses and various delicious Aretine dishes cooked by a family member.

 Chapter Five

Pleasure

And who better to begin a chapter on seasonal pleasures and tempting food than Pietro Aretino, who was born in a house but a short walk away from where I sit and write.

> Letters. Book One. No. 164
> To M. Agostin Ricchi

If science and doctrine were more valuable than life, I, my son, would exhort you to occupy yourself with them; but as living is worth more, I entreat you to come here to us, where without troubling your memory and without the devilishness of Aristotelian thought, you can apply your mind to being healthy, until the raging heat, which is so vexing to a person, subsides. For myself I am happier to see the snow fall from the sky than to be touched by sweet breezes. Certainly winter seems to me like an abbot who sails through life comfortably, all needs catered for, eating and sleeping and that other little matter and all very agreeably. The summer though is similar to a rich and haughty harlot who when satiated throws away the dregs, doing nothing other than filling and refilling the glass to drink again. And the fresh wine and her ornate rooms full of the ostentatious artifices of bows and fringes

❋ Beppina and the Kitchens of Arezzo ❋

bring to mind June and July, but they are not worth one mouthful of the *pan'unto* [lightly toasted bread, dipped in grease and fried] which one eats around the fire in December and January, gulping down glasses of *mosto* [unfermented wine] and whilst turning the roasting meat, picking at a little of the *carbonato* [thick *pancetta* wrapped round the meat], without bothering about burning one's mouth and fingers in this act of thievery. At night go to where the warming pan has done its work, then hug your companion, or curl up under the covers which will comfort you with their warmth. And the rain, the thunder and the fury of the *tramontana* wind will encourage you to stay asleep until daybreak. But who can endure the beastly whining of the fleas, the bugs, the mosquitoes and the flies, tiresome additions to the other annoyances of summer? Those which have you lying as naked as the day you were born on the sheets, and make you pass wind and cause your traitor of a servant to burst into laughter, and make you cry so hard that you think your eyes will close for ever, and will wake you suddenly from a good sleep, to sweat and drink and puff and blow and toss and turn and if it was possible you would run from yourself, such is the rage that destroys you to the point that you are melting with sweat. And if you were not being destroyed by the thought of eating the whorishly tempting melons which one longs for at this, their time of ripening, one would flee from the heat, like chattering teeth flee the cold. There are many who desire the summer for its fruit, praising the artichokes, the cherries, the figs, the peaches and the grapes; as if the truffles, olives and cardoons of the winter were not their equal. But one can chatter as well around a good fire as one can in the shade of a fine beech tree, because the shade desires more than a thousand pleasantries, it needs the song of the birds, the murmur of water, the breath of the wind, the freshness of the grass and similar prattle. But four dry logs have all

※ CHAPTER FIVE – PLEASURE ※

that is necessary for four or five hours of gossiping, with chestnuts on the embers and wine between one's feet. Of course we love the winter, which is the spring of the wise.

But returning to us, I tell you, you must come here, because I have arranged a small room where you can sleep without difficulty and call for little tarts in their thousands. I have nothing else to say to you, other than to greet Signor Sperone and Ferraguto on my behalf.

Pietro Aretino, Venice, 10th July 1537

One can look over Arezzo from the vantage point of a high window and observe the measured rhythms of its life, from dawn when the early market stallholders enter the city, to the hours after midnight when guards patrol the streets to see that all is well. In the theatre that is the old city, the citizens make their appearances; from the women who come to the city walls in August to harvest the wild capers that grow between the stones, to those who parade in the Corso in winter, wrapped in luxurious furs that hide smooth necks hung with inherited ropes of gold and antique coral; from lawyers in elegant suits to bands of school children with heavy bags on their backs and *carabinieri* riding shining motorbikes and until recently, well-groomed, magnificent horses with abundant manes and tails. And as we have seen, every week country people throng to the city's general market to buy and sell and enjoy the noise and novelty. As there ever were in the market place, now there are itinerant musicians and jugglers who perform outside cafés and *palazzi,* and on the weekend of the first Sunday of each month streets and squares in the *centro storico* are thronged with dealers and all manner of antiques and bric-a-brac for the Antique Fair which has taken place without fail since 1968. On occasion, the Orchestra Sinfonica Guido d'Arezzo plays in the Piazza San Francesco, medleys of popular pieces including music from Federico Fellini's films which brings to mind *Amarcord* – that exquisite homage to Fellini's home town, likenesses of which can be seen in Arezzo's beloved streets.

❋ Beppina and the Kitchens of Arezzo ❋

Every evening, in winter or summer the *Aretini* have enjoyed the *passeggiata*, an evening stroll in the Corso Italia, where the voices of the young amplified by the narrow street and high walls create an overwhelming roar. Curiously, this evening walk largely takes place in the narrowest part of the Corso. Although the city has three squares in its centre, one, the Piazza Grande, is hardly used for promenading. The other two, although provided with bars and café tables from which to watch the passing parade, have not really been at the heart of the *passeggiata*. In these squares an older generation talked and drank their *aperitivi* before at eight o clock, the city magically emptied when most returned home for dinner. The really old-fashioned Aretine families, the *Aretini da sempre*, I am told, were not much inclined to eat in restaurants. They and their fellow citizens are also, like most Italians, bound by intricate rules as to what is suitable and healthy to eat and drink at particular hours of the day and in what order. It is unthinkable to drink an espresso coffee before eating lunch or to consume refrigerator-cold mineral water in the heat of a summer's day. *'Fa male!'* ('Bad for you!') they sternly say about any such foolish notions. Many eschew an *aperitivo* and will only accept a glass of wine with their meals, at which time the wine will aid digestion and enhance the flavour of the food. One can only marvel at the innocence of the British Government who were convinced that 24-hour licensing would result in the measured consumption of alcohol common in wine-producing European countries. What the British left out of the equation is the upbringing of people who are schooled from infancy in the rules of appropriate eating and drinking. Italians regard their daily sustenance with a serious eye to its health-giving properties, in so doing, employing their appreciation and discernment of what is genuine and of good quality.

Today, the *centro storico* has become ever more lively, filled with the successful young who on Saturdays crowd such squares as that of San Francesco eating to their hearts' content at the Caffé dei Costanti and many other good venues there.

✳ Chapter Five – Pleasure ✳

On the home front, a friend, Gianpaulo, bottles vintage wine bought in *demigiani* from a farmer who produces but small quantities, and keeps it in the mediaeval cellars below his apartment. He makes his own olive oil from groves he owns in the country and stores it in large terracotta pots. The wood that he uses in his kitchen fireplace to grill the good meat bought from the city butchers, is sold by an old man who comes with a laden cart from the Casentino when the first chills of autumn arrive. Gianpaulo could buy wine by the bottle, use commercial olive oil and eat industrially produced food but he chooses not to do so because he values the flavour, the satisfaction and the pleasure he derives from living and eating in his traditional way. He and Beppina would not be strangers if they were to dine at the same table. Living in harmony with his surroundings and eating well is an art much practised by him and his fellow citizens, and by most Italians in their own particular local ways.

At Gianpaulo's invitation one late December we gather in a tiny restaurant, da Nonna Lola, on the mountain road between Arezzo and Anghiari. The dining room opens off a grocery store which the family have run for generations. The food will be simple but genuine, made from produce that they have grown and livestock that they have raised themselves. Enlarged family photographs in matching brown frames are hung on the walls: seventy or so years' worth of great-grandfathers in uniform, religious processions, group portraits of seemingly dozens of family members. In the shop there are photographs of unusually large *porcini* found in the forest that surrounds them. More startling is the photograph of freshwater clams fished out of the swift-running river Arno. The shop's counter is full of cheeses, *pecorino* of all ages and descriptions.

Gianpaulo has invited several friends to Nonna Lola's for a quiet winter lunch. There is Maurizio a local doctor and ex-mayor of Subbiano, and Giovanni one of the *assessori* (aldermen) of Arezzo's city council and his wife. They are all Aretino to the

❋ Beppina and the Kitchens of Arezzo ❋

core and we are here to eat the purest of old-fashioned Aretino food. There is no menu, the proprietor reads out what he has. We eat *maccheroni con ragù*, then *fegatelli*, liver still cooked in the fashion of Francesco Gaudentio in Arezzo in 1686, or *scamarrita*, neck of pork with *pulezze*, which in this instance are fresh wild greens gathered in the valley. There is a good red wine, naturally from the Colli Aretini, made by one of their friends, then traditional Christmas sweets, Vin Santo, made by our host, and grappa. I ask my usual question. What do they think is the most typical Aretino dish? There are interesting answers. The doctor says immediately that once upon a time it was *zuppa Tarlati*, the famous chicken soup. Gianpaulo and the *assessore* disagree, that belongs in books they say, it's not what we really eat. As we have seen, in Arezzo there are a few recipes such as the *zuppa* (see page 105) which came to light in the 1930s along with the general harking back to the great age of the fourteenth century and the warrior Bishop Guido Tarlati and many are the cookery books that claim such recipes to be fundamentally expressive of Arezzo. However, when asked, *Aretina* housewives invariably name other dishes such as *maccheroni co'l'ocio* to be truly the most loved and most typical of their domestic tradition of cooking. Politics, nationalism, personal identity and passion sometimes compete in the kitchen.

The *assessore* suggests *acquacotta* and *scottiglia*, but no, the doctor says, they are part of the Maremma tradition too, and not exclusive to Arezzo. The restaurant owner, agreeing with the many Aretine women whom I have asked, says firmly that *maccheroni co'l'ocio* is the classic dish. I say that geese are not that easy to come by these days so with what other sauce should the pasta be served. He smiles at my use of the Aretino dialect word for goose *ocio*, and says *nanà*, duck, or *lepre*, hare, all are genuinely a strong part of the Aretino tradition. He then gives the *assessore* his recipe for *tortelli alla Casentina*, which is also a fundamental dish, made with potato and onion stuffing, delicious, they both agree with a sigh.

❋ Chapter Five – Pleasure ❋

Gianpaulo mentions *galantina*, a rich complicated dish appreciated by Artusi, an emptied chicken or capon skin stuffed with a mixture of chopped chicken and other meats seasoned with Parmesan and spices, a mosaic of hard-boiled eggs, pistachios and on occasion truffles, which graced many a bourgeois dinner table for special occasions and still does. But galantine is French, it was created by Prévost the notable cook who worked for the Marquis de Brancas. When the French Revolution put an end to the Marquis, it did not put an end to a taste for good food and Prévost went on to sell galantines to the Parisians for years. The elaborate dish reached the height of fashion when Napoleon was rampaging through Europe, perhaps with a few tucked into his saddle bags. It is possible that the galantine was introduced to the grandees of Arezzo by his officers when the city was taken under the control of Napoleon's forces in 1799, a state of affairs that with a few interruptions was to last until 1814. However, 'galyntyne' also appears in *The Forme of Cury* which was compiled by the master cooks of King Richard II of England in *circa* 1390 and was later presented to Elizabeth I. In this ancient document, however, the recipes for galyntyne are for pork or lampreys covered with a sauce of moistened breadcrumbs mixed with vinegar and spices.

Then, Gianpaulo continues, there is *sformato al cibreo*. A spinach flan or mould served with a savoury sauce of chicken livers cooked with, among other ingredients, a glass of Vin Santo. The sauce is mediaeval in origin and also akin to an early Aretine recipe which appears in Gaudentio's *Il panunto toscano*. The *sformato* is from another Arezzo tradition, more town than country. Here we are returning to the world of Beppina.

The conversation goes around the room, the *assessore* asks a man eating alone what he would suggest, he is wearing a boiler suit, quietly reading his newspaper. He says *trippa*, tripe, then *scottiglia*. *Scottiglia* was the famous dish that was made up of many different cuts and sorts of meat all brought as gifts to one house where the meal was to take place. The *massaia* would then make a vast stew in the cauldron hanging over the wood fire and serve it to the numerous guests who had gathered for a *veglia* – an evening where people recited poetry, often Dante, sang traditional songs, told stories and jokes, and a little discreet courting was indulged in by the young people under the supervision of the elders. The *veglia* was an important part of country social life before the advent of modern amusements. *Trippa* is surely a Florentine speciality I suggest. Yes they say but we have it too and made with tomato as well. In Florence, the *assessore* says, they also eat tripe or rather the darkest part of it, the *lampredotto, in bianco*, simply boiled and put between a split *panino* to make a hefty sandwich. These are sold from stands dotted over the city, there is a large one behind the station. At Arezzo too such a stand is to be found in the Via Marco Perennio under the railway bridge.

What about puddings I wonder. Well there is *gattò*, another gift from the French and very popular at the festive meals of country people. This is akin to what used to be known in England as a Swiss Roll and consists of a light sponge sprinkled with the bright red liqueur, Alkermes, spread with chocolate cream or confectioner's cream then rolled up and sometimes covered with a layer of whipped fresh cream or powdered sugar. My friend Cristina has told me that *zuppa inglese*, a common or garden trifle, is the most typical of Aretino desserts today. When I mentioned *gattò* she said it was the same thing, which I suppose it basically is, and the *zuppa* has the added advantage of not including the rolling up of the sponge cake. It appears to me to be rather odd that today's typical Aretino desserts are basically the French *gâteau* and the British trifle. However, even Artusi included English plum pudding and other foreign puddings in his majestic collection of Italian recipes. The owner of da Nonna Lola brings two plates of seasonal sweetmeats to the table. *Panforte*, which is a speciality of Siena although it was made in Arezzo in the nineteenth century by several

Chapter Five – Pleasure

confectioners and still is today, and *biscotti di Prato*, to dip into the Vin Santo; they are however, both home-made.

The cook, the workman, the Alderman, the physician cum politician all have a firm opinion about food and its place in their affections and their culture, the room is alive with humour and enthusiasm. We are really at the warm heart of Arezzo. To sum up, everyone agrees that the well-cooked unpretentious meal that we have just eaten off plain, cream, round plates expresses perfectly the essence of Arezzo's traditional food. Artusi would be proud of us, and so would Pietro Aretino who, as we have seen in a previous chapter, in the luxury of his Venetian residence, amply lauded simplicity: '…death is the cook of elaborate food, and life the cook of that which is simple.'

19th of March. The Feast of San Giuseppe.
Tomorrow is the first day of Spring and already the air has a hint of warmth about it. As we leave the house to meet some friends the small adjoining square is crossed by a group of people heading for a doorway in a large palazzo whose windows are shuttered against the night. They are carrying parcels neatly tied with ribbon, cakes, *pasticcieria*, ice cream and one of them has a yellow begonia. A woman dressed in red presses a bell and a crackling sound comes from the intercom, they disappear through the high arched doorway; it is 8.30 pm. The windows in the seminary across the way are blank, a dim light shows through the grill above the door, there is no sign of the *frati*, they too must be eating.

As we walk down the narrow street that edges the ecclesiastical building and leads to one of the town gates more people are knocking on doors, they are also laden with cake boxes and flowers. We reach Alessandro and Anna Maria's apartment which is near the old city wall, then we all continue to walk to a restaurant on the Viale Giotto, the long pine-edged street which each Saturday morning houses the market. As we cross the

❈ Beppina and the Kitchens of Arezzo ❈

Piazza Guido Monaco the traffic has diminished, the pavements are empty, the *passeggiata* has ceased; everyone is at table. We have not eaten at this restaurant before but Alessandro says that they have good wine and a knowledgeable sommelier. The room prettily furnished with fresh yellow table linen is welcoming.

We start with pasta, *tagliatelle* made from chestnut flour which is served with a *porcini* sauce, and *tortelli* filled with *pecorino* cheese which are garnished with a little *purea* of *cannellini* beans and freshened with pieces of ripe *Camone* variety tomato. Alessandro says that the sun coming after the snow which has been laying for weeks on the hillsides will produce a huge crop of wild mushrooms. The snow seeping gently into the earth will benefit both the water table and the dormant *funghi*: much desired effects, as the last few summers have been far too dry, streams have ceased flowing and wild mushrooms were scarce. There were plenty imported from Eastern Europe, but as they say here, the flavour is not the same as that of the native Tuscan and Umbrian *funghi*. And there is always the suspicion which has invariably surrounded eating wild mushrooms, as Pietro Aretino expresses so well in a letter to a friend.

Volume 1 letter 208
To A.M. Matteo Durastante da San Giusto.

This is a word of thanks, such as a good man should proffer, and which I now render you for sending me the *funghi* which I was expecting. But I should thank you ten times over for sending me the quails and the thrushes which I did not expect. Because these are safer foods than those risky ones; and one can cook them in two turns of the spit, sandwiched between bay leaves and sausages in the good old rustic way, *a la Carlona*. [An expression that originally referred to Charlemagne who had the reputation for being a simple, genuine man. The modern usage usually means cooked in a hurried, even careless

✻ CHAPTER FIVE – PLEASURE ✻

manner.] A thing which one cannot do with the *funghi*, which you need to boil with two slices of crustless bread, and then fry in oil. And one does not eat them willingly except in the morning, because of the suspicion of poison from which at night one cannot easily defend oneself thanks to the sleep that teases even the eminence of the Medici. And I well understand the people of Chieti who make their confessions and take the sacrament before they even taste a mouthful of those mushrooms. It amuses me to see a gluttonous but also timid person who wants to eat a bellyful, and I laugh to see them grimace while the enticing scent assails their nostrils and fear grips their souls. But who does not know the little esteem which 'life' holds for anyone, you can put a piece of any sort of paltry food in your mouth, and then be snared by it.

Now, God protect you from this or any other kind of accident.

From Venice, 20th October 1537.

La Tagliatella has a menu which experiments with traditional Aretine recipes and also contains some dishes that are made strictly to the rules and would probably not be eaten with great enthusiasm by many foreign visitors to the city, it would however be to the visitors' loss. Here I am speaking of *grifi* and *trippa*, tripe. *Grifi* is a dish emanating from the city as opposed to those with rural roots, which perfectly expresses Aretine thrift, created by housewives who wasted nothing and made the most nourishing and tasty dishes from humble and often despised ingredients obtained at a low price from city butchers. *Grifi* are the fleshy muzzles and jowls of cows. The term is also used for the snouts of pigs which end up in brawn. The word *grufolare* means to grub around in the earth with the snout. *Trippa* consists of strips of tripe, the stomach lining of cows, whose fine flavour is often considered to be marred by its rubbery texture. Another traditional Arezzo dish is *nervi* which is made of the connective tissue from the thighs and legs of cows and a mixture of tripe and intestines. Again, a concoction not likely to attract kind comment. I ask the restaurant owner about some of these specialities and he cheerfully brings us *assaggi* so I can judge for myself. The *grifi* are a triumph of taste and texture; small pieces of soft gelatinous meat with a rich savoury flavour, a dark stew cooked slowly in red wine. The sample of *trippa* is also delicious, made much in the Florentine way with tomato, which seems to marry well with tripe.

Being close to Easter there is lamb baked in the oven with potatoes garnished with rosemary on the menu, and *Nodini di maiale* which are roundels of pork loin wrapped in *pancetta* and served on slices of toasted bread sprinkled with olive oil. The sommelier presents several bottles of his favourite wines for us to consider. Mostly from Tuscany they are the produce of young wine makers. We choose a bottle of I Greti made by newcomers to the area who have moved here from the Veneto. It is a dark, serious wine.

With dessert, a citrus mousse and a slice of *Torta del Riso* he serves a glass of a French dessert wine which he says is good but not great.

It is midnight by the time we leave the restaurant and wander back through the town. We turn into the Corso Italia, the venue of the *passeggiata*. The street is full of young people talking and laughing, standing in groups or walking along arm in arm. This is truly an impressive parade, there must be several hundred dressed in their best clothes which appear to us, huddled into our winter coats, to be too lightweight for the weather. The crowd of young people who have come from the outlying parts of the town and from villages in the surrounding valleys is good humoured, many of them have probably eaten in the large *pizzerie* which flourish in the streets behind the Corso. There is no drunkenness or rowdy behaviour, these boys and girls are simply there to enjoy themselves. At the end of the parade, which extends for nearly half the length of the Corso, a very

❋ Chapter Five – Pleasure ❋

small police car is parked. Three middle-aged officers sit and chat; we are sure that they will not have to go to the trouble of leaving the warmth of their panda car.

We wander slowly up the street, gazing into the shop windows and stopping to stand and talk, so we have joined the leisurely *passeggiata* too. On the left-hand side of the stone-clad street we reach the Palazzo Guazzesi, a building of the 1600s whose façade is decorated with a fine wrought iron balcony and a bust of a seventeenth-century scion of the Guazzesi family. Since 1912 the building has housed one of Arezzo's clubs, the *Circolo Artistico*. Alessandro and Anna Maria suggest we go in and look at the painted ceilings. We climb up the wide stone stairs stopping to admire an exquisite fresco of the Madonna and Child painted by Parri di Spinello. The palazzo façade hides the remains of a much more ancient structure, this fresco was made before 1453, the year of Spinello's death. As we enter the *piano nobile* we hear dance music, a small band is playing a quickstep. The painted ceilings are a delight, canopies of boçage and flowers with an over-painting of a net and lace cloth that seemingly is stretched across the shallow barrel vault. Past this salon there is the ballroom from where the music is coming. The room is darkened and there are tables and chairs set around the floor. Two or three couples are dancing and at the tables there are groups of carefully dressed and coiffured women. A few men are gathered around the bar. We walk through the rooms, another ceiling painted in browns and ochre is much more masculine as it features shields and lances. There is a library too where members can sit and study or read the newspapers. The main purpose of the club is to encourage the arts and over the years they have held many exhibitions of the works of Aretine and Tuscan artists. It is the custom to ask each exhibitor to donate a piece to the *Circolo* and as a result all the walls of the many rooms are hung with paintings, prints and also photographs.

The contrast between the noise of the throng of young people below laughing and talking as they parade up and down, the sound of their voices reverberating against the stone façades of the narrow street, and the discreet murmurs of the club members in their elegant salon is profound. Here is an example of the counting of the years in Arezzo, a moment in time when both the young and old of the city are entertaining themselves in their own appropriate ways: and these are just the latest generations of a city whose history stretches back millennia, a city where the great Maecenas was born into an ancient Etruscan family. And he, vital patron of the most glorious ancient Roman writers, also put his thoughts into written words, although only fragments of his writing still exist.

In the odd remaining pieces of Maecenas' *Symposium*, in a scene where Virgil and Horace are present, when the discussion turns to the power of wine, we read this: 'Just as that same liquor gives you a quick gaze, so it makes everything appear more attractive and restores the good things of sweet youth.' Many modern Aretines would heartily agree with him. Further to this, Roman period Arezzo was also the site of large potteries making highly refined tableware and recently, under the palazzo of the *Circolo Artistico*, the beautiful mosaic floor of an ancient Roman villa has been excavated. It was discovered during some work which our architect friend Alessandro was leading.

We leave the Palazzo Guazzesi and continue up the Corso to turn into the Via Cavour, here we pass the closed doors of the Church of San Francesco and the Caffé dei Costanti, legacy of Napoleon and some like-minded *Aretini*. As yet the tables have not been put out in front of the Caffé's large frontage, that will come after the Easter celebrations in a week's time. There are fewer people standing around talking now; we move on to the Piazza della Badia where there is the enormous Benedictine Monastery of Saints Flora and Lucilla. The building is much changed since mediaeval times and has been used for many purposes besides that of being a sanctuary for nuns. From the eighteenth and

❋ CHAPTER FIVE – PLEASURE ❋

nineteenth centuries the building with its beautiful Renaissance cloister designed by Giuliano di Maiano and the della Robbia of the Virgin and Child over the porch (heavily restored in the nineteenth century) served as the Granducal Post Office and the square is still known by some older citizens as the Piazza della Vecchia Posta. Sadly, it was damaged in the bombardment of Arezzo during the Second World War. We knew it when it housed some of the offices of the *Comune* and we went there with our country neighbour Orlando Cerotti in order to pay our property taxes. Now it is a school.

We stand at the corner of the piazza and admire the surrounding tall houses with their window boxes. Anna Maria has spent much of the day in her kitchen and makes us a gift of some *frittelle*, traditional fried cakes made for the Feast of San Giuseppe using lemon peel perfumed rice mixed with sugar, soft within and crisp on the surface. It is now after one o'clock, time to say goodnight and walk up the hill. As we pass the dark palazzo, where the gift-laden guests were entering at the same moment that we left for dinner, we hear music and laughter still coming from the ground-floor rooms. And as ever, Pietro Aretino with a magnificent flourish has apt words on eating with friends:

> To Brenzone

> The gift of the citrus, trout and truffles was not merely of gentlemanly, ducal or princely grace, it was regal, the stuff of emperors and popes; otherwise it would not be worthy, great or beautiful enough for the magnificence, the nobility and the excellence of the gallant, generous and sublime soul of the bountiful, brilliant, noble gentleman of Verona, Agostino Brenzone; orator, citizen and philosopher, majestic, just and wise in the way which one desires in a man who exemplifies the genius of nature, the nature of the spirit and the spirit of virtue in the study

Beppina and the Kitchens of Arezzo

of those admirable professions. And although I consider it a miracle that a person of such greatness would stoop to the pleasure of giving with such generous splendour, I give you thanks in two ways, one for receiving the gift and the other for the brilliance of it; I praise you for it and to show you with honest heartfelt affection, I promise you, God willing, to enjoy with my friends your precious gifts without which I would feel bereft. I avow that to eat in the company of affable companions doubles the flavour of the food, and we would be the poorer without friends, knowing that nothing gives more pleasure than friendship, that affection which today by way of virtue ties us together, and cannot be dissolved in eternity.

January, Venice, 1556

Aretino was a true epicurian!

Cristina, widow of a renowned Tuscan painter, is celebrated for her cooking. She lives in an artist's eyrie at the top of our building, the views of the city from her windows are impressive. A long loggia, its walls covered with frescoes painted by her husband Rossano houses a dining table large enough to seat a dozen guests. The walls of her sitting room are filled with his prints and paintings, portraits in which, with great subtlety of colour he has played with voluptuous forms. His drawings evoke the historic streets of Arezzo lined with tall *palazzi* and peopled with groups of old men of Tuscan character. Piles of books lie on the antique desks and side tables. Cristina belongs to one of the most ancient families of Arezzo. To listen to her talking about Arezzo is to reach into the heart of the city. When she was a small girl her aristocratic father would tell her stories about sixteenth-century Aretine knights who went to sea to fight Saracen pirates. As a child she thought these stories were conjured from his imagination and it was only upon cultivating an interest in the annals of her family and that of the city, by publishing family diaries of historic interest written by her

Chapter Five – Pleasure

ancestors, that she discovered one of her forbears actually was a Knight of St Stephen who around the turn of the sixteenth and seventeenth centuries commanded a ship and fought many battles with the Turkish and pirate vessels which abounded in the seas around the peninsula, contending with the trade vessels of Genoese and Venetian merchants. Far from inventing her bedtime stories her father was telling her of her family history, without mentioning the fact. Another member of this band of knights has a plaque dedicated to him on the wall of his birthplace in the then Borgo Maestro now the Corso Italia:

> Here was born and lived the Terror of the Turks. Marchese Alessandro dal Borro, a fierce defender of Tuscany.

Cristina learnt to cook in the best possible way, at her mother and grandmother's side. In this manner she is a repository of the genuine tradition of Tuscan Aretine cooking. She has never habitually used cookery books, but does own a copy of Artusi which she says is a reliable guide when trying an unfamiliar dish. Her culinary memories of life in Arezzo as a schoolgirl in the 1950s revolve around her family's garden where fresh, seasonal fruit and vegetables were grown. They kept chickens, too, for lunch on Sundays; the city elders of 1327 would have greatly approved. Near her home there was one of the oldest *pasticcerie* in Arezzo, Bruschi. Today they still make delicious cakes and serve excellent coffee. On a shelf in the bar there lie recipe books handwritten by their antecedents, photographs of the family and the bar hang on the walls. Cristina remembers eating their *gattò* with delight. She would also accompany her mother to the market in the Piazza Grande which still flourished in the 1950s; the piazza would be full of country people who brought small carts full of fresh produce to sell, fat hens, baby chicks, flowers, eggs and honey.

To celebrate her birthday Cristina has invited twelve guests, two of her six sisters, their husbands and various friends. There

❋ Beppina and the Kitchens of Arezzo ❋

is much talk and laughter, everyone has brought her a gift, flowers, wine, decorative candles and a designer friend has made her a beautiful transparent box its square frame covered with silk tulle appliquéd with velvet flowers and leaves. The evening begins with glasses of chilled white wine served with pieces of crystalline Parmesan of excellent flavour and *pecorino* from Pienza. We stand in groups looking at the lights of Arezzo below or linger in the long sitting room; a photograph of Rossano in a silver frame regards us with a smile.

At nine Cristina calls us to the table, we sit down without ceremony, the women on one side the men on the other. At the head sits her brother-in-law, a large man with leonine hair who is a professor at La Sapienza in Rome. Cristina appears carrying a massive bowl full to the brim with *penne* seasoned with a rich *cinghiale*, wild boar sauce, dishes are passed along the table to be filled and there is a momentary silence as we all start to eat. The pasta is luxuriant. With this dish Cristina has elaborated on the method and ingredients which underlie a traditional Arezzo speciality that was served to the farm workers in celebration at the *Battitura*, the threshing of the corn, *maccheroni co'l'ocio*, goose baked slowly in the stone farmhouse oven on a bed of chopped onion, celery, carrot, *prosciutto* and tomato preserve. The rich sauce formed by the *battuto* of vegetables and the pan juices is served with *maccheroni*, which in Arezzo means squares or wide strips of home-made pasta, while the meat itself appears as a main course with a *contorno* of salad or green vegetables. Tonight it is not goose but wild boar which Cristina has chosen for the main ingredient, marinated for hours in spiced wine. Made with goose, duck or wild boar this dish demonstrates the elegant economy of Aretino and Tuscan cooking. As in a French *pot-au-feu*, the dish provides two courses.

Cinghiale in Umido (Wild Boar Stew)

The most important thing for this recipe is that the piece

Chapter Five – Pleasure

of meat comes from a young animal, has been hung for several days and undergoes a thorough marinade for a day, better two days. Meat from an old male boar has a penetrating smell that takes a long and careful marinade to dispel, it is also more than likely to be very tough, probably better avoided.

For the marinade use red wine, a handful of coarse salt, cloves, sage, mint, a bay leaf or two. After the marinade, rinse the meat and dry it thoroughly. Cut it into pieces the size of two walnuts and sprinkle them with flour. Make a *battuto* of garlic, fresh sage leaves, pepper and salt and a little crushed *peperoncino*. Heat some olive oil in a large pan and brown the meat together with the *battuto*. When the meat is a good nut brown, lower the flame and add some red wine and a little *passato* of tomato mainly for its colour. Continue to cook very gently for about three hours adding a little more wine or stock as needed. If you intend to serve the sauce with *maccheroni* you should add a little liver towards the end of the cooking, chopping it into small pieces. Crumble a little of the meat, mix it with the liver and the sauce, and serve this with the pasta. Delicious. Then serve the *cinghiale* as the main course with white beans seasoned with the best Arezzo olive oil and abundant black pepper.

After the *penne*, and then the *cinghiale*, a platter of *arista* is served – roasted loin of pork, another triumph of Arezzo cooking. This dish has been cooked, served and eaten in Arezzo for centuries and stories as to the origin of its name have long been told. Our magisterial Artusi writes that the Byzantines, no mean connoisseurs of good food, who came from Constantinople to attend the Council of Florence in 1430 were so appreciative of the roast pork with which they were served that they termed it *aristos*, the very best, and the name stuck.

However there is good reason to believe that *arista* was well known in the latter part of the 1300s and probably long before. Franco Sacchetti, who was born on some unrecorded day between 1332 and 1334 and died in 1400, was destined to write some of the most entertaining stories about the habits of priests, bishops and gentlemen of his times. His collection of stories, *Il Trecentonovelle*, which he is thought to have been inspired to write when serving as *podestà* of Bibbiena in the Aretine Casentino valley, as well as being witty is a source of information on the food of Italy in the fourteenth century. Novella number CXXIV tells of a certain Noddo d'Andrea who had an enormous appetite and a strange ability to swallow extremely hot food as easily as if he was shoving his dinner down a well instead of his throat. The story which ends with his greedy mode of eating *maccheroni* being improved by his dinner companion, starts with Noddo sending, as was the custom at that time when houses were not equipped with ovens, a dish of *arista* and one of *busecchio*, tripe, to the village baker's oven to be cooked. So, with the date of the writing of *Il Trecentonovelle* in mind we might say that *arista* was eaten at the very least nearly forty years before the arrival of the Byzantine delegation to Florence and therefore the story of their christening the dish with a Greek name is an elegant myth. However, here there arises a further complication which may tend to favour a return to a Greek ancestry for Sacchetti's tale of the chimney-throated Noddo and his dish of *arista*. In Book I of Athenaeus' *Deipnosophists* – 'The Gastronomes', a certain Chrysippus tells of a shameless gourmand called Philoxenus who in order to accustom his hands to fierce heat would plunge them into extremely hot water and likewise would gargle with the same to prepare his throat for the hottest of food. He had persuaded the cooks to serve their dishes so hot that only he amongst the other diners was capable of eating the food in that state and as a result he could gobble it all up before his companions had a chance to eat. Strangely enough, after further discussions about other gourmands who desired necks as long as cranes to further prolong the pleasure of eating and who sheathed their tongues with membranes and wore finger

❋ Chapter Five – Pleasure ❋

guards to enable them to eat broiling hot food, the attention of Athenaeus turns to Aristoxenus, a Cyrenic philosopher who was noted for excessive luxury at his table and after whom a kind of specially prepared ham was named, *arista*, roast loin of pork – *Aristoxenus* – a specially prepared ham. Within close proximity in the pages of *The Deipnosophists* we have two incidents that were to be eventually included by Sacchetti in the tale of Noddo, again written a few lines apart. Their very proximity would suggest that this is not a simple coincidence.

The Deipnosophists or *The Sophists at Dinner*, a cookery book cum philosophical treatise on food, eating and diverse entertainments, was probably completed around 228 AD. Many other ancient classical works which have completely disappeared are mentioned in its pages including some of the first cookery books which were written as far back as the fifth century BC. How, as seems possible, did Franco Sacchetti read a copy of the treatise? The existing texts of *The Deipnosophists* are far from complete, large parts having been lost and paraphrased through its long history. However, it is known that a manuscript containing parts of the work was circulating in Italy in the fourteenth century and thus it is a possibility that Sacchetti did indeed have access to it.

Several hundred years later, the Aretino cook Giovanni Battista Magi in his journal, which he wrote in Arezzo from 1842 to

Giovanni Battista Magi's handwritten collection of recipes, prepared in Arezzo.

1885, gives a pretty recipe for *arista* in which he suggests piercing the meat here and there and stuffing the slits with garlic, rosemary and cloves as if embroidering a quilt before sprinkling it with salt and pepper and a little ground cinnamon. He then writes that the *arista* should be placed in the oven but not left there too long or it will become as hard as a bone.

Cristina has prepared the *arista* in much the same way as Magi, it is tender and perfumed with clove and cinnamon. The meat is carved into thin slices and irrigated with a sauce made from the pan juices. With it we eat a salad of red and green radicchio cut into wide ribbons, the slightly bitter flavour marrying well with the richness of the pork. We drink good local red wine. We finish our meal with a beautiful apricot *crostata*, soft lush jam corseted with a light pastry. There are some of the last dessert grapes of the season, *spumante* and Vin Santo. Again tradition is served.

It is late November and the conversation turns to the olive harvest. Everyone around the table is busy olive picking on the various pieces of land that they own around the city. Donato, a recently retired *Primario* at Arezzo's Hospital, and his wife Teresa plan to rise at 5 am the next morning to finish their harvest in time for their allotted slot at the *frantoia*, olive press. Today fewer of these professional people rely on the increasingly disappearing farm workers to harvest for them. Instead they are out there on the wooden ladders themselves, picking with freezing fingers. But the reward and the satisfaction is significant and pleasing, their own cold-pressed extra virgin olive oil which will last them for the whole of the year to come. This close tie to the countryside is fundamental to Arezzo – a relationship with the landscape that has formed the character of the city and its inhabitants.

The designer and the doctor's wife talk about ways of preserving olives for eating. The former relates how her mother-in-law taught her to put olives in a shallow earthenware bowl and entirely

Chapter Five – Pleasure

cover the surface with a thick layer of coarse salt. The bowls were then left in a cold place and after a few weeks had passed, the bitter juices of the olives being expressed, the fruit was ready; wrinkled but good to eat. Then she said she had learnt from a friend another method. This was to put about a kilo of olives into a sack with 100 grams of salt and leave the sack hanging from a tree, remembering to move the olives around every now and again. After a few weeks the olives would have lost their bitterness but in this instance retained their plump shape.

On this birthday evening we have eaten dishes with antique origins cherished over centuries by Aretine cooks and lovers of good food. The shades of Pietro Aretino, Francesco Gaudentio, Giovanni Battista Magi, Beppina and also Artusi might be smiling in the recesses of the kitchen, where Cristina follows in their footsteps or, indeed, they may be looking longingly over our shoulders as we eat. *Vivi Felice!* Live in happiness, they murmur.

The City and Fortress of Arezzo in the 1700s.

✺ Recipes ✺

The Essentials

1. Battuto, Tritato, Soffritto

Battuto or *Tritato* or *Soffritto*, from the words *battere* to beat or thresh, *tritare* to mince or hash, and *soffritto* to fry gently. These vital steps in the preparation of ingredients appear in many of the recipes in this book. Onion, carrot, celery and garlic are the basic ingredients, the *odori*, the flavour givers that are continually used in a *battuto* or *tritato/trito* as a basis for most Italian soups, sauces and *stufate*, stews. These ingredients are chopped up together finely using a *mezzaluna* or sharp knife. The purpose of chopping the diverse items together is to meld their flavours, they are then fried in a pan with olive oil until they are soft and golden, but never burnt. If the ingredients should burn it is best to throw them away and start again from the beginning, as the burnt taste will haunt the final dish in an unpleasant way. The basic mixture adds depth of flavour and texture to the recipe. Other ingredients such as black pepper, rosemary or fresh sage leaves are also often added to the fundamental ingredients according to what the particular recipe requires. After the *soffritto* is golden you then add the other ingredients in the recipe according to their prescribed order.

2. Pane e La Zuppa: Bread and its use in Soup

In Arezzo as in most of Tuscany bread is the traditional staple. It was the basis of all meals in poor country households. Stale bread was gracefully used up in that famous Tuscan delight *panzanella*, and all *zuppe* contain a slice of two-day-old or toasted fresh bread. *Inzuppare* means to soak. The bread is soaked in a ladleful of soup or sauce. Even the popular dessert *zuppa inglese* refers to the *langues du chat* biscuits or cake at the bottom of the trifle.

For the purposes of the recipes in the following pages, bread means Tuscan bread, a robust loaf with a strong structure that does not collapse into a mush as soon as it comes into contact with liquid. Outside of Tuscany this often presents a problem. Experiment with the *schiacciata* sold in many Britsh or US stores, use it stale or toasted, or try baking your own with strong flour. Remember the toast must be made at the last moment, as cold toast will not absorb the soup; old, cold toast has a penetrating flavour, if you make it hours before you are ready to spread on your toppings it will dominate their taste in a decidedly unpleasant way.

3. Utensils

There are two pans which are crucial when cooking pasta. One is a very large deep saucepan in which to boil the pasta, there should be sufficient room in the pan for the pasta to move easily in the water. The other is a large, deep, curved sided flat pan, big enough to cook the pasta sauce in and then tip in the drained pasta in order to mix the two together with the aid of two wooden forks. These pans are available in many stores and large supermarkets in Italy, and are a worthwhile item to buy when on a visit, if you enjoy cooking pasta. A truffle slicer is a very satisfactory tool as its use is not just confined to truffles, you can shave off elegantly thin slices of Parmesan with it too; perfect on top of a rocket salad.

❋ Recipes ❋

The Recipes

Broths and Sauces

Brodo di Gallina (Chicken Broth)

For four to six people you will need one free-range hen obtained from a decent butcher. Pallid supermarket chicken will not provide the same flavour. One onion, two cloves, one carrot, one rib of celery with its leaves attached, a bunch of parsley, a bay leaf, two cloves of garlic, one whole tiny tomato, nutmeg, four black peppercorns, salt.

Clean the hen and split it open. Peel the onion and stick the cloves into it. Put the hen and all the herbs and ingredients, except the salt and black pepper, into a large saucepan with two and a half litres of cold water. Set the pan on a low flame. Add a very little salt and the peppercorns, cover, then allow the broth to come to the boil very, very slowly. It should take around half an hour to reach boiling point, keep the broth boiling gently, the liquid hardly moving. Skim any froth off the surface from time to time. It will take about two hours for the hen to cook to the point when the flesh falls easily off the bone at just a poke of a wooden spoon. At this point, stir the broth, add an *ombra*, a shadow, of grated nutmeg and adjust the salt. Then pour the broth into another pan through a sieve. To make the broth even clearer, sieve again through a finer mesh or a piece of muslin. Shred the meat of the hen into pieces and serve this with pickled vegetables, artichokes, aubergines and peppers. Green olives too, will not go amiss.

Sugo di Pomodoro (Tomato Sauce)

This is a basic household recipe for the essential tomato sauce used to flavour all manner of pasta dishes, pizza, and composite meat or vegetable dishes where a tomato sauce is required.

To serve four people you will need one mild onion, one carrot, one rib of celery, four tablespoons of extra virgin olive oil, five large basil leaves, 300 g about 12 oz of fresh, ripe tomatoes deprived of their skins or decent Italian tinned chopped tomatoes. Salt and black pepper to taste.

Chop the *odori* (carrot, celery, onion) very finely together until they are almost a paste. Heat the olive oil in a thick-based saucepan and add the chopped ingredients to the oil, let them cook over a gentle flame until they have become soft but not brown. It is important that the *odori* are completely soft otherwise the sauce will be gritty. At this point add the basil leaves torn into pieces and the tomato, season with salt and pepper. Stir the mixture and let it simmer gently for about half an hour, if it should become too dry add more olive oil. The sauce should have an unctuous base not a watery one.

When cooking in the winter or in the north, when really well-flavoured ripe tomatoes are not readily available, there is another good method which will help to give a rich, sweet-flavoured sauce. Simply discard the onion and double the amount of carrot. Instead of chopping the carrot, grate it finely. Chop the celery finely too, add it to the carrot and sweat the ingredients in extra virgin olive oil until they are well softened but not brown. At this point add Italian tinned chopped tomatoes, the Cirio or Mutti brands, if available, are I have found, the best for the purpose. Cook the sauce gently until the juice has evaporated and the sauce is thick. Add more olive oil if needed, do not even think of using any other type of oil. The whole object of tomato sauce is to encapsulate the 'essence' of the best of tomatoes.

Sugo al Carne or Ragù
(Meat Sauce)

This is also a sauce that is fundamental to food in Italy, to be used with a variety of pasta, gnocchi, polenta and in composite dishes like *lasagne al forno*. There are probably as many recipes

✻ Recipes ✻

for *ragù* as there are cooks in Italy, most of whom have their own particular tastes and fancies and very often include what there is to hand in the way of meat, a little rabbit perhaps, a Tuscan sausage or two, pieces of chicken or duck and their livers too. The more variety of meat ingredients the richer and more complex the sauce will be. There are also distinct local variations, in Arezzo, *milza*, spleen is a favourite, in many parts of Umbria béchamel and black truffles play their part. In Bologna, *ragù* is sometimes garnished with the cooked yolks of unlaid hens' eggs.

To make a good Tuscan *ragù* you will need the following ingredients: one large onion, two medium carrots, two small ribs of celery and a few leaves, a small sprig of rosemary, 50 g / 2 oz of butter, 2 tablespoons of olive oil, 100 g / 4 oz of smoked *pancetta*, 350 g / 14 oz of beef or 200 g / 8 oz of beef and 150 g / 6 oz of minced lean pork, two Tuscan sausages skinned and crumbled, black pepper, be very parsimonious with salt as the *pancetta* and the sausages will have their own supply, then a tiny amount of Tuscan *droga*, which is a mixture of spices, chiefly clove, nutmeg and cinnamon and sometimes a little allspice. A glass of white wine or, better still, good Vin Santo. Two heaped tablespoons of *concentrato di pomodoro*, tomato concentrate sold in tubes, dissolved in a tea cup of hot water. You may also decide to include 40 or 50 g / 2 oz of dried *porcini*. In this case you must put them into a bowl, cover them with hot water and allow them to plump up. When they have done so, squeeze them dry and chop them roughly. Strain their dark brown liquid through a muslin or a piece of kitchen paper lining a sieve and use it if extra liquid is needed for the sauce. The purpose of straining the liquid is to remove any grit which tends to hide itself in the folds of the *porcini*.

Chop the onion, carrots, celery and rosemary (discarding the tough stalk) together finely on a large chopping board, season the mixture with black pepper. Heat the butter and oil in a large deep sided sauté pan, add the *battuto* (chopped vegetables) and the *pancetta* cut into dice. Let this mixture cook until the vegetables are well softened and golden but not brown. At this point add the minced meats and the crumbled sausages, mixing them in as you go. Keep cooking on a low to medium flame stirring all the while. Season with a pinch of spice, but do not overdo this, start with a scant quarter of a coffee spoon, too much will overpower the sauce. When the meat has become a light gold colour pour the wine or Vin Santo into the pan. Let it hiss and bubble and evaporate. Add the *porcini* now if you choose to use them and a little of their liquid. At this point add some of the tomato, enough to colour the meat and make the sauce liquid. Cook very slowly for about an hour adding more *porcini* liquid, tomato or olive oil if the sauce should catch. The consistency of the sauce should be thick and oily, never watery. Season to taste with salt.

Risotto and Soups

Risotto con Carciofi
(Artichoke Risotto)

To serve four people you will need six young artichokes, salt and white pepper, a walnut-sized knob of butter and two tablespoons of olive oil, one small white onion, the variety with silver skin, or failing that two shallots (do not use yellow onions as they are too robust for this dish), 300 g / 12 oz of Arborio rice, about a litre of stock, 50 g / 2 oz of freshly grated Parmesan and a little finely chopped parsley.

Strip off and discard the tough outer leaves of the artichokes. Slice them finely lengthways, throwing the slices into acidulated water as you go (use a little lemon juice), to prevent the artichokes from blackening. When you are ready to make the risotto drain the slices and dry with a cloth. If tender artichokes are not available in your area then clean the ones you have obtained and put them into a pan of boiling water for ten to fifteen minutes before slicing the leaves. Be careful not to overcook them as they may lose their flavour and substance.

❊ Recipes ❊

Chop the onion or shallots finely. Heat the butter and the olive oil in a thick-bottomed pan, add the onion and then the artichoke slices and let them cook on a low flame until they are pale gold but nowhere near brown. At this point add the rice and turn it about until it has become transparent. Season with salt and white pepper. For the next step there are two methods. One is to add a ladle of hot stock and keep stirring with a wooden spoon until the stock is consumed and it is time to add another ladleful, stirring all the while and so on until the rice is cooked. The other less time consuming method is to add most of the hot stock, keeping some in reserve. Stir it in well and cover the pan, cook over a low flame for about 20 minutes checking every now and again to see if there is sufficient liquid to soften the rice. Add more if necessary. When the risotto is done stir in abundant grated Parmesan and the finely chopped parsley. Serve the risotto in a hot bowl.

There are many variations of this risotto between Arezzo and Florence, some are simpler and use solely olive oil and no butter, others add strips of cooked ham to the chopped onion, and some use a little wine or Vin Santo poured over the rice and evaporated before the stock is added. I think the artichokes are best left to their own devices without too many competing additions. Artichokes are particular favourites in Arezzo as they are believed to be very beneficial to health especially that of the liver.

Risotto con le Zucchine
(Risotto with Zucchini)

To serve four people you will need one small white onion, 3 tablespoons of extra virgin olive oil, 20 g / 0.75 oz of butter, 400 g / 16 oz of small zucchini sliced into rounds half a cm / ¼ inch thick, the pale green ridged Florentine variety are best, half a glass of dry white wine, 400 g / 16 oz of Arborio rice, salt to taste, a generous litre / 2 pints of good chicken or capon stock, 50 g / 2 oz of freshly grated Parmesan, freshly ground white pepper.

Chop the onion finely and put it into a large pan with the olive oil, let the onion become transparent over a medium flame, add the butter and let it melt, now add the sliced zucchini stirring them around. Let them soften for a few minutes but do not let them brown, this would change the colour of the risotto and produce a bitter flavour. Season with salt. At this point add the white wine and let it evaporate. Next add the rice and stir it well into the zucchini mixture. Now add two or three ladles of hot stock, stir, cover the pan and let it cook over a low flame, check frequently that there is sufficient liquid to soften the rice, adding more if necessary. The risotto is done when the rice still has a little bite to it and the consistency is *all'onda*, the risotto is liquid enough to make a gentle wave in its bowl. About twenty minutes of cooking is generally enough, be guided by the instructions on the packet of rice. When the rice is done to your satisfaction, stir in the grated Parmesan and serve it up hot.

Risotto con la Zucca
(Risotto with Pumpkin)

To make sufficient for four people you will need 500 g / 20 oz of ripe, orange fleshed pumpkin, one litre of stock, 50 g / 2 oz of good butter, salt to taste, black pepper and/or a sprinkle of ground red pepper flakes, 400 g / 16 oz of rice, a generous amount of freshly grated Parmesan.

Carve off the hard pumpkin skin and slice the flesh into bite-size pieces. Put them into a pan with the stock and allow them to cook until they are almost tender. Chop the shallot into fine pieces. In another pan furnished with a thick base heat up the butter until it starts to bubble then add the shallot and the pepper flakes, stir the shallot around until it is transparent. At this point add the rice and stir this too until it is also transparent, a step known in Italy as to *tostare*. Then pour in the pieces of pumpkin plus the stock, stir all well together and leave to bubble gently for around twenty minutes. Stir occasionally, checking the consistency of the rice. Add a little more stock or water if necessary and towards the end of the cooking taste the risotto to see if there is sufficient salt and

❋ Recipes ❋

adjust accordingly. The rice should have retained a very slight bite to it and the liquid be sufficient to make a wave in the serving bowl. Stir in a little more butter and two tablespoons of grated Parmesan and serve the risotto hot.

Minestra di Pane
(Bread soup in the style of Cristina)

To serve five or six people you will need: 300 g of cannellini beans soaked overnight in cold water, 1 onion, 2 ribs of celery plus their leaves, a little parsley, 2 carrots, two potatoes, 2 zucchini, a handful of green beans, a quarter of a green cabbage, 3 leaves of Swiss chard, 5 or 6 leaves of *cavolo nero*, kale, 1 small round tomato, olive oil and salt as required.

In a large pan cook the beans in water, adding a clove or two of garlic, two sage leaves, one small round whole tomato, salt to taste and a large spoonful of olive oil. When the beans are tender put half of them through a food mill and reserve the rest whole.

In a shallow pan heat two large spoons of olive oil and gently cook the various vegetables cut into dice or disks. Start with the onion, celery and parsley: the *odori*. Then add the diced potatoes, roundels of carrot, the kale leaves torn into pieces with their stems removed, ditto the Swiss chard and the green French beans snapped in two, then the zucchini sliced in rounds. Do not let the vegetables brown or catch. Add a little water, half a glassful, from time to time and cook the vegetables for 40 minutes.

In another pan fry the green cabbage, the leaves torn up and without the ribs. Turn it in a little olive oil with the addition of some chopped garlic and then a little water. After a few minutes add the cabbage to the other vegetables.

Place the cooked vegetables into a large pan or casserole and add the liquidized beans and let the mixture cook for an hour over a low heat. When all is cooked and flavoured with pepper or peperoncino and salt, add the whole beans.

To serve, lay a slice of hot toasted bread in every dish and ladle on the soup. Add olive oil and a little chopped raw onion as you please.

Ribollita
(Re-cooked soup)

The next day lay slices of toasted bread in an oven dish, then ladle the remains of the soup over them, repeat this until the dish is full or the soup is used up. Put the dish into a very hot oven for ten minutes.

Zuppa di Fagioli
(Bean Soup)

To serve four people you will need: 300 g / 12 oz of fresh cannellini beans or 200 g / 8 oz if they are dried. Four ripe tomatoes with their skins removed, 25 g / 1 oz of lean *pancetta* cut into dice, one onion, one carrot, one celery rib, two cloves of garlic, a sprig or two of fresh rosemary, 2 tablespoons of olive oil, 4 slices of Tuscan bread toasted just before serving.

Cook the beans in a pan of salted water until tender, the time required depends on whether they are fresh or dried and soaked, you may also use tinned beans and their liquid.

Make a *battuto* of the onion, carrot, celery and garlic, i.e. you must chop the ingredients finely together on your chopping board. Pour the olive oil into the saucepan, let it heat up and then add the *battuto* and the chopped *pancetta*, stir them around until they are golden but do not allow them to become brown, add the sprig of rosemary as well and let it flavour the ingredients. Next add the tomatoes, skinned and chopped into small pieces and a little hot water if the mixture seems too dry and is in danger of sticking to the pan.

When the *battuto* and the tomato are thoroughly softened remove the sprigs of rosemary. Take the cooked beans and put about three-quarters of them with some of their water through the blender to make a fairly thick cream-like liquid. Add this to the pan and then pour in the remaining whole beans which will give the soup texture, adding a little of their liquid if necessary. Simmer the soup for a further ten minutes or so. In each soup bowl place a slice of hot toasted bread rubbed with garlic if you

Recipes

like it and then pour in a generous ladle of soup. Freshly ground black pepper and a few drops of best olive oil complete the dish.

Be careful when salting the soup as the *pancetta* will have its own supply and be sure to use good substantial bread.

Zuppa di Farro
(Spelt Soup)

Farro is an ancient type of grain, *Triticum spelta*, related to wheat, which is still much appreciated in Italy.

For six people you will need: 300 g / 12 oz of dried borlotti beans, one medium onion, two sprigs of rosemary, five or six sage leaves, two cloves of garlic, 300 g of *farro*, six slices of Tuscan bread, olive oil.

Set the beans in a pot of cold water and let them soak for five or six hours; when they are swollen, drain them but reserve the water in which they were soaked. Put the beans into a pan with fresh cold water to cover and let them cook gently for about half an hour or until they are almost tender.

Meanwhile chop up the onion, the sage and garlic finely together. Heat six tablespoons of olive oil in your soup pan and add the *battuto*, plus the sprig of rosemary, letting them soften in the oil. Then add the *farro* and stir it around, allowing it to soak up the oil and flavour. This step – *tostare*, toasting or roasting – is similar to stirring the rice into the oil or butter when making a risotto. When the *farro* is well mixed into the oil add some of the water that the beans were soaked in and let the soup simmer over a low flame for about an hour to an hour and a half until the *farro* is tender, adjusting the liquid as necessary. Halfway through the cooking add three-quarters of the beans. Pass the remaining beans through a mouli or blender and add them at the last moment to thicken the soup.

To serve, ladle the soup into bowls, pour a little of your best olive oil into each one and place a slice of hot toasted Tuscan bread rubbed with garlic at the side of each bowl.

Beppina and the Kitchens of Arezzo

There are many different versions of this soup to be found in Tuscany. Some people in the area employ more ingredients, adding, for example, marjoram and *pancetta* to the *battuto* and a little tomato to the body of the soup. I prefer the simpler more austere version above which exalts the quality of the oil and herbs and is to be found in many homes and eating places in Arezzo.

Zuppa Frantoiana
(Soup with Fragrant Olive Oil)

This soup, as its name suggests – *frantoia* – being an establishment where olives are pressed, is one in which the season's new olive oil takes pride of place. The strong flavour of the new, cold-pressed extra virgin olive oil is the star of the soup and it is pointless to make it unless you have such an oil to hand. Tuscan farmers taking their olives to the *frantoia* for pressing were, and in some cases still are, in the habit of tasting their oil as it oozes from the spigot by pouring a little on rough slices of bread toasted rapidly over the wood fires that burn brightly near the olive presses. The olive is a winter crop picked in November and December and the night vigil watching the oil emerging is a cold one. Over the years country women have elaborated the *bruschetta* or *fett'unta* as the simple dish is called around Florence into a *zuppa*, a soup in which bread is a fundamental ingredient. Many recipes, especially those emanating from Siena, use white beans, the ever delicious cannellini, but brown borlotti beans are better suited to *Zuppa Frantoiana* because of their rich colour and texture. As with many dishes of this nature there are a myriad variations on the ingredients employed, fruit of the imagination of the *massaia* and what was to be found at the opportune moment in her *orto*, her kitchen garden.

The following recipe is a good basis for a rich soup. For six people you will first need 300 g / 12 oz of dry borlotti beans or 600 g if they are fresh, one carrot, half an onion, a handful of celery leaves and sufficient water to cover the beans and the *odori* in a large saucepan.

✻ Recipes ✻

For the second stage you will need, 4 tablespoons of best olive oil, 100 g / 4 oz of smoked *pancetta* cut into dice, one carrot, three cloves of garlic, a small onion, abundant freshly ground black pepper.

For the third stage you will need a potato or two, perhaps a small amount of pumpkin or a carrot all chopped into rough pieces, some torn leaves of dark green cabbage, preferably the Tuscan variety, a level teaspoon of fennel seed, salt and pepper to taste.

To serve you will need two thick slices of firm bread per person, a cut clove of raw garlic, abundant new extra virgin olive oil.

Method.
1. Soak the dry beans for five or six hours, fresh beans, naturally do not need this step. Put the soaked or fresh beans, the whole carrot, onion and celery leaves into a large pan, cover with water, bring it to the boil then let the beans simmer until they are tender. Put the bulk of the beans and some of their cooking liquid through the mouli or food processor to make a broth. Reserve a few of the cooked beans whole to add at a later stage. Add more liquid if the broth is too dense.

2. Chop the garlic, onion and carrot finely together and sprinkle the mixture liberally with the black pepper, add the chopped *pancetta* to the pile on your chopping board. Take a large clean saucepan and in it heat the 4 tablespoons of olive oil. When the oil is hot, tip in the chopped ingredients and stir them around until the *pancetta* is golden and the other ingredients have started to soften. Do not let this *soffritto* burn.

3. At this point add the bean broth to the pan, stirring well and allow it to come to the boil. At boiling point add your choice of potato, pumpkin, carrot or even zucchini all cut into small chunks, then add the fennel seed and season to your taste

with salt and pepper. Lower the heat and let the soup simmer until the vegetables are tender. When this is so, add the whole beans and stir.

To serve
Toast the bread, rub one side with the cut garlic clove and pour on a liberal amount of the olive oil. Place one slice of this *bruschetta* in every bowl then cover with a ladleful of the soup. Put another slice of the toast on top and then more soup. Make sure that each bowl contains some of the whole beans. This is a substantial dish which totally depends on the quality and strong flavour of the oil that you use. The heat of the liquid will release the flavour and perfume of the oil giving you one of the greatest of culinary pleasures.

Antipasto and Frittata

Crostini Neri
(Chicken liver savouries)

To serve six to eight people as part of an antipasto course you will need one small white onion, one small carrot, half a celery stalk, two or three sprigs of parsley, three tablespoons of extra virgin olive oil, five chicken livers, a sprig of rosemary, one heaped teaspoon of tomato concentrate, salt and freshly ground black pepper, a glass of white wine.

Chop the onion, carrot, celery and parsley together very finely. Heat the olive oil in a sauté pan and add the chopped vegetables to it. Let them cook gently until they are thoroughly softened but not burnt. At this point add the whole chicken livers and the sprig of rosemary. You must be absolutely sure that all traces of the green bile duct are removed from the livers, otherwise their extreme bitterness will ruin the dish. Let the livers cook through gently then remove them from the pan and chop them until they are the texture of a coarse porridge. It is best to chop the livers after their initial cooking as this gives a better texture, chopping them in their raw state can result in them disintegrating into a mush. Remove the sprig of rosemary and return the chopped liver to the pan. Next add the tomato concentrate, season with salt and pepper and stir in a little of the wine. Let the mixture cook gently for about ten minutes adding more wine if the mixture starts to catch. Any wine left over belongs to the cook!

Spread the mixture onto small rounds or squares of good strong bread. Allow one or two per person. If you are using untoasted bread, dip one surface into a bowl of hot stock, this will help the liver mixture spread. Otherwise cover hot fresh toast with the paté. Remember, *crostini* made with old toast is unappetising, the warm mixture will not meld with the cold dry toast.

This is a classic recipe for which the ingredients should be easily available outside Italy. In Arezzo these *crostini* are made with the addition of *milza* which is spleen. Spleen comes in flat sheets about 2 cm / ¾ of an inch thick and firstly it must be blanched in boiling water for about five minutes. Its surface is covered with a thin grey membrane which has to be scraped off before the spleen is chopped finely and added to the *soffritto* in the pan. Spleen is very dark when cooked and has a rich meaty flavour. Sometimes *crostini* are made solely with *milza*. However, given the difficulty of obtaining spleen in a British or US butcher or supermarket, this delicious treat, however unlikely sounding that might be, is probably best left to be eaten in Arezzo.

Fegatini al Burro
(Chicken Liver with Butter)

This is a simpler way to use chicken liver on *crostini* but it is also rich and delicious. You will need three large chicken livers, a little white wine, 75 g / 3 oz of unsalted butter, a handful of capers, and about ten to twelve small rounds of good bread.

Poach the livers gently in the white wine making sure that you do not overcook them and make them hard. Next, in a shallow bowl mash the livers into the butter as evenly as you can to make a smooth *paté*. Spread this onto the pieces of bread and top each *crostino* with a caper.

Crostini con Acciughe
(Crostini with anchovy)

This is a very quick and delicious recipe that fits in well with a first course of mixed appetisers like black olives, preserved artichokes, the hard-boiled eggs in the recipe below and a little grilled aubergine or bell pepper.

Simply take as much unsalted butter as you need and mix into it thoroughly some anchovy paste, when the colour of the butter is a pale beige you will know that you have added sufficient anchovy. Spread this onto small pieces of good strong bread and top each with a slice of gherkin or a caper.

Uova soda con Salsa Verde
(Hard-Boiled Eggs with Green Sauce)

Mix a handful of finely minced parsley, a dozen chopped capers and one minced anchovy with olive oil to make a thick paste and spread over 4 hard-boiled eggs split in half lengthways.

Insalata d' Ovoli
(Ovoli Salad)

The ovolo (*Amanita caesaria*), said by the Emperor Nero to be the food of the gods, is one of the most prized of wild mushrooms and makes an exquisite salad. It is a bright orange-coloured *fungo* and egg-shaped before it unfolds.

Take as many of the exquisite *ovoli* as you have been lucky enough to obtain from a reliable source. Slice them

✻ Recipes ✻

lengthways as finely as possible with a very sharp knife, arrange on a serving dish and sprinkle with a little juice from a ripe lemon, rather more of the very best olive oil and cover with fine flakes of best Parmesan cut with the aid of a truffle slicer.

One may eat this delicacy as an antipasto at Sansepolcro, in the Province of Arezzo, at the Ristorante da Ventura which is situated in the same street as the Pinacoteca, the art gallery. A perfect luncheon after a morning of looking at the even more exquisite Piero della Francesca *Resurrection*.

The *ovolo* however, is a relative of the deadly *Amanita phalloides*. At this point it is vital to remember that one should never be tempted to eat any mushroom picked in the wild without first asking an expert if the mushroom is edible. A mistake can be fatal.

Insalata di Fave Fresche e Pecorino
(Fresh Broad Bean and Pecorino Cheese Salad)

When the first broad beans are ready to be picked their arrival is often celebrated in Aretino houses by placing a dish of them still in their pods on the table when the cheese is served. The fresh slightly bitter flavour of the new beans marries well with soft young *pecorino,* as do ripe pears in their season.

This salad is based on the same principle. Take 250 g / 10 oz of tiny tender broad beans and place them in a bowl with 150 g / 6 oz of firm *pecorino* which has been seasoned for about seventy days (not too fresh and soft or hard and seasoned) cut into small dice. Add enough of the very best olive oil, the *Aretini* say it has to be from the groves around Arezzo, to irrigate the ingredients well without leaving pools of oil in the bottom of the bowl. Season with a little salt and freshly ground black pepper.

Serve as an antipasto or at the end of a meal instead of a conventional cheese course.

Beppina and the Kitchens of Arezzo

Frittata di Fagiolini
(A Frittata with Green Beans)

To serve two people for lunch or as part of an antipasti for more guests, lightly boil a large handful of green beans, drain them well and cut them into two or three pieces. Heat a spoonful or so of olive oil in an omelette pan and spread the beans evenly across the surface. When the oil is very hot add four eggs beaten up with 25 g / 1 oz of grated Parmesan, salt and black pepper to taste. Lower the heat and let the eggs cook through, if the pan is small and the *frittata* thick, cover it with a plate until the eggs are firm. Unlike the classic omelette, *frittate* are not runny in the centre, you should be able to cut them into slices as one would a pie. In this way they make an excellent addition to an antipasti, perhaps accompanying artichokes preserved in olive oil, olives, *ventricino*, a type of salami spiced with *peperoncino*, and some thinly sliced *prosciutto*.

Frittata con Spinaci
(A Frittata with Spinach)

To serve two people you will need a cupful of cooked spinach which you must drain well and chop very finely with a sharp knife. Four large fresh eggs, a scant 50 g / 2 oz or of grated Parmesan cheese, salt and freshly ground black pepper. Olive oil. In a bowl beat up the four eggs and add to them the chopped spinach and the Parmesan, season to taste with salt and pepper and stir the mixture carefully until the ingredients are evenly distributed. Put a little olive oil into your omelette pan and heat until the oil begins to smoke. At this point pour in the egg mixture and let it cover the pan. Reduce the flame and cook the *frittata* until all the egg mixture has set through. If the pan is small and the *frittata* thick you may lower the heat yet more, cover the pan with a lid and cook until the *frittata* is completely set. Slide the cooked *frittata* onto a board and let it cool. It will make a good luncheon dish whether tepid or cold.

Recipes

You may also cut the *frittata* into wedges and serve it as part of a selection of antipasti. The underside of the *frittata* will be golden and the top pale yellow. To make a prettier dish, slice the *frittata* into wedges and turn over each alternate wedge so that you have a dish of contrasting colours.

Frittata con la Salsiccia
(A Frittata with Sausages)

To serve two people you will need two Tuscan sausages, four eggs, salt and pepper, a little olive oil.

Skin the sausages and crumble the meat into small pieces with your fingers. Put the sausage meat into an omelette pan with a very little olive oil and cook it over a lively flame until the meat turns colour and starts to brown. Meanwhile beat up the eggs with a little salt and freshly ground black pepper. When the meat is done tip the eggs into the hot pan and let them set. Cook over a lowered flame until the *frittata* is cooked through. If you wish, tip out the *frittata* onto a plate then replace it top side down into the pan so that both sides are golden.

Alternatively cook the sausage meat in a separate pan, make a classic omelette with the eggs and use the piping hot sausage as a filling.

Frittata con i Porri
(A Frittata with leeks)

For two people you will need two small leeks, four eggs, salt and pepper, a little olive oil and a small amount of water.

Wash and trim the leeks cutting off most of the green part and slice them finely into rounds. It is best to use small leeks as they are more tender and will cook faster. In an omelette pan set the leeks to cook over a slow flame in a little olive oil and a few drops of water. Do not let them brown and if they show signs of sticking add a little more water. Meanwhile beat the eggs together in a bowl and season them to your taste with salt and pepper. When the leeks are tender, distribute them evenly over the pan, raise the heat until the oil is sufficiently hot and pour in the eggs. Let the *frittata* cook through on a very slow heat covering the pan with a plate if the pan is small and the egg mixture deep.

Frittata di Ceci
(Chickpea Frittata)

For two people you will need six tablespoons of well-cooked chickpeas, 2 tablespoons of milk, 4 eggs, olive oil, salt and freshly ground black pepper.

Sieve the soft chickpeas and remove any tough outer skins. It is important to use well-cooked chickpeas otherwise the *frittata* will have a gritty texture. In a bowl beat up the eggs with the milk. To this mixture add the chickpea purée, a little salt and abundant black pepper. Mix the ingredients until they form a rather liquid batter.

Take an omelette pan and in it heat a tablespoonful of olive oil, when the oil is smoking pour in the batter and let it cook over a lower flame until it is crisp on one side and set on the other.

To turn the *frittata* in order to crisp both sides, take a large plate and slide the *frittata* onto it. Then tip the *frittata* pale side down back into the pan. Let the second side take on some colour. The smaller the pan you use the thicker the *frittata* will be. If you choose to make the thick version you may need to cover the pan with a lid and let the *frittata* cook through slowly over a yet lower flame.

This *frittata* is excellent cut into wedges and served as part of an antipasto.

Frittata di Pomodori Acerbi
(A Frittata with fried Green Tomatoes)

For two people you will need two unripe tomatoes cut into segments, a little white flour or maize flour, olive oil, four eggs, salt and pepper.

✳ Recipes ✳

Dip the tomato segments into the flour and fry them in a separate pan with a little of the olive oil until the tomatoes are tender on the inside and crisp outside. Meanwhile beat the eggs and season with the salt and pepper. Take an omelette pan and lightly cover the base with oil, let it become smoking hot, add the cooked tomato segments then pour on the beaten eggs. Let them cook through as for a normal *frittata*.

Finta Trippa
(Faux Tripe)

This is a very simple country dish in which a *frittata* mimics a Tuscan way of preparing tripe, which is to cut it into strips and cook it in a tomato sauce. The dish of course lacks the inimitable flavour of tripe but it does make a pleasant alternative to the classic omelette. It also makes a very good first course to serve to those who do not eat carbohydrates as the strips of *frittata* are also reminiscent of pasta.

For a *frittata* for two people you will need four fresh eggs, salt and black pepper, 2 heaped tablespoons of finely grated Parmesan, 2 tablespoons of milk, one dessertspoon of olive oil.

For the sauce you will need one carrot, one rib of celery, one small mild onion, one clove of garlic, a few sprigs of fresh parsley, salt and black pepper and a tiny pinch of dried pepper flakes, two tablespoons of olive oil and 300 g / 12 oz of chopped tomato, either tinned or fresh. If using fresh tomatoes make sure they are very ripe, remove their skins and seeds and squeeze away any excess liquid, weigh them after discarding the skins and juice.

First of all make the *frittata* in the usual way. In a bowl beat up the eggs with the milk and Parmesan, add the salt and pepper to taste. Heat the oil in a large flat pan and when it is very hot pour in the egg mixture swirling it so that it covers the base of the pan; the *frittata* should be roughly a quarter to half a centimetre thick. Lower the heat and let the *frittata* cook until it is set all the way through. When this is so, slip the *frittata* onto a plate, then tip it into the pan again pale side down in order to brown it. After a minute or two slide the *frittata* out of the pan onto a board which you have covered with a piece of kitchen paper to soak up any excess oil, and let it cool.

To make the sauce chop the *odori*, that is the carrot, celery, onion, garlic and parsley together finely. Season this mixture with salt and freshly ground black pepper and the tiny pinch of red pepper flakes. Heat the oil in a deep sided, flat and clean pan which is large enough to take both the sauce and the strips of *frittata*. Add the chopped *odori*, stir the mixture around until it has thoroughly softened but do not let it burn; if you neglect this latter step the sauce will be unpleasantly gritty. At this point add the tomato, stir, lower the heat and let the sauce simmer for about fifteen to twenty minutes. If it shows signs of being too dry add a little more tomato or a small amount of olive oil.

When you are ready to serve the *finta trippa* cut the cooled *frittata* into strips about the width of tagliatelle and around four to five inches long. Add the strips to the sauce and stir them around gently allowing them to heat through. Serve very hot piled onto a serving dish or arrange on individual plates, in either case add a good sprinkling of freshly grated Parmesan cheese.

Uova col Pomodoro
(Eggs with Tomato)

For two people, three ripe fleshy tomatoes, one large clove of garlic, two tablespoons of extra virgin olive oil, three or four basil leaves, four fresh eggs, salt and black pepper to taste.

Put the tomatoes in boiling water for a minute or so to loosen the skins, remove the skins and cut up the tomatoes discarding the seeds and as much excess moisture as possible.

Heat the olive oil together with the sliced clove of garlic and let it sizzle until the garlic is golden but far from brown. When this is so, add the tomato pulp and the basil leaves and let them cook for five to ten minutes until the tomato is cooked

❋ Recipes ❋

through and not watery. There should be enough oil in the pan to prevent the tomato from sticking to the surface. At this point break four eggs into the pan on top of the bed of tomato, season with salt and pepper, cover the pan and let it cook gently until the whites are firm.

You can also beat the eggs in a separate bowl and stir them into the tomato as you would when making a *piperade*. Just as delicious but with a very different appearance.

Pasta

Gnocchi del Casentino
(Gnocchi in the Casentino manner)

For four people you will need 400 g / 16 oz of fresh ricotta, 600 g / 24 oz of raw spinach, 3 eggs, 50 g / 2 oz grated Parmesan, a little flour, a sprinkling of ground nutmeg, salt and black pepper, a pan full of stock.

Wash the spinach and place it in a large covered pan with just the water that clings to its leaves. Wilt the spinach over a medium flame then drain it extremely well pressing the excess water out with your hands. Chop it very finely with a *mezzaluna* or very sharp knife.

In a large bowl mix the ricotta and spinach together, add the Parmesan, the nutmeg and salt and pepper to taste. Bind the mixture with the beaten eggs adding a little at a time to avoid the mixture becoming too moist. If the mixture should be too wet add a very little flour. Form the ricotta mixture into small balls the size of a walnut. Bring the stock to the boil and throw in the gnocchi a few at a time, they will sink then rise to the surface which means that they are done. Scoop them out with a slotted spoon and reserve. Serve them in bowls with a little of the stock and a sprinkle of grated Parmesan or eat them dry simply turned in a pan with a little hot butter and a sage leaf or two. They may also be served with a *ragù*, meat sauce.

❋ Beppina and the Kitchens of Arezzo ❋

Pappardelle all'Aretina

Artusi gives a similar recipe to this one, but he includes butter and *milza*, spleen, in the sauce, which latter is something that is much appreciated in Arezzo and which adds a very particular savoury flavour. He makes the comment that it is not a fine dish but rather one to suit a family meal. He uses the word *pappardelle* instead of *maccheroni* to describe the pasta. *Pappardelle* is a term that appears now on some restaurant menus and the type sold commercially is a wide ribbon pasta with edges that are deckled. There have been debates amongst the authoritative writers on Aretino food as to the authenticity of *pappardelle*. Some say that *maccheroni* is the genuine Arezzo name for the pasta, one which everyone recognises. Indeed, according to some of the stories of Sacchetti in his *Il Trecentonovelle*, people have been happily eating *maccheroni* since the late 1300s at the very least (see page 208). The genuine Arezzo variety should be home-made and come in the form of squares about 8 cm in size or long strips of about 6 cm in width. On the other hand, Artusi writing in Florence at the end of the nineteenth century – which makes the recipe old but not ancient – says that to make *pappardelle all'Aretina* one should 'Roll out a sheet of dough made with eggs as thick as required for *tagliatelle* then with a scalloped edged pastry wheel cut strips wider than a finger's width.' In his recipe for *pappardelle colla lepre* he suggests using home-made *pappardelle* or strips of bought pasta. However, the sauce given below is just as delicious with *tagliatelle* or *farfalle* or *penne*.

To serve four people: one duck, a little olive oil, 100 g / 4 oz of *prosciutto crudo*, one celery stalk, one carrot, one shallot, a few sage leaves, a small bunch of basil, one glass of white wine, 700 g / 28 oz of chopped tomato, grated nutmeg, salt, freshly ground black pepper, 400 g / 16 oz of pasta, abundant grated Parmesan.

Wash, dry and quarter the duck, pepper and salt the pieces and let them brown in a large pan with a little olive oil. When the duck is golden on all sides add the *prosciutto*, celery, carrot, shallot, sage, basil and parsley which you have chopped together on your chopping board to make the usual *trito* or *battuto*. Turn the duck in the *trito* so it takes on its flavours. After a few minutes tip any excess fat out of the pan. After this pour on the glass of white wine and let it sizzle and evaporate. Add the tomato and a good sprinkle of grated nutmeg and salt and pepper to taste.

Cover the pan and let it cook over a low flame for about an hour and a half or until the duck is tender. Remove the duck pieces from the pan and reserve in a warm oven. Stir the remaining sauce well and make sure that it remains hot.

Cook the pasta in salted boiling water until it is al dente, drain it well. To serve, take a large warm bowl and in it mix the pasta into the sauce with the aid of two forks. Add abundant grated Parmesan sprinkled throughout the bowl and over the top. For the main course serve the pieces of duck with a green salad or *fagiolini verdi*.

Spaghetti al Basilico
(Spaghetti with Basil)

To serve 4 people take a posy of fresh basil, 50 g / 2 oz of grated Parmesan or *pecorino* cheese, salt and black pepper. 400 g / 16 oz dry weight of spaghetti.

Chop the basil into the smallest fragments you can. Mix it with the grated cheese and season with salt and abundant black pepper.

Cook the pasta *al dente*, drain well into a serving bowl, add the basil mixture and mix well. The heat of the pasta will melt the cheese and make the scent of the herb sing.

Spaghetti al Olio e Aglio
(Spaghetti with Olive Oil and Raw Garlic)

To serve four people you will need 400 g / 16 oz of spaghetti, six fat cloves of garlic and a generous handful of parsley chopped together finely, two overflowing tablespoons of your best extra virgin olive oil, a generous 50 g / 2 oz of freshly grated Parmesan, freshly ground black pepper. Put the garlic and parsley mixture into a bowl and add the two tablespoons of olive oil, stirring it well. Boil the pasta in a large pan of salted boiling water until it is *al dente*, be guided by the timing suggested on the packet, drain it well and tip it into a large warm serving bowl. Pour the sauce over the pasta mixing it well in with two forks. Add a little more oil if need be. Serve with abundant grated Parmesan and freshly ground black pepper. Simple and effective.

Tagliatelle con i Carciofi
(Tagliatelle with Artichokes)

To serve 4: Four young artichokes, 50 g / 2 oz of cooked ham, 200 ml / ⅓ of a pint of cream, 1 clove of garlic, 2 tablespoons of olive oil, salt and pepper, abundant freshly grated Parmesan.

Clean the artichokes of their tough outer leaves and slice them finely vertically with a very sharp knife. As you cut them put each slice into a bowl of water acidulated with a little lemon juice to prevent them from blackening in the air. When you are ready to cook them, dry the artichokes well with a cloth or kitchen paper.

Take a large deep sauté pan big enough to toss the cooked pasta together with the artichokes and in it heat the oil with the sliced garlic. Add the slices of artichoke to the oil and cook over a slow flame until they are soft, seasoning with salt and pepper, at this point add the cooked ham cut into small strips.

Cook the tagliatelle in the usual way in boiling salted water, drain it thoroughly and add it to the pan of artichokes, pour in the cream and mix all the ingredients together over a raised flame. Serve the pasta either in its pan or in a large bowl, sprinkling it with a generous amount of freshly grated Parmesan.

✻ Recipes ✻

Fish

Arezzo is as about as far away in Italy as one can be from the sea. Here, although today one can buy sea fish at the fish market and in the supermarkets, it is the fish from Lago Trasimeno and the fresh water fish and eels from the Casentino Valley and the River Arno that really represent the roots of the fresh fish eating tradition in Arezzo. In the Statute of 1327 the attitudes of the *Aretini* towards fish are made very clear.

> *IV 77. The punishment for those who sell fish against the rules of the Statute*
> Every person who brings fish to be sold into the City of Arezzo, must bring good fresh fish not stale fish, and he who buys fish from the lake with the scope of bringing it into Arezzo and selling it there, he must sell it himself alone and there must not be another citizen or person of the area selling with him or instructing him to sell the fish, under the pain of forty *soldi* for each person and each occasion. [No middlemen then!] Whoever can make an accusation can denounce the transgression and expect half of the fine. Every fish seller must sell the fish on the day on which he brought it to sell and these days must be from the feast of St Michael in the month of September [29th] until the Calend of May [1st]. The aforementioned fish must be sold from the morning to the hour of Nones [15.00] under the above rule; but at all other times the fish must only be sold until the third hour [9.00] under the pre-mentioned fine. Otherwise the family of the *Podestà* can take, scatter and throw away in the Square the stale fish or those unsold during the prescribed hours; except in Lent, at which time anyone may sell good fish during the entire day on which he brought them.

Before the marshes of the Val di Chiano were drained in the early nineteenth century by Vittorio Fossombroni – a

Beppina and the Kitchens of Arezzo

statue to him erected in 1863 still decorates the Piazza San Francesco – the people of the *palude*, wetlands, caught and ate the numerous frogs, eels and coarse fish that were to be found there. Some of the oldest recipes of the area are for ways of cooking frogs and also eels, simple dishes making the most of what came easily to hand. Perhaps for this reason for many years middle class *Aretini* rather despised fish as a food. They prided themselves on eating game and meat and preferred to forget the humble dishes obtained from the marshes. It was the custom years ago I am told, when the rivers ran clear, for the men and the children of country households in the Casentino Valley to go fishing on Saturday or Sunday; they would return home with a bucket full of eels which the housewives would cook. Simply cutting up and frying the eels in oil with a few sage leaves and when the eels were golden adding a little tomato preserve sharpened with a sprinkling of *peperoncino*. A famous restaurant, the Antica Trattoria al Principe, is to be found at Giove, a few kilometres north of Arezzo. The restaurant is situated near the Arno and here you may taste this traditional dish of the Arezzo landscape, *anguilla al tegamaccio*. Here they serve eel in individual pottery dishes with olive oil, tomato, *peperoncino* and parsley. The rich flesh of the eel marries perfectly with the spiced sweetness of the sauce.

Trote Affogate
(Drowned Trout)

For four people you will need four cleaned trout, a little flour, two tablespoons of olive oil, two cloves of garlic, a small bunch of parsley, one glass of white wine, salt and pepper to taste.

Wash and dry the trout and dip them lightly into flour. Chop the garlic and the parsley finely together. Heat the olive oil in a flat pan and add the parsley garlic mixture, let it become golden but not brown over a medium flame. Add the

❋ Recipes ❋

trout to the pan and let them become golden on both sides. At this point add the glass of white wine and let it evaporate. Season with salt and black pepper. Cook the fish gently for about 15 minutes, serve on a platter covered with the hot sauce that is left in the pan.

Trote al Forno
(Baked Trout)

Scale, open and clean the trout (or have the fishmonger do this).

Take fresh sage leaves, young rosemary leaves, garlic and parsley and chop them up together on a chopping board until you have a fine mixture, season this with salt and black pepper.

Put some of the stuffing in the cavity of each trout and secure the opening with a toothpick. Put the fish in an oiled oven dish then sprinkle them with a little more olive oil and bake in a pre-warmed oven at 170 °C / 325 °F / Gas Mark 3 for 30 minutes. Serve hot with lemon wedges.

Trote Farcite
(Stuffed Trout)

To serve four people you will need four fresh cleaned trout, three cloves of garlic, two handfuls of flat-leafed parsley, a teaspoon of dried oregano, a quarter-teaspoon of *peperoncino* (dried red pepper flakes) which substance is sometimes called *zenzero*, ginger, in Arezzo, salt and freshly ground black pepper, around 40 g / 1 ½ oz of butter.

Chop the garlic together with the parsley finely. Add to this *trito* the oregano, the *peperoncino*, mixing all the ingredients together well. Season with salt and pepper.

Stuff the cavities of the trout with this mixture, secure with a toothpick and cook them in a large pan of bubbling butter until the fish is golden on both sides, firm of flesh but never dry.

Beppina and the Kitchens of Arezzo

Trote coi Funghi Porcini
(Trout with Fresh Porcini)

To serve four people: Four cleaned trout. 150 g / 6 oz of *pancetta* cut into tiny dice, two cloves of garlic, a handful of parsley, a young rosemary stalk, salt and black pepper, 50 g / 2 oz of butter, flour sufficient to coat the fish, one fat shallot, 250 g / 10 oz of fresh *porcini*.

Make a stuffing by chopping up together 100 g / 4 oz of the diced *pancetta*, the garlic, parsley and rosemary. Season the mixture with a little salt and pepper. Stuff the interiors of the fish with this *trito* and fix the cavities with a tooth pick. Dip the fish lightly into the flour immediately before you cook them.

Chop the remaining *pancetta* together with the shallot. In a large pan melt the butter and cook the *pancetta* and shallot mixture in it until it has softened. Add the floured trout and cook them on both sides until they are justly golden. At this point add the fresh *porcini* which you have sliced very finely with a sharp knife. Let the fish and *funghi* cook together gently until the trout is firm and the *porcini* have given up their liquid. This liquid will serve to augment the butter in the pan and provides a small sauce. Serve very hot.

Trout cooked in this manner uses the good produce of the Casentino Valley in a luxurious and delicious manner. The white wine of the Val di Chiana is a good accompaniment to the dish. Arezzo over the centuries has been well nourished by the bounty of these two surrounding valleys.

Baccalà in Umido
(Salt Cod in Tomato Sauce)

Baccalà has for centuries been eaten by town and country people on Fridays and Fast Days when the Catholic Church stipulated that the only flesh to be consumed was that of the fish. Although this regulation no longer stands many people in Arezzo still honour it and some *alimentari* stock ready cooked *baccalà* on Fridays.

✻ Recipes ✻

To serve six people you will need a kilo or 2 lb of the prepared fish. Today in Italy it is possible to buy *baccalà* which has already been soaked to rid it of its salt and is therefore ready to be cooked. Otherwise this essential step requires soaking the fish in a full bowl of water under a gently running tap which thus constantly renews the water, for at least 24 hours. Then you need a large plate full of flour, four cloves of garlic, four tablespoons of best extra virgin olive oil, the pulp of five large very ripe tomatoes deprived of their skins or the equivalent weight in Italian tinned tomatoes – about 400 grams (16 oz). Abundant freshly ground black pepper, a handful of chopped parsley and possibly a very little salt. Taste the dish at the end of the cooking before you add any salt, as the fish will probably have enough of its own.

First trim the fish of any skin and bone. Cut it into convenient pieces about two inches by three and dip the pieces into the flour, covering all sides. In a large deep frying pan heat the olive oil and in it place the garlic which you have chopped up roughly; let the garlic take on some colour but do not let it burn. Now add the floured pieces of fish and let them become golden brown on both sides At this point add the tomato and stir it around evenly in the pan. Sprinkle on the black pepper and the chopped parsley. Lower the heat and let the fish cook gently until the sauce has become dense.

A variation to this recipe is to add a large yellow onion sliced into rings along with the garlic, let them become golden and then continue with the recipe above.

Tinca con i Piselli
(Tench with Peas)

Here is a charming recipe from the 1705 cookery manuscript of Francesco Gaudentio who on the 21st of December 1686 came to Arezzo as cook to the new Jesuit college.

Put fresh peas into a pan with chopped shallots, perfumed

herbs, a few cloves of garlic, pepper and salt and let them cook. When they are half done add the tench, which you have cleaned and scaled and blanched in boiling water as I have already said, and let it cook through along with the peas: add a few gooseberries, and if at the end you want to give the broth a little colour with egg yolk or saffron, you may.

This recipe might well be translated into modern terms using butter to fry the *battuto*, mint and basil for scent, and a little saffron tinted water to soften fresh picked garden peas, a piece of firm white fish, and perhaps two or three very ripe sweet gooseberries as garnish.

Tonno con Fagioli e Cipolla
(Tuna with White Beans and Onion)

To serve four people or more if including this as part of a course of mixed antipasti you will need 500 g / 20 oz of cooked cannellini beans, 250 g / 10 oz of Italian tinned tuna, preserved in olive oil. *Ventresca,* which is cut from the thickest belly part of the fish, is best as the tin will contain large pieces of tuna not trimmings. Then you will need four or five tablespoons of really good extra virgin olive oil, abundant freshly ground black pepper, a little salt, one large red onion, a handful of chopped parsley.

Drain the beans well of their liquid and put them into a serving bowl. Drain the tuna and arrange it on top of the beans in the middle of the bowl. Sprinkle on the spoonfuls of olive oil. Season with abundant black pepper and a little salt. The crystalline Maldon salt suits well. At the last minute, slice the red onion into fine rings and arrange over the beans and tuna then sprinkle on the chopped parsley.

This is a very simple but delicious dish. If you warm the beans before using them this will serve to enhance the scent of the olive oil. Draining the tuna of the oil in which it was preserved and using fresh oil improves the flavour too.

✳ Recipes ✳

Meat and Game

Very often in Arezzo meat dishes which include fennel seed are termed *in porchetta*, that is, cooked in a similar manner to the exquisite whole pigs stuffed with garlic and the stalks and seeds of wild fennel, which are baked in huge ovens and sold from vans in the city's market. There are usually queues of people waiting to buy a slice or two of the succulent meat cut with sharp cleavers from the whole carcass of the pig; the crackling is crisp and the salty fennel and garlic stuffing mixed with the chopped pig's liver is a much appreciated treat. Clearly it is not possible to cook such large animals in a domestic setting but it is possible to use a similar flavouring. The majority of the recipes in this section are for pork; it is a favourite in Arezzo for reasons of tradition and economy, it was the only meat that was available in any quantity to country people, and every scrap of the animal could be used either fresh or preserved; in the careful Tuscan way nothing was wasted. Besides this, it is also delicious. The recipe below although called *alla cacciatora*, is flavoured with fennel seed.

Braciole alla Cacciatora
(Hunter's Pork)

For four people you will need, four pork chops, 3 tablespoons of extra virgin olive oil, one onion, one carrot, one rib of celery, five cloves of garlic, 2 or 3 tablespoons of *passata di pomodoro*, salt, black pepper and 2 teaspoons of fennel seeds.

Chop the usual suspects, the onion, carrot and celery into a fine mixture, aka a *battuto*. Heat the oil in a frying pan and add the whole cloves of garlic, bruising them slightly to release their flavour, then add the *battuto*, stir all together and cook gently until the ingredients are golden but not burnt, in this way the carrot will caramelise slightly and become sweeter. Now add the chops, turning them until both sides have taken on colour. Stir in the tomato, add salt and pepper and sprinkle on the fennel seeds. Let the chops cook over a low flame until cooked through but do not overcook them or they will harden.

Passata di pomodoro is preserved or canned tomato which has been processed into a fairly smooth sauce. It provides the dish with a more velvety texture than that obtained with whole or chopped tomatoes.

Bracioline di Maiale
(Pork Chops in Red Wine)

To serve four people you will need four thick pork chops, 2 or 3 tablespoons of extra virgin olive oil, 2 cloves of garlic, 2 level teaspoons of fennel seed, half a glass of red wine, salt and freshly ground pepper.

Cover the base of your pan in olive oil and in it heat the garlic cut into slices and the fennel seed, raise the heat, add the pork chops and briefly let them take on a golden colour on both sides. Add the red wine and let the chops cook through slowly over a low flame, adding a little more wine if the chops are in danger of becoming too dry. Season with salt and black pepper. Serve with a simple dish of *fagioli bianchi*, cannellini beans soaked and cooked until tender with a few sage leaves. Present the beans in separate bowls with the addition of abundant freshly ground black pepper and a splash of your best olive oil.

Bracioline di Maiale con Cipolle
(Pork Chops with Red Onions)

For four people, 4 pork chops, four red onions cut into medium thick slices, 25 g / 1 oz butter, salt and black pepper, a little water as required.

In a lidded pan large enough to take the chops in one layer, melt the butter and put the sliced onions in a layer on top of it. Lay the pork chops on top, season with salt and pepper, cover the pan and cook over a very slow flame until the meat is tender,

Recipes

shake the pan now and again, adding a spoonful or so of water to prevent the onions sticking.

Polpette con l'Ortica
(Meatballs Flavoured with Nettles)

Put on your gardening gloves and gather two handfuls of young nettles which, needless to say, you have let grow in your garden to attract butterflies. Wash the nettles well then simmer them in boiling water until they are wilted. Drain them thoroughly, by this time gloves will no longer be necessary as their sting will have disappeared at the first touch of the boiling water, chop the nettles finely.

In a bowl place 250 g / 10 oz of lean minced beef, a teacupful of grated Parmesan, salt and grated nutmeg to taste, then the chopped nettles. Mix the ingredients together and add a beaten egg to bind the mixture. Form into small balls or patties and fry in hot olive oil until they are cooked through and golden on the outside.

L'Arista
(Roast Loin of Pork)

A roast loin of pork done in the expert Aretino manner is well worthy of praise and is very popular.

You will need one loin of pork of about 750 g / 1 ½ pounds in weight. If possible buy the loin without the bone and remove the skin and most of the fat as this particular pork roast does not have crackling. For the seasoning you will need two or three plump cloves of garlic, salt and black peppercorns, a few cloves, a sprinkling of grated nutmeg and a few sprigs of new rosemary. Crush the garlic with a knife and break the peppercorns and cloves roughly in a mortar; they need to be cracked rather than ground to dust. Mix these with a little salt and the grated nutmeg then insert the mixture into small cuts that you have made here and there over the surface of the pork. Take a few sprigs of rosemary, preferably from the tender new growth of the plant, and lard the pork with these at odd intervals too. After you have larded it, roll the loin in the remains of the crushed spice mixture.

Put the seasoned pork into an oven dish and irrigate it with good extra virgin olive oil; roast it in a slow oven, 170-180 °C / 350 °F for two hours. If you pour half a glass or so of white wine over the meat halfway through its cooking, the joint will provide its own delicious sauce.

Arista makes an excellent Sunday lunch served with a light red wine, preferably one from the Colli Aretini. As Artusi rightly remarks, the meat tastes even better cold, carved into thin slices. In this way the savour of the spices is accentuated and contrasts well with the flavour of the pork.

Agnello alla Casentinese
(Lamb with Spinach)

This is a dish that comes from the great Casentino valley which for centuries has provided Arezzo with good things to eat.

To feed four people you will need one small onion, 25 g / 1 oz of *pancetta*, a sprig of rosemary, 2 tablespoons of extra virgin olive oil, 500 g / 20 oz of lean leg of lamb cut into pieces, half a glass of white wine, one 280 g / 11 oz tin of chopped tomatoes, 1 kilo / 2 lb 4 oz of young spinach leaves, salt and freshly ground black pepper.

Chop the onion, the *pancetta* and the rosemary, discarding the woody stalk, together on your chopping board, sprinkle the mixture with black pepper. In a large shallow pan heat the olive oil and add the onion mixture. Let it take on colour in the oil but do not let it burn. When this *battuto* is golden add the pieces of lamb and turn them around until they too have taken on colour. At this point add the wine and let it hiss and evaporate. Next, add the tomatoes and stir them evenly into the pan. Leave the lamb to cook on a gentle

Recipes

flame until it is cooked through and tender. Clean and rinse the spinach and put it into a large saucepan with just the water that clings to the leaves and a little salt. Cover the pan and cook over a medium flame until the spinach has wilted. When this is so, drain the spinach in a sieve or colander and squeeze away any remaining liquid with your hands. Add the spinach to the lamb and stir it into the sauce. Serve very hot with abundant black pepper and a good Aretino red wine.

Arrosto d'agnello all'Aretina
(Lamb Roasted in the Arezzo Manner)

In this recipe, which is included in *L'arte di mangiar bene*, Artusi begins by saying that lamb is at its best in December and by Easter is about to start its decline. Today much lamb, the most expensive meat on the market, is actually bred for the Easter trade to provide Italians with delicate young legs and shoulders for their Easter Sunday luncheons. In the nineteenth century, lamb, as Artusi puts it, was wont to have the smell of the stable about it and his recipe gives a remedy for this inconvenience.

Take a leg or shoulder of lamb and bathe it with a mixture of salt, pepper, olive oil and a small amount of vinegar. Pierce it here and there with the point of a knife and let it soak up the flavour of the liquid for a few hours. In Artusi's day vinegar was often used to dissipate disagreeable smells and flavours. Put the leg on the spit, he continues, and using a branch of rosemary baste it often with the oil and vinegar mixture until the lamb is cooked. This will result in a not unpleasing flavour. If you like rosemary he adds you can stud the lamb with small pieces of it, removing them before sending the joint to the table.

Whether delicate or tending towards the mutton side in flavour, lamb is still well served by rubbing it with olive oil, sprinkling it with coarse salt and studding it with rosemary before roasting it in the oven. A few drops of balsamic vinegar sprinkled on halfway through the cooking also do no harm.

STRACOTTO
(BEEF STEW)

This is a rich stew cooked until the meat falls apart, overcooked as its name suggests.

To serve four or five people you will need three large cloves of garlic, 50 g / 2 oz of *pancetta* cut into dice, a level teaspoon of freshly ground black pepper, 1 kilo / 2 lb 4 oz of beef, 2 tablespoons of olive oil, one onion, one carrot, one rib of celery, salt, a large glass of the best red wine, a good Chianti is very suitable, 500 g / 1 lb 2 oz of ripe skinned and chopped tomatoes, or the equivalent of Italian tinned tomatoes, a little good stock as needed.

First of all chop the garlic and mix it with the *pancetta* adding the ground black pepper. Make slits here and there all over the piece of beef and stuff them with the above mixture. Tie the beef with string to preserve its shape. Then in a large heavy bottomed pan, big and deep enough to take the beef comfortably heat up the olive oil and add the *odori*, the onion, carrot and celery which you have chopped up finely. Let them soften but not burn. At this point put the beef into the pan and seal it on all sides. Pour on the glass of Chianti and let it fume. After the wine has finished bubbling add the tomatoes. Add a little salt. Cover the pan and let it cook extremely slowly over a very low flame for at least four hours. Add some hot stock from time to time if necessary. The *stracotto* is ready when it is tender enough to fall apart.

To serve, remove the meat from the pan and slice it with a very sharp knife. Arrange the slices on a serving dish and keep them warm. Raise the heat under the pan and boil the sauce briskly until it has reduced. Spoon a little of this sauce over the meat and serve immediately. It is good with *spinaci con pinoli*, spinach flavoured with pine kernels (for this recipe, see page 258). As an accompanying wine choose the same Chianti with which the dish was cooked.

Recipes

Per fare stufato di Vaccina Vitella, Castrato Selvaggina and similar
(Gaudentio's Stew of Various Sorts of Meat)

This recipe, although written in the late 1600s by Francesco Gaudentio, is remarkably similar in its method to those written by Artusi and Beppina.

Take the chosen meat, wash it in water with the addition of a little vinegar as one washes meat for roasting. Dust it with salt and pepper and put it into a stew pan in which you have placed a little lard. Take an onion and pierce it with cloves and pieces of cinnamon stick. Fry the meat in the lard turning it often, then add the spiced onion and half a glass of white wine. Finish the cooking and serve it up in its own broth or dry with pungent potherbs like onion and garlic or possibly lemon or orange.

Fagiano Tartufato
(Pheasant with Truffles)

This is a dish that exquisitely demonstrates the opulent sensibilities of many Aretines and is often served on Christmas day for the main festive meal which, these days, is taken at lunch time.

For this dish you will need a hen pheasant about 800 g / 1 lb 12 oz in weight that has been hung until tender but not high, 150 g / 6 oz of fat and lean *pancetta* chopped into small dice, 150 g / 6 oz of grated black truffle, a glass of cognac.

Make a stuffing of the chopped *pancetta* and grated truffle mixing them with the cognac. Fill the interior of the pheasant with this stuffing and leave the bird over night to absorb the truffle aroma.

Cover the breast of the bird with slices of fat *pancetta* and place it in a deep, lidded pan with some olive oil and a few fresh sage leaves. Let the bird cook covered in a 170 °C / 325 °F oven for about twenty minutes. After this remove the lid and baste the bird first with half a glass of white wine then with the pan juices. Replace lid and roast until tender, about another 30 to 40 minutes depending on the size.

Remove the bird from the pan and cut it into pieces, discarding the slices of *pancetta* and reserving the stuffing. Arrange the pieces in a lidded ovenproof serving dish and keep them warm. Over a low flame deglaze the pan with a second glass of cognac and strain the resulting sauce into a clean saucepan. Add the stuffing to this, stirring it well in, and then add a quarter litre/half a pint of cream. Simmer the sauce stirring all the while for a couple of minutes then pour it over the pieces of pheasant. Scatter abundant slices of black truffle over the dish and return it to a medium oven for a few minutes before serving.

This dish deserves a serious red wine.

Anatra in Finocchiata
(Duck with Fennel Seed)

For four people you will need one duck about 1 kilo / 2 lb 4 oz in weight, 200 g / 8 oz of *pancetta* cut into cubes, 3 cloves of garlic, a small handful of fennel seeds, olive oil and salt and pepper as needed.

Wash and dry the duck and stuff the interior with the chopped *pancetta*. In a mortar crush the garlic, some rough salt (Maldon or sea salt is good for this, fine table salt is not suitable), together with black pepper corns and the fennel seed. Rub the duck with some of the oil and sprinkle it generously with the fennel mixture, pressing it into the skin. Place the duck in an oven dish, add a little more olive oil, and roast in a pre-heated 200 °C / 400 °F oven, for about an hour and a quarter.

Pollo in Umido
(Chicken in Tomato Sauce)

One chicken cut into eight pieces or a mixture of drumsticks and pieces of breast, 2 cloves of garlic, one medium carrot, a sprig of

fresh rosemary, 2 tablespoons of olive oil, salt and pepper to taste, a glass of white wine, 150 g / 6 oz of chopped tomatoes (better genuine Italian tinned tomatoes than tasteless fresh ones).

Chop the garlic, carrot and rosemary (discarding the stalk) together on a board.

Heat the oil in a large shallow pan and add the chopped ingredients plus the pieces of chicken. Let them become golden over a medium flame. Season with salt and pepper. When the chicken has turned colour add the glass of white wine to the pan, stirring as you go let the wine evaporate then add the juicy chopped tomato. Let the chicken simmer until it is tender, adding a little water if the dish threatens to dry out. A nice variation is to add a little *peperoncino*, red chilli pepper flakes, to the initial chopped carrot and garlic.

Pollo al Ginepro
(Chicken with Juniper)

Stuff a plump chicken with two fat slices of *pancetta* chopped into dice, four bruised cloves of garlic and eight slightly squashed juniper berries. Douse the chicken with olive oil, sprinkle on salt and black pepper and roast in a 170 °C / 325 °F oven for two hours, this slow roasting at a low heat results in tender flesh. Do not forget to bring the chicken to room temperature before consigning it to the oven.

Faraona al Ginepro
(Guinea Fowl with Juniper.)

1 fowl, 60 g / 2 1/2 oz of butter, 8 juniper berries, two tablespoons of olive oil, one glass of white wine.

Mix half the butter with the juniper berries and place this inside the cleaned bird. Heat the rest of the butter and the oil in an oven dish (which can be used on top of your cooker over a gas or electric ring) and brown the bird in this until it is golden on all sides. Pour over the wine which you have heated in a small pan. Put the fowl into a pre-heated 200 °C / 400 °F oven and roast for 50 minutes.

Piccioni alla Cristina
(Pigeon as Cooked by Cristina)

Take one cleaned good quality pigeon per person, reserve the hearts and livers, being careful to remove all trace of the bitter gall bladder. Stuff the interiors with a generous handful of fresh young sage leaves, two large cloves of garlic deprived of their skins lightly crushed but not cut into slices and a little salt and black pepper. In a large deep thick-bottomed pan heat a small amount of olive oil, about two tablespoons for four pigeons plus a tiny knob of butter. Place the birds into the hot oil and stir them around constantly over a medium high flame, let them become golden on all sides but do not let them burn. This process should take about forty minutes and the pan should remain uncovered. Next, splash a small glass of good quality cognac over the birds and let it fume. At this point add a few cherry tomatoes to the pan and stir them around too, their purpose is solely to add a little extra flavour to the pan juices, not to be served up with the birds. At this point lower the flame and cover the pan, leave the pigeons to cook for another thirty minutes, checking frequently to see that the pan is not too dry. Before serving raise the heat again, splash on a little more brandy and let it evaporate whilst stirring the pigeons. The birds may be cooked and set aside and this last step accomplished when you are ready to serve them. The birds may also be split into quarters and served to more than four people if they form just one of a selection of dishes.

Accompaniments to the pigeons:
1. Take the whole hearts and livers of the pigeons and fry them in a little butter and olive oil, splash them with a little Vin Santo, season with salt and freshly ground black pepper and cook until they are done but not hard. Remove them from the pan and chop

❋ Recipes ❋

them into a rough paste. Spread this on hot slices of toasted bread and serve alongside the pigeons, allowing two *crostini* per person. 2. Have ready some boiled potatoes cut into wedges. Heat up the juices in the pan in which the pigeons were cooked, add the potatoes to these and stir around, allowing the potato to soak up the flavour of the birds and the tomato.

Vegetable Dishes

Carciofi alla Massaia
(Artichokes in the Country Manner)

Four young artichokes, 3 cloves of garlic, 2 tablespoons of olive oil, salt, pepper and a pinch of dried oregano, water as needed, 50 g / 2 oz of chopped tomatoes, a little lemon juice and a handful of chopped parsley.

Trim the artichokes, discarding the hard outer leaves, halve them lengthways and cut the halves into slices with a sharp knife. Put the slices as you cut them into a bowl of water acidulated with a little lemon juice. This step will prevent the artichokes blackening. In a large pan heat the olive oil and let the crushed garlic turn a pale gold in it, no darker or the garlic will become bitter. Add the drained and dried artichoke slices, toss them around in the oil and season with salt, pepper and oregano. Add a little hot water to irrigate the pan and simmer until almost tender, add a little more water if the dish becomes dry. Add the chopped tomato, stir it in and let the dish cook until the sauce has reduced. To serve, sprinkle on a little lemon juice and a handful of finely chopped parsley.

Fagioli con Rigatino
(Beans with Rigatino – the Aretino word for Pancetta)

Two tablespoons of olive oil, two cloves of garlic, one small onion, a handful of parsley, salt and pepper, 50 g / 2 oz of *pancetta* cut into small cubes, one fat tomato skinned and 500 g / 20 oz of cooked cannellini with some of their cooking water. You can use the tinned variety at a pinch.

Chop together finely the garlic, onion and parsley and sprinkle the mixture with salt and black pepper. Heat the olive oil in a large pan and add the *soffritto*, let it become transparent over a medium heat but do not allow it to brown, add the chopped *pancetta* and the quartered tomato. Cook for a few minutes until the *pancetta* has become golden then add the cooked cannellini and their liquid, this should be a little more than sufficient to prevent the beans sticking to the pan. Simmer for half an hour to let the beans take on the other flavours and the liquid is reduced.

Fagioli all' Olio
(Beans with Olive Oil)

300 g / 12 oz of dried cannellini beans, three cloves of garlic, a few sprigs of fresh sage, one rib of celery, water as needed.

Place the dried beans in a large pan, cover them amply with water and let them soak overnight.

In the morning, half fill a clean pan with the beans and enough of their water to cover them. Add the whole garlic cloves, the sage and the celery. Bring the pan to the boil then let them simmer slowly, adding more hot water if they are in danger of drying out. Only when they are halfway tender add some salt, then continue the cooking until the beans are done. Serve the beans with a little of their liquid in small bowls adding a generous swirl of the best olive oil, better that it comes from the hillsides around Arezzo, and a sprinkling of freshly ground black pepper. This is the classic Aretino way of cooking beans.

They are excellent on their own with a piece of Tuscan bread to sop up the juice or as an accompaniment to grilled meat. Dina, who sold these beans ready to eat in the *alimentari* at the end of our street, says that the beans cook

up better when there is a large quantity of them, as it makes their sauce more unctuous.

Fagiolini Verdi con Pomodoro all'aretina
(Green Beans with Tomatoes in the Arezzo Manner)

For four people you will need 500 g / 1 lb 2 oz of small green French beans, 500 g / 1 lb 2 oz of ripe skinless tomato pulp, better fresh although you can use Italian tinned chopped tomatoes, two cloves of garlic bruised and sliced, a few fresh sage leaves, 4 tablespoons of olive oil, salt and black pepper to taste.

Wash and trim the beans, cutting any oversize ones into two pieces. Put the olive oil into a large flat pan, heat and add the crushed garlic and the sage leaves. Let the garlic become golden but not brown. At this point add the beans together with the tomatoes, stir well and season with salt and freshly ground black pepper. Cover the dish and let it simmer over a low flame for about thirty minutes or until the beans are tender. Stir occasionally and add a little water if the mixture starts to catch. Serve very hot with more black pepper.

Fresh sweet tomatoes are the making of this dish, take ripe ones, put them into boiling water for a few seconds then slip off their skins. Chop them roughly before combining them with the beans. If you do not like the flavour of sage, add sprigs of fresh basil during the last minute or so of cooking, in this manner the scent will be stronger. Artusi has a version of this recipe in *La scienza in cucina e l'arte di mangiar bene* where he uses whole garlic cloves and fresh tomato, but he does not use sage or any other herbs.

Fagioli all' uccelletto
(Beans with Fresh Sage and Olive Oil)

This is a recipe that emanates from Florence but is to be found in many homes and restaurants in Arezzo. Artusi gives what I think is the most appetising version of the dish, allowing the beans to imbibe the flavour of the olive oil before adding the tomato.

To serve six people you will need: 500 g / 1 lb 2 oz of cooked cannellini beans, a handful of fresh sage leaves and four tablespoons of good extra virgin olive oil, a scant tea cup of *passato di pomodoro*, salt and black pepper.

Drain the cooked beans well. Put the olive oil into a large pan with the sage leaves, let the oil heat and when it bubbles fiercely and the sage frizzles, add the beans, turn them with a wooden spoon and season with a little salt and abundant black pepper. Lower the heat and allow the beans to soak up the flavour of the sage-perfumed oil, then a few minutes before serving stir in a small amount of the tomato sauce. As with many Tuscan recipes the success of the dish depends on the quality and flavour of the olive oil used in its making.

Spinaci con Pinoli
(Spinach with Pine Kernels)

For this recipe you will need 1 kilo / 2 lb 4 oz of young spinach, 3 cloves of garlic, bruised then finely sliced, 3 tablespoons of olive oil, 25 g / 1 oz of sultanas which you have plumped up in a little hot water, 50 g / 2 oz pine kernels, salt and black pepper.

Rinse the spinach and put it into a large pan with just the water that clings to the leaves and a little salt. Cover the pan and allow it to cook over a medium flame until the spinach is wilted. Drain the spinach well and press out any excess water with your hands then chop it roughly with a sharp knife.

In a large sauté pan heat 3 tablespoons of olive oil, add the bruised and sliced garlic and let it take on some colour, do not however let the garlic brown and burn. Add a handful of sultanas and then the chopped spinach and mix it all well into the garlicky oil. In a separate non-stick pan heat the pine kernels tossing them around until they are golden. It is not necessary to add oil as they have plenty of their own. When the pine kernels have changed colour and released their scent add them to the spinach. Serve

Recipes

hot with abundant freshly ground black pepper. Red pepper flakes added to the olive oil and garlic are a good variation on black pepper but in this case omit the sultanas.

Cavolfiore in Padella
(Cauliflower Turned in the Pan)

For this recipe, which lends interest to this bland vegetable, you will need one firm cauliflower, and, as my Egyptian friends say, it must be as white as the moon. You may also use a green Roman cauliflower – both work well in the recipe and give equally good but different flavours. You will also need 3 tablespoons of decent extra virgin olive oil, do not contemplate using any other type of oil. A scant half-teaspoon of dried red pepper flakes, 2 tablespoons of finely chopped parsley, salt.

Clean the cauliflower of its outer leaves and thick lower stalk then divide the head into florets of about the same dimensions. Put them into a saucepan with a little salt and cover with boiling water. Let the florets cook until just tender, neither mushy nor crisp. Drain thoroughly in a colander. In a large flat pan with deep sides heat the olive oil and into it sprinkle the red pepper flakes. When the oil is hot tip in the cooked cauliflower and turn it around in the pan. Crush it roughly with a wooden fork and stir in the chopped parsley. Let the dish cook briefly over a low flame turning it constantly until the vegetable has soaked up the piquant oil. At this point you may either season it with a little salt and serve immediately or put the pan aside and simply reheat when you are ready. This dish, which again depends on the quality and flavour of the oil used, goes very well with roast chicken or grilled Tuscan sausages.

Zucchine con Pomodoro
(Zucchini with Tomato)

Take 500 g / 1 lb 2 oz of small zucchini, preferably the pale green ridged variety called *Fiorentino* in Italy, 250 g / 10 oz of ripe tomatoes, ideally the San Marzano variety or a tin of genuine Italian tomatoes, 2 tablespoons of extra virgin olive oil, salt and pepper to taste, mint or *nepitella*, a variety that grows wild in Tuscany and is much appreciated for the grilling of *porcini*.

Skin the tomatoes after placing them in boiling water for a minute or so. Crush their flesh and add it to a pan in which you have heated the oil. Let the tomatoes cook for about 15 minutes. Wash, top and tail the zucchini and cut them into slim rounds. Add the zucchini to the tomato mixture and let them cook gently until they are tender but not mushy. Throw in a sprig of mint towards the end of the cooking or add a sprig of *nepitella* or perhaps a tiny amount of dried *nepitella* which can be bought in Tuscan food shops.

This is good with grilled meat.

Zucchine di Magro
(Zucchini for Fast Days)

This is a dish of stuffed zucchini that Giovanni Battista Magi would have prepared for a Friday or a fast day. One of the greatest influences on cuisine in Catholic countries has always been the church. There are foods suitable for feast and normal days when meat is permitted and fast days when only fish, vegetables and on some occasions cheese were allowed.

Take some fat pale green zucchini, trim the stalk end and core the centres with an apple corer. Chop the flesh finely and mix it with some tinned tuna preserved in olive oil. Reduce this mixture into a fine paste with a pestle and mortar or in a food mixer. Add your seasonings, a little finely chopped garlic, grated lemon peel, thyme and marjoram, parsley and basil. In a small bowl mix together the tuna and zucchini flesh and the seasonings with a beaten egg, a small amount of breadcrumbs then add salt and pepper to taste.

Stuff the zucchini with the mixture, place them in an oven dish, add a generous amount of olive oil and let them bake until tender.

✻ Recipes ✻

Rocchi di Sedano all'Aretina
(Celery in the Arezzo Manner)

In the Arezzo countryside the word *rocchi* was used to describe the pork sausages that were made when a pig was slaughtered in December or January. *Rocchio* literally means a cylindrical block of wood, hence a sausage shape. The word is also used to denote a string of dried figs: *un rocchio di fichi secchi*. Here it is used to describe ribs of celery which in some venerable recipes were first cut into segments then boiled and drained and two or three pieces were pressed together to make a sausage shape. I suggest using small celery hearts instead of the stringier ribs.

For four people you will need six to eight small celery hearts, 300 ml / half a pint of *sugo*, meat sauce (see pages 216–17) or the same of tomato sauce (see pages 215–16), two eggs, olive oil, 100 g / 4 oz grated Parmesan, salt and black pepper.

Wash and trim the celery hearts and boil them in a pan of boiling salted water. When they are almost tender, drain them thoroughly, pressing the water out with your hands. Let the celery cool. Beat up the eggs in a bowl with a pinch of salt, dip each heart into the egg and fry them until they are golden in a little olive oil. (You may also dip the celery into a light batter made with eggs, a little flour and milk but this results in a heavier dish.) When each heart is fried to a nice gold colour, blot it on some kitchen paper and lay it in an oven dish into which you have poured some of the sauce. Spoon the rest of the sauce over the celery, sprinkle with grated Parmesan, season with salt and black pepper. Place the dish in a medium oven until the celery is completely tender and the cheese melted. Serve very hot.

Lenticchie Stufate
(Stewed Lentils)

For six people you will need 400 g / 16 oz of dried lentils, 4 tablespoons of olive oil, one carrot, one celery stalk, two cloves of garlic, 50 g / 2 oz of *pancetta* chopped into dice, a glass of *passato di pomodoro*, smooth tomato pulp, salt and freshly ground black pepper, about half a litre / 1 pint of good stock.

The night before you intend to cook the lentils place them in a large pan and cover them with abundant cold water, leave them to soak until the next day. When you are ready to cook, drain the lentils, rinse them well in fresh water and drain them again thoroughly. Chop the carrot and the celery and garlic finely together with a sharp knife or a *mezzaluna*, mix this *battuto* with the diced *pancetta*. In a large saucepan heat the olive oil, add the mixture and let it take on colour over a medium heat, make sure that it does not burn. At this point add the lentils. Next add the glass of tomato pulp and a ladle of hot stock. Stir the pan and let it cook covered over a low heat, adding from time to time some more stock to prevent the lentils from sticking, check and stir frequently. Cook for about an hour until the lentils are very near soft, they can then be left to stand until they are served.

Lentils cooked in this way are traditionally eaten with slices of *cotechino*, a fat pork boiling sausage easily found in butcher shops and supermarkets in winter in Italy. This dish is an indispensable part of a New Year's Eve dinner, when it is said that the more lentils you eat the more money you will make in the coming year!

Tarts and Moulds/Pies

Tortino di Patate
(Potato Tart)

To serve six people you will need one kilo / 2 lb 4 oz of floury potatoes, a little salt, two Tuscan sausages, 100 g / 4 oz of freshly grated Parmesan, one egg, salt and black pepper to taste, a sprinkle of grated nutmeg. A knob of butter with which to oil a flat round oven dish about 35 cm / 12 inches in diameter, a terracotta dish would be most suitable.

Peel the potatoes and boil them in salted water until they are

❋ Recipes ❋

completely tender, drain them well, then in a large bowl mash them thoroughly making sure that there are no lumps. Skin the Tuscan sausages, if you do not have these use Toulouse sausages. It is important for the success of the recipe that the meat in the sausages is coarse ground, ordinary finely ground British sausages do not have the right texture for this tart. After skinning the sausages crumble the meat up into tiny fragments with your fingers. Mix these into the mashed potato until they are evenly distributed. Next add the beaten egg, the grated Parmesan, salt and pepper and a sprinkle of nutmeg stirring all together into a firm consistency. Oil the dish with the butter then spread the potato mixture evenly over it, the tart should be about around 3 cm / 1 inch thick. Decorate the surface with the tines of a fork. Put the tart into a pre-warmed 170 °C / 325 °F oven for half an hour. If at the end of that time the surface is not a satisfactorily golden colour, dash it under a hot grill for a moment or so. Serve the tart very hot.

This a is comfortable domestic dish which although simple is absolutely delicious and makes a good alternative to pasta. Its success depends on using good quality sausages without additives and the best Parmesan cheese. My neighbour Mariella excels in making it.

Patate e Funghi al Forno
(Potato and Wild Mushroom Pie)

You will need 3 cloves of garlic, a bunch of flat leafed parsley, salt and pepper to taste, olive oil, 500 g / 1 lb 2 oz of waxy potatoes, 400 g / 16 oz of *porcini* (ceps or *Boletus edulis*) or *gallinacci* (chanterelles or *Cantharellus cibarius*).

Make a *battuto* with the garlic and parsley, chopping the ingredients finely with a *mezzaluna* or a very sharp knife. Season the mixture with salt and freshly ground black pepper,

Oil the base and sides of a deep oven dish, a terracotta one if possible. Slice the potatoes into rounds about ½ cm / scant ¼ in deep, cut the *porcini* into thick slices, or if you have chanterelles tear them into convenient pieces. Put a layer of potato slices in the bottom of the pot then a layer of *funghi*, sprinkle with a little of the garlic mixture then another layer of potato and so on until the pot is full. On the top make a layer of whole *funghi*. Sprinkle with olive oil and bake in a medium oven, 180 °C / 350 °F for about one hour.

In the absence of *porcini* or chanterelles you can make this dish with field mushrooms mixed with dried *porcini* that have been soaked in hot water for a few minutes to plump them up. A pleasant dish; however, it is not the same thing at all.

Sformato di Spinaci con Cibreo
(Spinach Pudding with Chicken Liver Sauce)

The *sformato* was a type of dish much appreciated in the nineteenth century and often served at the tables of the *alta borghesia* in Arezzo, it is a dish that Beppina would most certainly have eaten.

Step one: the *sformato*
Wilt 500 g / 1 lb 2 oz of spinach, drain it well and chop it extremely finely with a *mezzaluna* or a sharp knife. Make a rich béchamel with 50 g / 2 oz of butter, 50 g / 2 oz of flour and half a litre / a scant pint of milk, salt, white pepper to taste and a powdering of nutmeg. Stir in the chopped spinach, four beaten eggs, and 75 g / 3 oz of finely grated Parmesan. Pour the mixture into a buttered mould and bake in a medium oven in a *bain marie* for an hour and a half. Remove from the oven and leave the mould to cool.

Step two: the sauce
To make the sauce cut 300 g / 12 oz chicken livers into small pieces and dip them in flour. Make absolutely sure that there is no trace of the green bile duct on the livers, this would ruin the entire dish as it is extremely bitter. Chop a medium onion very finely and sweat it in a pan with some melted butter until the onion is soft. Add the chicken liver to the pan and cook gently

✶ Recipes ✶

for five minutes, add a sprinkling of pepper and a small glass of Vin Santo then cook for a further five minutes until the Vin Santo has mostly evaporated leaving a thick sauce, stir all the while. Do not overcook the liver or it will become hard.

When the spinach pudding has become cold tip it out of the mould onto a serving dish and return it to a hot oven for a few minutes to heat through. Whilst this is going on you have been making the sauce. To serve, pour the sauce over the *sformato*. You may also bake the *sformato* in individual moulds.

Tortino di Carciofi
(Crustless Artichoke Tart)

Three tender artichokes, four large eggs, a little cream, salt and pepper, olive oil.

Trim the artichokes discarding the outer tougher leaves and the stem. Cut them into four and cut the four quarters into thin slices. Gently fry the slices in some olive oil until they are tender. Drain and arrange the slices in a small buttered oven dish. Beat up the eggs and cream in a bowl, season with salt and pepper and tip over the artichokes. Bake in a medium oven for 30 minutes. A nice luncheon dish served with a green salad.

Dessert

The pleasure of sweet things.

To A M. Gianfrancesco Pocopanno

The fruits of your genius and of your garden were such sweet food to my intellect and to my taste, that until now I have never tasted their equal. Certainly the Sonnet is delightful, but the pears (save for the grace of the bergamot and the *carovelle*) [a type of pear with the scent of muscatel] surpass any other flavour or scent. It has been some time since I have received such a pleasing gift, or one which has so delighted me. So for the memory of the trees that produced them and in recollection of you who sent them, I would like to say that if rich Brescia had nothing else so beautiful, so noble, your gifts would still make the city famous. (*I frutti del vostro ingegno e del vostro orto, mi sono stati si soave cibo a l'intelletto e al gusto, che altro tale non ho provato fin qui. Certamente il Sonetto e dolce, ma le pere (salvo la grazia de le bergamotte e de le carovelle) trapassano il segno d'ogni sapore e d'ogni sugo. Egli e qualche giorno che non ricevei dono si grazioso, ne che piu mi dilettassi. Onde per memoria de l'arbore che li ha produtti, e per ricordanza di voi che mi gli avete mandati vo' dire che se la ricca ricordanza di voi che me gli avete mandati, vo' dire che se la ricca Brescia non avesse mai altro di bello, ne di gentile, che cosi fatte cose sono atte a darle il nome I famosa.*)

Pietro Aretino, Venice, 15th December 1537
Lettere Libro Primo, Lettera 292

Pinocchiata

To make this you will need a 100 g / 4 oz of pine kernels and the same amount of granulated sugar, about 3 tablespoons of red wine, two whole cloves and a knob of butter.

Oil a flat baking dish with the knob of butter. Toast the pine kernels by shaking them around in a non-stick pan until they start to turn colour and give up their scent. They do not need any oil as they have plenty of their own. Set the pan to one side of the stove. Put the red wine and the cloves into a thick-bottomed stainless steel pan. Next add the sugar and let it dissolve gently over a medium to hot flame, swirl the pan to help the sugar dissolve. When this is so let the sugar boil. As you are using wine rather than water to make this caramel you will not be able to see when the mixture becomes a light gold, the point at which the caramel is ready.

✳ Recipes ✳

So in this case when the sugar has dissolved and you start to boil it, time yourself, three minutes should be sufficient. Now, take the pan off the heat and stir in the toasted pine kernels. Return the pan to the heat and bring to the boil once more. At this point pour the mixture out onto the oiled oven dish and smooth it down into an even layer with a wooden spoon. Let it cool thoroughly then break the *Pinocchiata* into rough pieces. This is a delightful sweet to serve at the end of a meal, perhaps with another dessert and coffee. The method is similar to that of making praline which instead of being broken into rough pieces is crushed and used to sprinkle on desserts and ices. Praline is usually made with almonds and hazel nuts. Seemingly *Pinocchiata* is simple to make, the recipe comes from domestic kitchens not those of great restaurants but it actually needs practice to achieve. Take great care not to burn yourself, the caramel will be exceedingly hot.

Mele Cotte al Rosmarino
(Apples with Rosemary)

For two people you will need two Rennet apples, 50 g / 2 oz of butter, a few sprigs of fresh rosemary taken from the soft new growth at the tips of the branches, 50 g / 2 oz of granulated sugar, a scant tablespoon of water.

Peel and core the apples and slice them into segments. Melt the butter in a sauté pan with half the rosemary and cook the apples over a gentle heat until they are nearly soft. Meanwhile in a small thick-bottomed pan dissolve the sugar into the water by swirling the pan over a medium heat, when the sugar is dissolved then let it boil until you have a light golden caramel sauce. This will take three or four minutes. Do not let the caramel get too dark or it will be bitter.

Arrange the apple slices on two plates, scatter on a little more fresh rosemary and mizzle the caramelised sugar over the plates. The flavour of the apples mixed with the rosemary is uncommonly delicious.

Torta di Mele
(Apple Cake)

To make this cake you will need 150 g / 6 oz of self-raising flour or 150 g / 6 oz of plain flour plus 15 g / ½ oz of baking powder, the grated peel of one lemon, one cup of milk, 100 g / 4 oz of sugar and one egg, 2 Rennet or Cox's apples.

Sieve the flour into a mixing bowl and sprinkle in the grated lemon peel evenly. Mix the milk into the flour. Beat up the egg and stir the sugar into it. Add this mixture to the flour and milk and mix thoroughly until you have a soft dough. Peel the apples, slice them into small pieces and stir them into the soft dough. Spoon into a buttered mould and bake in a pre-heated 180 °C / 350 °F oven for thirty minutes.

Torta di Mele al burro
(Apple Cake with Butter)

For this richer version you will need 300 g / 12 oz of self-raising flour or plain flour and 15 g / ½ oz of baking powder, 150 g / 6 oz of butter, 200 g / 8 oz of sugar, 2 eggs, 4 Rennet or ripe Cox's apples peeled and cut into dice.

Cut the butter into the flour, rubbing it well with your finger tips until it has the consistency of breadcrumbs. Mix the sugar into the beaten eggs. Add this liquid to the flour and mix into a fairly stiff dough, adding the diced apple as you go. Roll out and shape the dough to fit a buttered baking dish. Bake the cake in a pre-heated 180 °C / 350 °F oven for 50 minutes.

Composta di Pesche al Vino
(Compote of Peaches and Wine)

Taken from the *Libretto di cucina di Gio Batta Magi, Aretino 1842–1885*. Take as many peaches as you need and put them into boiling water to loosen their skins. Slip off the skins, cut the peaches in half and remove the stone. Dip the peaches into sugar and place them in a deep wide bowl. Arrange

❋ Recipes ❋

them in layers dusting a little more sugar on them as you go, place ripe strawberries or raspberries in the spaces. Cover the bowl and leave it for half an hour. Next, take some good Chianti or Rosso di Montepulciano, pour the wine over the peaches, cover the bowl and let them marinate for three hours. Giovanni Battista Magi wrote that they may best be served in a crystal bowl.

Composta di Pesche
(Peach Compote)

Take some very ripe peaches, cut them in half and remove the stone. Place them cut side up in an oven dish equipped with a lid. Sprinkle the peaches generously with sugar and in the hollow where the stone lay pour a little red wine or *amabile* Vin Santo. Pour a little more wine around the peaches then cover the dish. Put it in a moderate oven and let it cook until the peaches are tender. Giovanni Battista Magi placed his in the ashes of the kitchen fire and adds that the peaches are to be served cold.

Ricotta all'Aretina
(Creamed Ricotta)

To make this for four people you will need 400 g / 16 oz of fresh ricotta, an overflowing liqueur glass of good rum, some wild strawberries or a few ripe raspberries, a little castor sugar. In a serving bowl stir the rum into the ricotta until you have a smooth cream with no lumps. Put this to cool in the fridge. When you are ready to serve arrange the fruit on top of the cream and sprinkle on a little of the castor sugar. When there is no fresh fruit you can also use a sprinkling of the best grated chocolate.

❋ Acknowledgements ❋

Firstly, I would like to express my fond gratitude to those Aretine friends who over many years have entertained me with fine food and good conversation and who have shared their knowledge and experience of the culinary traditions of Arezzo – Donato and Teresa Angioli, Attilio Brilli, Fiammetta Brilli, Liliana and Roberto Calcini, Gianpaolo Gamurrini, Cristina Naldi de Giudici, Alessandro and Anna Maria Melis, Mariella Morandi.

For their help and advice in my historical research for this book I would also like to thank Attilio Brilli, Lauretta Carbone, Cristina Naldi de Giudici, the family of Guido Gianni-Trippi, Rosaria Valenza at the Biblioteca Area Umanistica, Università di Siena, Arezzo, and the staff of the Biblioteca, Città di Arezzo, and Andrew Wright and his colleagues at the University of Sydney, Australia.

In addition, many thanks to Susan Palmer at the Sir John Soane's Museum, London, for providing information of a matter of considerable historic interest to Arezzo. Thanks also to my agent, Charlotte Seymour at Andrew Nurnberg Associates, Catheryn Kilgarriff at Prospect Books, Tom Jaine and Brendan King, my very careful editor.

Finally, thank you my darling husband John for all your loving help and support.

❋ Select Bibliography ❋

Acton, Eliza. *Modern Cookery for Private Families* (London: Longmans, 1845).
Armandi, Luigi. *Arezzo: anno 1900 e dintorni* (Arezzo: Compugraf, 2000).
Artusi, Pellegrino. *La scienza in cucina e l'arte di mangiar bene* (Florence: Landi, 1891). See also edition edited by Piero Camporesi (Turin: Einaudi, 1970).
Athenaeus of Naucratis. *The Deipnosophists* (tr. Charles Burton Gulick), 7 vols. (London: Heinemann, 1927). Online edition at www.perseus.tufts.edu
Audot, Louis Eustache. *La Cuisinière de la campagne et la ville ou la nouvelle cuisine économique* (Paris: Audot, 1818).
Beeton, Isabella. *The Book of Household Management* (London: S. O. Beeton, 1861). See also edition with introduction by Kathryn Hughes (London, Cassell, 2000).
Berti, Luca 'Gli stemmi civici di Arezzo fra storia e fantasia', *Bollettino d'informazione. Brigata Aretina degli Amici dei Monumenti,* 29, (1993): 25–30.
Bozzi, Ottorina Perna. *Vecchia Brianza in cucina* (Milan: Martello, 1968).
Brilli, Attilio. *Arezzo: visioni e vedute* (Perugia: Banco Popolare Dell'Etruria, 2000).
— *Arezzo: la città e i suoi ritratti* (Città di Castello: Edimond, 2005).
Carloni, Giuseppe. *Dall'Arno al Tebro* (Pistoia: Bracali, 1889).
Cleugh, James. *The Divine Aretino* (London: Blond, 1965).
Corrado, Vincenzo. *Il cuoco galante* (Naples: Raimondiana, 1773).
del Vita, Alessandro. *Guida di Arezzo* (Arezzo: Società Tipografica Aretina, 1923).
Droandi, Attilio (tr.). *Statuto del comune di Arezzo, 1327.* (Arezzo: Alberti, 1992).
Dubois, Urbano & Bernard, Emilio. *La cucina classica* (Milan: Società dei Cuochi, 1877).
Durante, Castore. *Herbario nuovo* (Rome: Bonfadino & Diani, 1585).
Fantoni, Giovanni. *Delitti, arresto e morte del capo assassino Federigo Bobini, detto Gnicche* (Florence: Salani, 1871).
Ferraro, Giuseppe (ed.). 'I Vini d'Italia giudicati da papa Paolo III (Farnese) e dal suo bottiglieri Sante Lancerio', *La Revista Europea,* 7 (1876) part 2: 87–116.
Francatelli, Charles Elmé. *A Plain Cookery Book for the Working Classes* (London: Routledge, Warne & Routledge, 1852).
Franciosi, Giannina. *Arezzo* (Bergamo: Istituto d'Arti Grafiche, 1931).
Frati, Ludovico (ed.) *Libro di cucina del secolo XIV* (Livorno: Giusti, 1899).
Gaudentio, Francesco. *Il panunto toscano* (1705). MS 450, Biblioteca Città di Arezzo. See also *Francesco Gaudentio: Il panunto toscano,* ed. Guido Gianni & Adele Zito (Rome: Trevi, 1974).
Gianni, Guido. *Il sapore di Arezzo* (Rome: Trevi, 1976).
— *Antica gastronomia aretina* (Rome: Trevi, 1981).
— *La cucina aretina* (Padua: Franco Muzzio Editore, 1990).
Gianni, Guido (ed.). *Quando la cucina si chiamava 'casa'* (Cortona: Ingrocart, 1991).
Goethe, Johann Wolfgang von. *Italienische Reise* (Munich: Beck 1988). See also *Italian Journey 1786–1788,* tr. W. H. Auden & Elizabeth Mayer (London: Penguin, 1982).
Goro, Dati. *Istoria di Firenze* (Florence: Manni, 1735).
Greci, Pier Francesco. *Cucina rustica nell'aretino* (Arezzo: Centro Studi Aretini, 1978).
Guerrini, Olindo. *L'arte di utilizzare gli avanzi della mensa* (Rome: Formiggini, 1918).
Hieatt, Constance B. & Sharon Butler (ed.). *Curye on Inglysch: English Culinary Manuscripts of the Fourteenth Century (including The Forme of Cury)* (Oxford: OUP, 1985).

❊ Select Bibliography ❊

Latini, Antonio. *Lo scalco alla moderna* (Naples: Parrino e Mutii, 1692).
Maestro, Martino. *Libro de arte coquinaria*, ed. Luigi Ballerini & Jeremy Parzen (Milan: Guido Tommasi, 2001).
Mangani, Lorella & Giuseppe Martini (ed.). *Francesco Redi Aretino, atti del convegno di studi* (Arezzo: Accademia Petrarca, 1999).
Mayhew, Henry. *London Labour and the London Poor*, vol. 1 (London: Woodfall, 1851).
Nocentini, Tiziana. *La Bastanzetti e l'industria aretina tra Ottocento e Novecento* (Florence: Polistampa, 2010).
Pasqui, Ubaldo & Ugo Viviani. *Guida illustrata, storica, artistica e commerciale di Arezzo e dintorni* (Arezzo: Viviani, 1925).
Paturzo, Franco. *Arezzo medievale* (Cortona: Calosi, 2002).
Pisanelli, Baldassare. *Trattato della natura de' cibi et del bere* (Venice: Alberti, 1586).
Prato, Katharina. *Manuale di cucina per principianti e per cuoche pratiche*, tr. Ottilia Visconti-Aparnik (Graz, Libreria Styria, 1892).
Procaccioli, Paolo (ed.). *Edizione nazionale delle opere di Pietro Aretino* (Rome: Salerno, 1997).
Pulci, Luigi. *Morgante*, ed. Franca Ageno (Milan: Mondadori, 1994).
Redi, Francesco. *Esperienze intorno a diverse cose naturali, e particolarmente a quelle che ci son portate dall'Indie* (Florence: Nave, 1671).
— *Bacco in Toscana* (Florence: Matini, 1685).
— *Libro di ricordi di Francesco, figliuolo di Gregorio Redi*. MS 299, Biblioteca Città di Arezzo.
— *Lettere di Francesco Redi gentiluomo aretino*, 2 vols (Naples: Stasi, 1779).
— *Lettere di Francesco Redi* (Florence: Stamperia Magheri, 1825).
Reeve, Mrs. Henry. *Cookery and Housekeeping: A Manual of Domestic Economy for Large and Small Families* (London: Longmans Green, 1882).
Righi Parenti, Giovanni. *La cucina toscana* (Rome: Newton & Compton, 1995).
Romer, Elizabeth. *The Tuscan Year, Life and Food in an Italian Valley* (London: Weidenfeld & Nicolson, 1984, 1993, 2018).
Sacchetti, Franco. *Il Trecentonovelle*, ed. Valerio Marucci (Rome: Salerno, 1996).
Scapecchi, Piero & Learco Nencetti (ed.). *Cioccolata, squisita gentilezza* (Florence: Vallecchi, 2005).
Tafi, Angelo. *Immagine di Arezzo* (Arezzo: Banca Popolare dell'Etruria, 1978).
Thornton, Peter. *The Italian Renaissance Interior, 1400–1600* (London: Abrams, 1991).
Tognarini, Ivano (ed.). *La guerra di liberazione in provincia di Arezzo 1943–44* (Arezzo: Amministrazione Provinciale, 1987).
Ude, Louis Eustache. *The French Cook: A System of Fashionable and Economical Cookery, Adapted to the Use of English families* (London: Ebers, 1818).
Viviani, Ugo. *Vita, opere, iconografia, bibliografia, vocabolario inedito delle voci aretine e libro inedito dei 'Ricordi' di Francesco Redi* (Arezzo: Viviani, 1924).
— *Arezzo e gli aretini* (Arezzo: Viviani, 1922).
Wheeler, Mortimer. *Rome Beyond the Imperial Frontiers* (London: Bell, 1954).
Zoi, Piero (ed.). *Libretto di cucina di Gio Batta Magi* (Arezzo: Letizia, 1989).

❋ List of Illustrations ❋

Cover.   South side of the Piazza Grande by Giovanni Marchig, 1932.

Page 14.   The walled city of Arezzo in the early nineteenth century from Antonio Ferrini's *Descrizione geografica della Toscana* (Florence, 1839), plate following page 51: 'Veduta della città d'Arezzo'.

Page 17.   Pietro Aretino. Frontispiece from *Le lettre di M. Pietro Aretino, di nuovo con la gionta ristampate, e con somma diligenza ricorrette* (Venice, 1538).

Page 23.   Pellegrino Artusi. Drawing by Elizabeth Romer, from a photograph of Artusi, 1891.

Page 26.   'Galantina di Fagiano alla Vallière', from *La cucina classica* (Milan, 1877), by Urbano Dubois & Emilio Bernard, Vol. 1, page 283, plate 28 (169).

Page 27.   'Galantina di Pollo all'Inglese', from *La cucina classica* (Milan, 1877), by Urbano Dubois & Emilio Bernard, Vol. 1, page 283 plate 28 (170).

Page 37.   Printer's flower from the first edition of Artusi's renowned cookery book, *La scienza in cucina* (Florence, 1891), dedicated to his two cats, Biancane and Sibillone. Drawing by Elizabeth Romer after Artusi.

Page 39.   Title page of the 1877 edition of *La cucina classica* (Milan, 1877), by Urbano Dubois & Emilio Bernard.

Page 59.   A 'cucina economica' cast and assembled in 1890 by the Arezzo foundry of Bastanzetti. Drawing by Elizabeth Romer after an illustration in Tiziana Nocentini's *La Bastanzetti e l'industria aretina tra Ottocento e Novecento* (Florence, 2010), page 23, plate 24.

Page 64.   'Sformato di Tafacche'. A recipe for a flan written by 'Sig. Tafacche', from Beppina's collection of handwritten recipes.

Page 68.   'Manzo alla Moda'. A recipe for beef stew with Marsala wine, from Beppina's collection of handwritten recipes.

Page 78.   Recipe for a dish of potatoes and a 'Tortino', from Beppina's collection of handwritten recipes.

Page 79.   'Frittata Ripiena'. A recipe for a filled omelette, from Beppina's collection of handwritten recipes.

Page 84.   'Anisette'. Recipe for an aniseed liqueur from Beppina's collection of handwritten recipes.

❈ List of Illustrations ❈

Page 86. 'Biscottini'. Recipe for dainty biscuits from Beppina's collection of handwritten recipes.

Page 107. 'Here is November'. Drawing by Elizabeth Romer of a relief in the doorway of Santa Maria della Pieve, Arezzo.

Page 113. Design for a decorative silver wine fountain. Drawing by Elizabeth Romer after a sketch by Teofilo Torri (1554–1623), in Lynda Fairburn's *Italian Renaissance Drawings: From the Collection of Sir John Soane's Museum* (London, 1998), Vol. 2.

Page 116. Title page of the first edition of Francesco Redi's poem *Bacco in Toscana* (Florence, 1685).

Page 119. Francesco Redi. Drawing by Elizabeth Romer after the frontispiece of the first edition of *Bacco in Toscana* (Florence, 1685), which reproduces a portrait of Redi by Justus Sustermans.

Page 140. Title page of *Il panunto toscano*, ms. 450, Biblioteca Città di Arezzo. Photograph by John Romer.

Page 141. The emblem of Arezzo. Drawing by Elizabeth Romer.

Page 144. The Piazza Grande in the mid-nineteenth century. Lithograph by Franklin B. Hallman, from Henry Gally Knight's *The Ecclesiastical Architecture of Italy* (London, 1844).

Page 147. The shooting of the brigand Gnicche. Frontispiece of Giovanni Fantoni's *Delitti, arresto e morte del capo assassino Federigo Bobini, detto Gnicche* (Florence, 1878).

Page 162. A grape picker on a piece of ancient Roman Aretine ware. Drawing by Elizabeth Romer, of a vase fragment in the Museo Archeologico Nazionale Gaio Cilnio Mecenate, Arezzo.

Page 209. Handwritten title page of Giovanni Battista Magi's *Libretto di cucina*, from *Libretto di cucina di Gio Batta Magi* (Arezzo, 1989), edited by Piero Zoi & Piero Ricci.

Page 211. The city and fortress of Arezzo in the 1700s, from a fresco *en griseille*, artist unknown.

Index of Recipes

Appetisers
Crostini con Acciughe 228
Crostini Neri 226
Fegatini al burro per crostini 227-8

Pasta and Rice
Gnocchi del Casentino 235
Pappardelle all'Aretina (Artusi) 34
Pappardelle all'Aretina 236-7
Pappardelle colla Lepre (Artusi), 236
Risotto con Carciofi 218-9
Risotto con la Zucca 220-1
Risotto con le Zucchine 219-20
Spaghetti al Basilico 237
Spaghetti al olio e aglio 237-8
Tagliatelle con i Carciofi 238

Sauces
Salsa (Beppina) 84
Sugo al Carne/Sugo al Ragù 216-8
Sugo di Pomodoro 215-6
Mostarda (Gaudentio) 138-9

Soups
Brodo de Polastri 102-3
Brodo di Gallina 215
Minestra di Pane 221
Minestra di Patate (Beppina) 80-1
Ribollita 222
Zuppa di Fagioli 222-3
Zuppa di Farro 223-4
Zuppa di Pollo all'Aretina 104
Zuppa di Pollo all'Avignonese 106
Zuppa Frantoiana 224-6
Zuppa Tarlati 105-6

Egg dishes
Finta Trippa 233-4
Frittata con i Porri 231-2
Frittata con la Salsiccia 231
Frittata con Spinaci 230-1
Frittata di Ceci 232
Frittata di Fagiolini 230
Frittata di Pomodori Acerbi 232-3
Frittata Ripiena (Beppina) 79
Uova alle Svedese (Beppina) 79
Uova col Pomodoro 234-5
Uova soda con Salsa Verde 228

Fish
Baccalà in Umido 242-3
Tinca con i Piselli 243-4
Tinca (Gaudentio) 134-5
Tonno con Fagioli e Cipolla 244
Trote Affogate 240-1
Trote al Forno 241
Trote coi Funghi Porcini 242
Trote Farcite 241

Lamb
Agnello alla Casentinese 248-9
Arrosto d'agnello all'Aretina 249-50
Polpette di Agnello (Guerrini) 75

Pork
Braciole alla Cacciatora 245-6
Bracioline alla Cacciatora
  (Beppina) 67
Bracioline Buonissime (Beppina) 67
Bracioline di Maiale 246
Bracioline di Maiale con Cipolle 246-7
Cinghiale in Umido 206-7
Fegatelli (Gaudentio) 154
L'Arista 247-8
Sanguinaccio (Gaudentio) 135-6
Sanguinaccio (Romer/Cerotti) 136
Salsicce alla Montanara 181-2

Beef and Veal
Bragioline con Salsa (Beppina) 67
Bue alla California (Artusi) 69-70
Carne Battuta per Farne Polpette

Index of recipes

(Gaudentio) 77
Carne Battuta per Farne
  Riempiture (Gaudentio) 76-7
Carne sotto l'aceto (Beppina) 73-4
Fricandò (Beppina) 66
Manzo alla California (Beppina) 69
Manzo alla California (Bozzi) 70-1
Manzo alla Moda (Beppina) 68
Polpette con l'Ortica 247
Polpette di Lesso (Beppina) 74
Polpettone alla Casalinga (Beppina) 75
Polpettone Grosso (Gaudentio) 77
Scaloppe alla Milanese (Beppina) 65-6
Stracotto 250
Stufato di Vaccina Vitella
  (Gaudentio) 251
Tortino (Beppina) 78
Vitello alla Schnitzel (Beppina) 66
Vitello in Fricandò (Beppina) 64-5

Fowl and Game

Anatra in Finocchiata 252
Cappone in Cazzeruola (Beppina) 71
Cappone Coperto (Gaudentio) 139
Cappone in Galantina (Artusi) 72-3
Fagiano Tartufato 251-2
Faraona al Ginepro 253-4
Piccioni alla Cristina 254-5
Pollo al Ginepro 253
Pollo in Umido 252-3
Cinghiale in Umido 206-7

Vegetable Dishes

Budino di fagiolini (Beppina) 82
Carciofi alla Massaia 255
Carline 182-3
Cavolfiore in Padella 259
Fagioli all'Olio 256-7
Fagioli all'uccelletto 257-8
Fagioli con Rigatino 255-6
Fagiolini Trifolati (Beppina) 81
Fagiolini Verdi con Pomodoro
  all'Aretina 257
Flan de Zucchette (Beppina) 82
Lenticchie Stufate 261-2
Patate e Funghi al Forno 263-4
Pomodori (Gaudentio) 131-2
Pomodoro alla Salsa di Tartufi
  (Corrado) 131
Pulezze con le salsicce 179-80
Rocchi di Sedano all'Aretina 261
Sformato di Spinaci con Cibreo 264-5
Sformato di Taffache (Beppina) 63-4
Sformato di Zucchini Passati
  (Beppina) 83
Spinaci con Pinoli 258-9
Tortino di Carciofi 265
Tortino di Patate 262-3
Tortino di Zucchini (Artusi) 83
Vegetable Pottage (Francatelli) 48-9
Zucchine con Pomodoro 259-60
Zucchine da Magro 260

Salads

Insalata d'Ovoli 228-9
Insalata di Fave Fresche e Pecorino 229

Desserts, Pastries and Liqueurs

Anisette (Beppina) 85
Biscottini (Beppina) 85-6
Composta di Pesche (Magi) 269
Composta di Pesche al Vino (Magi) 268
Crostata (Beppina) 89
Gelatina Spiritosa (Beppina) 84
Mele Cotte al Rosmarino 267
Pan di Caffè (Beppina) 89-90
Pinocchiata 266-7
Ricotta all'Aretina 269
Torta di Mandorle (Beppina) 90
Torta di Mele 268
Torta di Mele al burro 268
Tortino (Beppina) 78

General index

A Plain Cookery Book for the Working Classes (Francatelli), 48
abbucciato aretino (pecorino cheese), 14
Accademia del Cimento, 115, 120
Accademia della Crusca, 28, 115
acquacotta (soup), 53, 54, 194
Acton, Eliza, 32-3
Albergotti, Francesco, 11, 12
Alfredo (butcher) Arezzo, 22
Alkermes (Tuscan liqueur), 165, 196
Amarcord (Fellini), 191
amber & ambergris, 120, 125
anatra domestica in umido (stewed duck), 34
Andrea Corsi (grocer) Arezzo, 40, 43
Anghiari, Tuscany, 100, 143, 193
Anguilla al Tegamaccio, 240
Antica Trattoria al Principe (restaurant), 240
Aretino, Pietro, 11, 12, 16-7, 55, 56, 57, 63, 128, 166-70, 189-91, 197, 198-9, 203-4, 211, 266
Arezzo City Library, 128, 139-40
Ariadne (goddess), 116
arista (roast loin of pork), 15, 34, 71, 177, 207-10, 247-8
Aristoxenus (philosopher), 209
Arno (river), 24, 93, 143, 193, 239-40
arrosto morto (pan roast), 61
arte di utilizzare gli avanzi della mensa, L' (Guerrini), 46
Artusi, Pellegrino, 20, 23-38, 40, 42-44, 46, 48, 60, 62, 60-70, 72-3, 78, 81-3, 91, 102, 114, 195-7, 205, 207, 211, 236, 248, 249, 257
Athenaeus, 151, 154-5, 208-9
Austro-Hungarian Empire, 87
Audot, Louis Eustache, 31, 32

avanzi (leftover food), 46
Avignon, 100, 101, 106

baccalà (salt cod), 133, 151, 158, 177, 242-3
Bacchants, The (Epicharmus), 155
Bacchus (god), 115-7
Bacci (family), 111, 166
Bacco in Toscana (Redi), 115-6
Bacon, Francis, 114
Badia al Pino, Arezzo, 147
Baldi, Lorenzo, 140
Bar Pasticceria Stefano (bar), 40
Bardot, Brigitte, 163
battitura (threshing), 206
battuto (chopped ingredients), 34, 78, 83, 104, 121, 150, 206, 207, 213, 217, 222-4, 237, 244, 245, 248, 262, 263
Bayer e C. (food company), 41
Beeton, Isabella, 32-3
Benedetti, Carlo de, 40
Beppina, 12, 15, 19-21, 23, 38, 40-1, 43-6, 51, 60-5, 67-73, 75-6, 78-84, 86-91, 113, 145, 151, 173, 184, 193, 195, 211, 264
bergamot orange, 120
Bianco Vergine del Val di Chiana (wine), 159, 175
Bianco, Simon, 168
biancomangiare, 34, 103
Biancane and Sibillone (Artusi's cats), 24
Bibbiena, Scuola di San Andrea, 59
Biblioteca Città di Arezzo (Arezzo City Library), 128, 139-40
Bigerade orange, 120
Birds' nests (Chinese), 117
biscotti di Prato (biscuits), 197
biscottini (biscuits), 85-6

❋ General index ❋

blancmanger, 103
Boccaccio, 167, 172
Bologna, 29, 34, 46, 102, 217
Book of Household Management, The (Beeton), 32-3
Borro, Alessandro dal, 205
Borgo di Santa Croce, Arezzo, 145
Borgo San Piero (bar) Arezzo, 186
bramagere, 103
Brancas, Louis de (Marquis), 195
Brenzone, Agostino, 203
Brillat-Savarin, Jean Anthelme, 41, 94
broccoletti di rapa (turnip leaves), 180
Bronzino, Agnolo, 173
Brunelleschi, Philippo, 89
Brussels, Belgium, 171, 175, 178
Buitoni, Giovanni Battista & Giulia, 40-1, 43
Buratto (King of the Indies), 97, 99
Burro di zangola (churned butter), 65
busecchio (tripe), 208

cacciucco (fish stew), 28
Caffé dei Costanti, Arezzo, 22, 148, 164, 165, 192, 202
California (Lesmo, Brianza), 43, 69
Camaldoli Monastery, 15, 100
Cantina dei Vini Tipici dell'Aretino (winemaker), 175
cantuccini (biscuits), 111
capon, 71, 72-3, 118, 123, 124, 139, 168, 195, 219
carbonai (charcoal burners), 54
carbonata (crisply fried pieces of pancetta), 168, 169
carciofi (artichokes), 82, 124, 218, 238, 255, 265
carline (cardoons and thistles), 54, 182, 183
Carnevale (carnival), 177

Castro (river), 148
Casentino Valley, Tuscany, 15, 22, 53, 93, 126, 143, 159, 171, 193, 208, 239, 240, 242, 248
Cathedral at La Pionta, Arezzo, 99
cedronella (herb), 55, 56
cenci (fried sweet biscuits), 177
Censis (State census), 19
Cerfone (river), 143
Cerotti (family), 9, 10, 136-7, 157, 203
centro storico (historic centre of Arezzo), 15, 20, 22, 107, 149, 153, 160, 165, 184, 191, 192
Chianti (wine), 111, 159, 175, 250, 251, 269
Chimera (sculpture), 99
China illustrata (Kircher), 118
chocolate, 40, 117, 119-20, 122-3, 125-6, 196, 269
Chrysippus, 208
Church of San Francesco, Arezzo, 19, 22, 24, 111, 127, 165, 170, 202
Church and College of Sant' Ignazio, Arezzo, 128, 183
ciabatta (flat bread), 174
cider (beverage), 117
Ciggiano, province of Arezzo, 116
cima di rapa (turnip leaves), 180
Cimabue, 167
Cioccolato, 126
Circolo Artistico (Arts club), 201-2
ciambellone (sponge cake), 150
Città di Castello, Umbria, 143
clostridium perfringens, 76
Codex Bologna, 102
Codex Casanatense, 102, 103
Codex Riccardiano, 102
Coldiretti (national farmer's association), 14, 19, 150, 179

General Index

colonnaccia, Arezzo, 147
coloniali (colonial goods), 43
Columbus, Christopher, 166
Collegio S. Caterina, Arezzo, 59
conchiglie (pasta), 178
Conti Borghini Baldovinetti de' Bacci Venuti (wine producer), 111
Convent of Santa Maria Novella, 124
Cookery and Housekeeping (Reeve), 88
Corrado, Vincenzo, 91, 131
Corso Italia, Arezzo, 22, 40, 146, 149, 157, 191, 192, 200, 202, 205
Cortona, Tuscany, 143, 153, 163
cotechino (sausage), 76, 262
cuoco galante, Il (Corrado), 91, 131
crema pasticcera (confectioner's custard), 31
Crème de Poulet à la Reine, 101
croissant, 101
crostini (appetiser), 35, 45, 79, 124, 173, 183, 226, 227, 228, 255
cucina classica, La (Giardini), 39
cucina economica (cooking stove), 59, 87
Cuisinière de la campagne et la ville, La (Audot), 31, 32

d'Andrea, Noddo, 208-9
Dante, 28, 196
Dati, Goro, 93, 94
Decameron, The (Boccaccio), 167
Deipnosophists, The (Athenaeus), 151, 154-5, 208-9
dextrose, 178
Dominican Republic, 126
Duomo (Arezzo), 127, 145, 166, 170, 177
Duomo (Florence), 89
Durante, Castore, 91, 131
Durastante, Matteo, 198

eggah (egg dish), 15
Egypt, 9, 38, 259
Epicharmus, 155
Esperienze intorno a diverse cose naturale (Redi), 117
Etruscan culture, 38, 99, 160, 162, 172, 202
EU regulations, 171

fagiano (pheasant), 26, 251,
farfalle (pasta), 178, 236
farro (grain), 223
Fascists and Fascist Party, 98, 185
Fattoria di Piscinale, Arezzo, 140
Fattoria di San Fabiano, Arezzo, 111-2
Feast of St Andrew, Arezzo, 108
Feast of San Giuseppe, 197, 203
Feast of St Michael, 109, 239
Feast of the Immaculate Conception, 151
fegatelli (spiced liver), 15, 37, 130, 146, 153-5, 194
Fellini, Federico, 191
fennel, 15, 37, 68, 77, 118, 133, 135, 149, 153, 154, 174, 225, 245, 246, 252
Ferraro, Giuseppe, 45
filone (bread), 174
finocchiona (salami), 174
Fonderia Agenzia Generale di Arezzo, 74
Fonderia Bastanzetti Arezzo (foundry), 58-9, 87
Forlimpopoli, Romagna, 24
Forme of Cury, The, 196
Fossombroni, Vittorio, 239
Francatelli, Charles Elmé, 33, 48, 51, 53,
Franceschi, Angiolo, 74

General Index

frantoia (olive press), 210, 224
Fraternità dei Laici (charity), 60
Frati, Ludovico, 102
French Cook, The (Ude), 33
Frittata (egg dish), 15, 79, 136-7, 168, 226, 230-4
frittelle (fried cake), 203

galantina (stuffed chicken), 26, 27, 72, 73, 124, 173-4, 195
Galenic tradition, 125
Galileo, Galilei, 115
Galyntyne (lampreys with sauce), 195
Gammurini, Gian Francesco, 140
gateau à la Noisette (cake), 31
gattò (cake), 165, 196, 205
Gaudentio, Francesco, 42, 76, 78, 121, 128-9, 131-2, 134-5, 137-41, 154, 183, 194, 196, 211, 243
Genoa, 34
gergo francioso (culinary jargon), 28
Gherardi, Mario, 21
Giacomo Konz & C (grocer), 40
giallini (fungi), 149
Giannarini, Giulio, 42
Gianni, Guido, 65, 140
Giardini, Giacomo, 39
gigotto (lamb dish), 39
ginseng (root), 119
Giostra del Saracino, Arezzo, 95-100, 103, 148
Giudici, de (family), 127
Glasse, Hannah, 33
Gli Svizzeri (Konz & C) Arezzo, 40
Gnicche (Federico Bobini), 145-8
gobbi fritti (fried cardoon), 54
Gower Peninsula, Wales, 36
Granducal Spezieria and Fonderia, 119-20
grifi (muzzles), 54, 199, 200

grissini (bread sticks), 19
Grossetto, Tuscany, 151
Guerrini, Olindo, 46, 74-5, 76, 91, 102
Guido d'Arezzo (monk), 166

Henry II (Holy Roman Emperor), 101
Herbario nuovo (Durante), 91, 131
Homer, 94
Horace, 202
horsemeat, 54, 97,

ice factory, Arezzo, 59-60
Impruneta, Florence, 89
in porchetta (cooking method), 245
Italian Journey (Goethe), 171
Italy (Unification of), 20-1, 23, 25, 28, 32, 160

Jesuits, 42, 117, 128, 135, 137, 140, 141, 243

Kircher, Athanasius, 117-8
Krapfen (doughnuts), 31
Kugelhupf (cake), 31

La Primizia (green grocer), 188
Lo Scalco alla Moderna (Latini), 131
La Tagliatella (restaurant), 199
lampredotto (dark tripe), 54, 196
Lancerio, Sante, 45
Latini, Antonio, 131
Legend of the True Cross (fresco cycle), 111
Liebig (food company), 41
Lesso Rifatto all'Inglese (Toad in the Hole), 32
libbra (pounds), 62-3
Libretto di cucina (Magi), 268

❋ General index ❋

Libro de arte coquinaria (Martino), 91, 135
Libro di cucina del secolo XIV (Frati), 102
Logge del Grano (market) Arezzo, 14-5
Lo scalco alla moderna (Latini), 131
Loro Ciuffenna, Arezzo, 168
lunar calendar, 9
luppoli (hop shoots), 51

maccheroni (pasta), 206, 207, 208, 236
maccheroni co'l'ocio (pasta dish), 54, 194, 206
maccheroni con ragu (pasta dish), 194
Madonna del Conforto, 164
Maecenas, Gaius, 202
Magalotti, Lorenzo, 120
Magi, Giovanni Battista, 90, 209-10, 211, 260, 268-9
Maiano, Giuliano di (architect), 203
maize, 50, 51, 180, 184, 232
Manhattan, 114
Maremma, maritime region of Tuscany and Lazio, 53, 194
Martino, Maestro, 91, 135
Massetani, Giuseppe, 127
Mayhew, Henry, 49-50
Medici, Alessandro de, 97
Medici, Catherine de, 101
Medici, Cosimo III de, 97, 114, 119
Medici, Ferdinand II de, 114-5
Medici, Gian Gastone de, 122
Medici, feast, 1688, Arezzo
Mediterranean diet, 176
mela roggia (apple), 15
Mesopotamia, 38
mezzadria (farming system), 51
Milan, 21, 34, 39, 43-4, 50-1, 64-5, 70
milza (spleen), 173, 217, 227, 236
minestra (soup), 48, 61, 80, 221
minestrone, 184
Miniati, Arnoldo, 13
Minuit, Peter, 114
Modern Cookery for Private Families (Acton), 32
Monastery of Saints Flora and Lucilla, Arezzo, 202
Montepulciano, Tuscany, 116, 269
Monterchi, Tuscany, 143
Moreau, Jeanne, 163
Morgante maggiore, Il (Pulci), 155-6
Morpurgo, Salomone, 102
Mussolini, Benito, 98

Naples, 34, 40, 131
Napoleon, 22, 60, 63, 97, 127, 144, 163-5, 174, 195, 202
nepitella (mint), 56, 260
Nero (Emperor), 228
nervi (cartilage and tendons), 54, 199
Nestlé (food company), 40
New Year's Eve dinners, Arezzo, 76, 124, 262
Nodini di maiale (pork dish), 200
Nonna Lola (restaurant), 193, 196

Occhini, Pier Lodovico, 97-8
oncia (ounces), 62-3
Orchestra Sinfonica Guido d'Arezzo, 191
Order of St Stephen, 97, 205
orecchiette (type of pasta), 181
ovolo (wild mushroom), 228-9

Padovano, Federigo, 56-7
Palazzo Guazzesi, Arezzo, 201-2
Palazzo Orsini, Rome, 167

General index

Palestine lime, 120
pancetta (pork belly), 15, 37, 70, 169, 180, 181, 190, 200, 217, 222-3, 224-5, 242, 248, 250, 251-2, 253, 255-6, 261-2
Panforte (sweetmeat), 196
panini (filled rolls), 172, 174, 187
panunto toscano, Il (Gaudentio), 121, 128, 139-41 154, 183, 195
panzanella (bread salad), 172, 173, 214
Papal States, 25, 100-1, 106
pappardelle (type of pasta), 15, 34, 35, 150, 236
pappardelle alla lepre, 15
Partisans, 185
passeggiata (evening stroll), 192, 198, 200, 201
pastasciutta (pasta), 40, 61
Pasticceria Bruschi (bar and bakery) Arezzo. 205
pastina (tiny type of pasta), 41, 42
pecorino (cheese), 14, 15, 56, 57, 74, 137, 150, 152, 156, 159, 172, 178, 193, 198, 206, 229, 237
pellagra (disease), 50, 51
peperoncino (hot red pepper), 152, 174, 181, 207, 221, 230, 240, 241, 253
peposo (picquant beefstew), 89
Perelli, Eugenia, 21
Pertini, Sandro, 185
Peruzzi (family), 170-1, 175, 177, 181, 183
pesto all Genovese (sauce), 172
Petrarch, 97-8
Petrini, Carlo, 14
pezzuoli (napkins), 122
Philoxenus, 208
piatti poveri (simple food), 54-5

Piazza d'Azeglio, Florence, 24, 27
Piazza della Repubblica, Florence, 22
Piazza Grande, Arezzo, 96, 98, 144, 145, 148, 192, 205
Piazza San Agostino, Arezzo, 148-9
Piazza San Francesco, Arezzo, 22, 191, 240
Piazza Vasari, 144, 145, 147, 164
Piero della Francesco, 111, 127, 165, 167, 229
Pineider (stationers), 21
Pisanelli, Baldassare, 91, 121
Pitti Palace, 115, 123
Poggio di Poti (spring), Arezzo, 144
plum pudding, 31, 47, 196
Pocopanno, Gianfrancesco, 265
polpette (meat balls), 46, 74, 75, 76, 77, 123, 173, 247
polpettone (meat loaf), 46, 75, 77, 145
pomi d'oro (tomatoes), 131
Pope Clement V, 100
Pope John XXII, 100
Pope Paolo III, 45
Pope Pius XI, 114
Porta del Foro, Arezzo, 99, 159
Porta San Clemente, Arezzo, 127, 164
Porta Santo Spirito, Arezzo, 58, 159
Prato, Il, Arezzo, 93-4, 110, 145
Prato, Katharina, 87
Pratobevera, Eduard, 87
Presciani, Lorentino, 163-4, 166
Prévost (chef to the Marquis de Brancas), 195
Priapus (god), 56
primizie (spring produce), 187
prosciutto (dry-cured ham), 34, 66, 72, 74, 82, 145, 146, 172, 177, 184, 187, 206, 230, 236
Pulci, Luigi, 155

✳ General Index ✳

pulezze, 179, 180, 181, 194
pusu (herb), 119

RAI TV, 28
Rearing horse (coat of arms of Arezzo), 112-3
Redi, Giovanni Battista, 58, 123, 124, 138, 141
Redi, Francesco, 42-3, 58, 114-28, 137, 140-1
Redi, Ignazio Maria, 140
Redi, Maria Diomira, 124
Redi, St. Margherita, 114
Reeve, Mrs Henry, 88
Ricchi, Agostin, 189
rigatino (a type of pancetta), 37, 169, 181, 255
Ristoro di Mauro, Cristofano di, 162
rizzole (rissoles), 39
rocchio di fichi secchi (string of dried figs), 261
Romagna, 24, 25, 46
Roman Empire, 38,
Rome, 21, 22, 93, 114, 139, 140, 141, 151, 161, 163, 166, 169, 206
Rome Beyond the Imperial Frontiers (Wheeler), 161
rosbiffe (roast beef), 31
rosella (berry), 43
Rossi, Mattei (stationer) Arezzo, 24
Rovere, Vittoria della, 122
Ruffilli, Francesco, 29

Sabatini, Marietta. 29
Sacchetti, Franco, 208, 236
St James's Gazette, 47
Saint Peter's, Rome, 114
Sallei, Giovanni, 140
San Donato (Saint Donatus), 96, 99, 164

San Marzano (tomato), 260
Sandrini, Vincenzo, 120
San Polo massacre, Arezzo, 185
Sansepolcro, 40, 143, 229
Sansovino, 116
Sarra, Girolamo, 55
Sassafras (deciduous tree), 118
Savona ware (ceramic), 58
Scheiger, Joseph dei Nobili von, 87
schiacciata (flat bread), 214
scienza in cucina e l'arte di mangiar bene, La (Artusi), 20, 23, 31, 42, 249, 257
scottiglia (stew), 194, 195
Seville orange, 120
sformati (flans), 62, 81
Siena, 100, 126, 196, 224
Signorelli, Luca, 167
silphium (spice), 38
silver wine fountain (design), 115
Slow Food, 14
Soane, Sir John (museum), 112
Società per le Cucine Economiche (charity), Arezzo, 60
soffritto (base for sauces), 66, 74, 76, 82, 105, 121, 213, 225, 227, 256
Soyer, Alexis, 33
spaghetti alla carbonara (pasta with eggs and pancetta), 169
Spinello, Parri di (painter), 201
star anise, 118
Statute of the *Comune* of Arezzo 1327, 23, 96, 106, 108, 110, 239
Stecchetti (pseudonym of Olindo Guerrini), 46, 74-5, 76, 90, 102
Symposium (Maecenas), 202

Tarlati, Guido (Bishop of Arezzo), 98, 100, 102, 108, 194
Teatro Petrarca, Arezzo, 22, 148

General Index

Tegoleto, Arezzo, 146
Tiber Valley, 15
Tiber (river), 93, 143
Torri, Teofilo, 112, 113
transhumance, 53
Trasimeno (lake) 36, 143, 239
Trattato della natura de' cibi et del bere (Pisanelli), 91, 121
Trattoria Mazzoni, Arezzo, 103
Trecentonovelle, Il (Sacchetti), 208, 236
Tregozzano, province of Arezzo, 116
trippa (tripe), 54, 123, 195-6, 199, 200, 233, 234
tritato (in food preparation), 213
truffles, 33, 72, 131, 159, 190, 195, 203, 214, 217, 251
turnips, 49, 107, 180
Tuscan sausage, 78, 152, 178-9, 181-2, 217-8, 231, 259, 262, 263
Tuscan Year, Life and Food in an Italian Valley, The (Romer), 9, 136

Ude, Louis Eustache, 33
Uffizi Gallery, 114
Umbria, 9, 143, 198, 217
Unification of Italy, 20-1, 23, 25, 28, 32, 160
utensils, for cooking, 214

Val di Chiana, Tuscany, 22, 143, 159, 175, 185, 242
Valdarno, Tuscany, 143
Valtiberina, Umbria, 143
vanilla, 31, 120, 125
Vasari, Giorgio, 111, 112, 144, 160, 167
Vecchia Brianza in cucina (Bozzi), 70
veglia (entertainment), 196
Venice, 11, 17, 55, 57, 129, 163, 166, 168, 191, 199, 204, 266
Vernacoliere, Il (periodical), 167
Vestri Cioccolato (confectioners), 126
Victoria, Queen, 46-7, 48
Vienna, 101
Villa degli Orti, Arezzo, 114, 126, 140
Villa di Piscinale, Arezzo, 127
Vin Santo (sweet wine), 62, 90, 111. 113, 175, 194, 195, 197, 210, 217, 218, 219, 254, 265, 269
Virgil, 202
vitalba (briony), 51
Viva Maria uprising, Arezzo, 163-4
Vormio, Olao, 118

Wheeler, Mortimer, 161-2
World War, First, 12
World War, Second, 180, 203
workhouse, 50

Ximenez, Francesco, 118

Zanobi, Raffaello di, 144
zuppa di pane (bread soup), 53
zuppa di verdure (vegetable soup), 184
zuppa impero (trifle), 102
zuppa inglese (trifle), 31, 102, 196, 214
zuppa regina (chicken and bread soup), 34, 48
zuppa Tarlati (Bishop Tarlati's Soup), 100, 103, 105, 194